D0397795

10-29-08

To Donna,
With friendship and
encouragement always!

[signature]

SUCCESS IN ACTION

SUCCESS IN ACTION

THE DIRECT PATH TO

YOUR HIGHER POTENTIAL

by Dan Thurmon

Foreword by John Goddard

Action Press, a subsidiary of Motivation Works, Inc.
Atlanta, GA

Library of Congress Cataloging-in-Publication Data
Thurmon, Dan.
    Success in Action / by Dan Thurmon. 1st. ed.
    p. cm.
    LCCN: 2005927664

    ISBN 0-9766663-0-8
    1. Self-Help   2. Communication   3. Interpersonal Relationships

Editor: Michael Carr
Jacket Design: Tony Brischler
Interior Design: Leslie Rains
Photography: Tom Abraham

Printed in the United States of America

ENDORSEMENTS

"For more than five years Dan Thurmon's presentations have been an integral part of our communication strategy and culture. In fact, we've hired Dan more than any other speaker, hands down! His new book, *Success in Action*, conveys the same powerful message he brings to the stage, and it will help you to positively transform your life."

—Randy Merritt,
Executive Vice President, Corporate Sales and Marketing
Shaw Industries, Inc.

"There are lots of self-help books you could read, but this is one you *should* read. Dan Thurmon knows what he writes and talks about: he lives life boldly and is a first-class guide to show you how to live more passionately and successfully. His engaging stories and practical insights make *Success in Action* an enlightening and entertaining read. I highly recommend it!"

—Mark Sanborn
Author of *The Fred Factor*

"Dan Thurmon is a genius . . . this is a terrific book that'll educate you, inspire you, and transform your thinking in abundant ways."

—Nido Qubein
Chairman, Great Harvest Bread Company
President, High Point University

"Dan Thurmon is a master performer—our employees continue to request him more than any other speaker. Now, he has channeled the energy and excitement of his amazing live performances through his compelling book, *Success in Action*, which will inspire you to redesign your life."

—Jack Middleton
President and Chief Executive Officer
Southern Motor Carriers

DEDICATION

This book is dedicated to the memory of Merck Smith, a dear friend who lived a life of honor, love, and action. Thanks, Merck, for teaching me the importance of using the gifts we are given. Thanks for showing me, through your relationship with your darling wife, Toni, it is possible to remain newlyweds for a lifetime. And thanks for encouraging me to be at my best, always. You never know who is in your audience.

TABLE OF CONTENTS

TABLE OF CONTENTS (CONT)

*Teaches you how to use hours more effectively and expand
every moment to "warp" time to your advantage.*
> The Greatest Bank in the World
> Time Flies
> First Things First
> Let's Have the Time of Our Lives
> Warping Time
> Learning at the Speed of Freefall
> Seven Powerful Priority Parachutes

*Encourages you to stop procrastination by "putting an end
to putting it off."*
> Life's "Snooze Button"
> Procrastination Quiz
> The Price We Pay For Procrastination
> Why We Procrastinate
> Procrastination Prevention

*Explains how you can turn calculated risks into cultivated
outcomes to deliver the performance of your life.*
> The Globe of Destiny
> The Perception of Risk
> Strategies for Increasing Your Risk Tolerance
> The Rewards of Risk Taking

*Gives you the insights and tools to welcome change as an ally
instead of avoiding it as an adversary.*
> Change Perspectives
> Myths about Change
> Why People Resist Change
> Mastering Change

*Demonstrates how you can use failures to "grow" forward
with confidence.*

TABLE OF CONTENTS (CONT)

FOREWORD

As we move into the 21st Century, a revolution in human awareness is taking place. The accelerating pace of change, coupled with the need to make important lifestyle and career decisions, have prompted an increasing number of people to redefine the exact meaning of success in their lives. They are redirecting their talents, skills and energies toward improving—more productively—their personal and professional environments. They understand that goal-setting and goal achievement are active processes, demanding perseverance and commitment that ultimately produce immensely rewarding results.

One of the special virtues of this book, in my estimation, is that it so effectively instructs readers how to transform their goals into concrete actions. Dan Thurmon has captured the essence of success in action. He uses an entertaining but balanced approach, which vividly demonstrates that your success is not determined just by the circumstances in which you find yourself, but by your thinking, choices and actions.

I first met Dan through my adopted niece, Reneé, who had attended one of Dan's seminars. She was greatly impressed with his charismatic delivery style and by the fact that he had referenced my original list of 127 life goals in his presentation. After a brief chat, she asked Dan if he would like to meet me. This resulted in an enjoyable get-together in my California home. It didn't take us long to realize we were true kindred spirits with the same philosophy of life.

What amazes me about Dan is his dynamic energy, boundless enthusiasm and intense focus. His zest for life springs off every page! He is an old soul in a young, athletic body, imbued with broad insights far beyond his age. I know you will be inspired by what you read. It is an enthusiastic book with a "do it now" quality. It is not a book to read through quickly—it is filled with too many thought-provoking ideas—

so you will want to revisit it on many occasions to soak up its wisdom.

Its literary style and universal content make it a must read for all ages. I mean that! It's impressive instructions will help you blast out of stale routines and soar—faster than you might think—toward realizing your dreams. If you've attended any of Dan's seminars, you will see immediately how this book amplifies and extends his on-stage message.

As one who has been hooked on reading since age ten, I can tell you I have read numerous books on self-improvement and success throughout my lifetime. Several of them have been memorable and influential, but this is one of the best of them! Its practicality, straight-forwardness, and call-to-action focus make this book a treasure trove of life-enriching information.

If you're like Dan and me—and the people who are mentioned in this book—you're constantly striving to upgrade the quality of success in your life. So, as its title suggests, use this invaluable book as a catalyst for your own Success in Action!

John Goddard
Explorer and Author of *The Survivor: 24 Spine-Chilling Adventures on the Edge of Death*

INTRODUCTION

In perhaps the most famous scene from the mockumentary film *This Is Spinal Tap,* Nigel Tufnel (played by Christopher Guest), lead guitarist of the fictional British metal band Spinal Tap, explains to journalist Marty DiBergi (Rob Reiner) why the band's sound is so unique and powerful. You'll need to imagine the accent for full impact. Nigel: "If you look at the amp, you'll see that all of our numbers all go to eleven. Most blokes will be playing at ten with everything turned all the way up, and where can you go from there? Nowhere. Exactly. But when we need that little extra push, you know what we do? We go to eleven." Unable to grasp the reporter's logic that you could just make number ten louder and accomplish the same thing, Nigel reiterates, "These go to eleven. That's one louder, isn't it?"

Nigel's approach to music resembles my approach to life. Go to eleven. Go just one more past where you set out to go. Go just a little further than everyone else, and you will stand out by far. When delivering a speech, instead of giving my audiences an energy level of ten, I go to eleven. When lifting weights in the gym, instead of doing ten repetitions, I go to eleven. When passing flaming torches or knives with my juggling partner, Philip Solomon, instead of concluding our routine with ten throws to each other, we go to eleven. Why? Well, that's one more, now, isn't it?

This book is all about action, and it is my passionate desire that it will assist and inspire you to "go to eleven." Increasing your level of commitment even by just one more increment will result in multiplied rewards. Sometimes the eleventh attempt, the eleventh hour, the eleventh idea, or the eleventh plan will be the one that catapults you to success.

This book is designed to both inspire you and assist you in getting past obstacles that have, until now, prevented you from being your best and bringing out the best in others. I am so convinced that positive, prudent, purposeful actions are the keys to your success that I have infused this book with a variety of tools to engage your participation. I don't expect you to do everything on your first reading, but the more you commit to this interactive process, the greater your results will be. The time to take action is in the flow of your reading. As I say in my speeches, "If the ball is in your hand, throw it!" In other words, when the ideas are fresh and the opportunity is at hand, you are poised and ready to make a breakthrough! Follow through to keep your momentum moving forward. I will help you to do just that, with specific actions to take at the end of each chapter, in the sections titled "Action Assignments."

Each of these eleven chapters is packed with actions you can take to increase your success and happiness. The chapters can be read independently or sequentially; however, for continuity's sake, I recommend starting with Chapter One and reading them in order.

You will find that the principles outlined in each chapter can be applied equally to both personal and work-related goals. To me, the two are inseparable when it comes to pursuing the kind of success you deserve. If this book helps you to take the first step and then the next step toward realizing your dreams, it will have served its purpose. And now let's go to eleven—together.

CLEAR FOR TAKEOFF

To know oneself, one should assert oneself. Psychology is action, not thinking about oneself. We continue to shape our personality all our life.

—Albert Camus

Success in life is determined not by your circumstances, but by your actions.

—Dan Thurmon

On March 9, 1994, I awoke to an overcast morning and breathed a sigh of relief. After stumbling to the phone, I called the automated weather information line at the airport: ceiling of thirteen hundred feet—definitely not a good day for flying. Thankful for the reprieve, I phoned my instructor, Mark Milam, to confirm that my lesson was off.

"No, come on in," he said. "We're just going to stay in the pattern today, so we won't need more than a thousand feet. The weather's perfect."

My heart skipped—there was no backing out. Today I would fly my first solo—the culmination of commitments I had made to my teacher and to myself.

Commitments are how we define our character, and they come in varying degrees. I have always been fascinated by flight. As a child, flying was often the subject of my dreams and fantasies. So when I was formulating my "life list" of experiences and goals I expected to achieve, learning to fly was a natural choice. I wrote down the goal and committed to following through on it at some point later in life. While this was an important step, it was only the first level of commitment.

The next level of commitment is when you begin to take action. My pursuit of a pilot's license began five years after I made my list. My wife, Sheilia, gave me her full support to go after my dream. We were newly married, with no children yet, so I sensed that this was my window of opportunity. I saved some money, met an instructor at the local airport, bought my books and other materials, and took my first lesson.

By that cloudy morning, I had logged just over nine hours in the pilot's seat. And during every flight, I had the reassuring presence of my instructor in the seat to my right. It had been comforting to know that even if I made a mistake or forgot a procedure, he would be right there, lending his calm expertise to prevent a mishap.

Takeoffs and landings are the most important and potentially dangerous parts of any flight. It is said that the key to a successful career as a pilot is to have your take offs and landings come out even. This was the focus of our lesson, and why we stayed "in the pattern." This meant that we would take off and then turn left four times, making the box that defined the flow of traffic before landing. We would climb to 1,000 feet, the clouds practically on top of us, and then descend to the runway, performing touch-and-go's, following each landing with an immediate takeoff run. I was doing all the flying. After I repeated the procedure eight times, Mark instructed me to land the airplane, then taxi back toward the runway.

Once we were stopped, my instructor did something that made me extremely uncomfortable: He got out of the plane. "Now just do the same thing again, Dan. Then come back and pick me up. Okay?"

This was the moment I had been nervously anticipating, but I didn't think it would come so suddenly. Not today, after only nine hours of practice. Surely he really didn't think I was ready to go solo.

"Are you sure?" I asked.

"Sure, I'm sure. I haven't lost a student yet. Don't screw up my record."

His confidence in me was reassuring, in a way. He thought I was ready. And at that moment, so did I. I pushed the throttle, guiding the plane toward the runway. I radioed the tower, requesting permission to take off. "Gwinnett tower, Cessna six seven three one eight ready for immediate departure, runway seven."

"Six seven three one eight, you are clear for takeoff."

That cinched it. Even the guy in the tower thought I was ready to solo. So I taxied the plane onto the runway and followed the routine we had practiced, all the while talking to myself. Wearing a microphone and headset allows you to speak and hear your own voice amplified. The words are only broadcast when you push the button. To me, this version of an amplified pep talk was useful, and the words flowed spontaneously.

"Okay, Dan, you're going to fly a plane today," I said to myself. "You know how to do it. Let's get going now. Push the throttle. Oh, yeah, that sounds good. Hold the centerline. Watch your airspeed. Oil pressure okay. Relax . . . Yeah, right! Speed's increasing. Approaching sixty knots. Begin to rotate, pull back . . . and . . . we're off the ground!"

It was at this moment that I realized a third and final level of commitment. The instant the wheels left the runway, my first thought was, *Why did you do that? There's no way out of this now.* Then the realization hit me. *Now I* must *follow through with this goal. It's a matter of life and death. There is no turning back.* Suddenly, all my senses were peaking, and I found a warehouse of new motivation to succeed. So I kept talking, only now the talking unconsciously became more like singing.

"I'm flying a plane . . . flying a plane! It's hard to believe, but I'm flying a plane. Climbing to five hundred feet. Time to turn . . . Here we go. Make the call." Then I composed myself and, in my best pilot's voice, broadcast to the tower.

"Gwinnett tower, six seven three one eight turning left crosswind runway seven." Climbing and singing, I reached pattern altitude, just below the clouds. Another call. "Gwinnett tower, six seven three one eight turning left downwind runway seven."

The airport was laid out perfectly just outside my window. The proximity looked right. I had gauged my turn to be the appropriate distance from the runway: not too close, not too far. I kept an eye out for traffic as my plane drew parallel to the spot where I hoped to land. Just two more turns. A little more singing.

"Carb heat out. Throttle back to seventeen hundred rpm," I said to myself. "Looking good . . . now some flaps. Ten degrees . . . Here we go."

The increased flaps and reduction of speed started my descent, and after a few eternal seconds, it was time to turn again.

"Gwinnett tower, six seven three one eight turning left base, runway seven."

"Add more flaps. Twenty degrees now. I am coming down, down,

Flying high—a spontaneous celebration of the successful first solo flight

down. Keep the airspeed up," I murmured. Out my window, I could see my runway alignment. It was time for my last turn.

"Gwinnett tower, six seven three one eight turning final, runway seven."

And I did. Watching the runway lights that serve as a guide, I could judge that my approach path was slightly high. "Add flaps. Thirty degrees. And let that nose come down," I cautioned myself. The lights turned from both white to white and red, indicating I had fixed my angle of descent. The next moments seemed like slow motion as I glided down toward the ground. "Watch your speed. Keep it down the middle . . . Get ready to level out above the runway, right about . . . now," I instructed myself.

The plane remained above the ground for a few more seconds, then lost the speed and the will to fly. I eased down to the runway and heard that wonderful squeak of rubber on asphalt. I had done it! I had followed through on my promises to my instructor and myself. What a relief. What a moment. I taxied the plane around to Mark, who was watching with a big smile on his face. I opened his door so he could climb in to complete the lesson and I could take him back to the flight school.

"That was great," he said. "Few people ever have the experience of flying solo. And today you did. Now do it again. Then come back and pick me up." He closed the door. My lesson was not over.

I did three more takeoffs and landings. They came out even. Each time I expected the lesson would end, but Mark would ask for one more run. Each landing became easier and more fun. The singing continued, but the voice steadied a bit with repetition. My confidence grew. I am grateful for the way my teacher pushed me when he knew I was ready. He also knew how to keep me focused on just the next moment.

I learned a great lesson that day about commitments. I entered a new dimension of my life's narrative, a dimension that said that commitments come in stages. First comes mental commitment, which reveals your aspiration. Then the process moves to physical commitment, when you move beyond good intentions and take action. But, the final level of commitment is when there's no turning back. When the wheels leave the runway, the challenge comes clearly into focus, and new resources become available to you. Once you've pushed yourself to a new level of personal performance, you'll never be satisfied with the way you were.

The day of my first solo, I also learned a lot about myself. The knowledge was acquired, not simply through reflection or self-examination, but through action. As I write this book, my sincere hope is that as you prepare for your own personal takeoff, you will find the courage to commit completely to a new adventure. It is a voyage of self-discovery through action. The knowledge you gain will change the way you think, and *if* you make the commitment to follow through, you will forever be a different person.

Halfhearted attempts don't create lasting change. In fact, they often leave us further from our goal than when we started. That's because when we attempt something with partial commitment, it usually doesn't work. Then the experience of failing creates a higher mental hurdle and undermines all future attempts. We have, in a sense, demonstrated to ourselves that we cannot change, improve, grow. As a result, we resolve to avoid future attempts altogether, sometimes indefinitely.

You have started reading this book because you sense there is more to life than you are currently experiencing. And you are absolutely right. Your potential is infinite, and no matter where you are in your life situation, there is always an action you can take to improve. This book will help you stay focused on your intuitive understanding that you have a right to more joy, fulfillment, accomplishment, and satisfaction. Furthermore, it will guide you through a process to create lasting change, so you can get your wheels off the runway and soar.

At this moment, I am sure you have a wide variety of commitments in place. Some of these are at the first stage—you've made a decision that you would like to accomplish something, change something, or learn something new. You're sure about it, and you've even expressed it in writing or in conversation. That's fantastic, but it's just the beginning. In my life, for example, I've made the decision that I am going to learn to speak Spanish. I've written it down. I can see it becoming a reality. But I'm not doing anything significant to move that goal forward. This initiative is simply marking time at level one.

To reach level two, I could begin to take action. I've done that in the past to small degrees. I've taken a night class at a local school. I've listened to instructional tapes. And from time to time I watch the *telenovelas,* the soap operas on the Spanish TV station, for a few minutes to see if I understand anything they are saying. I still have no clue. Those previous attempts were ways to test the water and confirm that the goal appeals to me. It does, and I really do want to learn. I would love to be able to communicate with the increasing number of Spanish-speaking people I encounter. That's the key. I want it, but so far I've been unwilling to take meaningful action and reach the third level of commitment.

I think that the only way to learn a new language is to commit completely, to the point that there is no turning back. Take my friend Jill Steinberg, who, after graduating from college, decided she wanted to learn Spanish. What did she do? Jill moved to Spain. Her intentions were to teach English while learning the language. Unlike my halfhearted wish to learn Spanish, her action was compelling. As a result, Jill is now fluent in Spanish, while I am as monolingual as ever.

It is unlikely that I will move to Spain anytime soon. So what other actions could I take that would elevate my commitment? Here are some options:

- Take an extended vacation to Mexico.
- Enroll in a "total immersion" learning program.
- Take a speaking engagement six months from now that requires me to deliver a part of my program in Spanish.
- Adopt a Spanish-speaking child (or become a Big Brother).
- Become involved in the Spanish-speaking community with volunteer work.

You can easily see that these actions are quite different from buying Spanish tapes or taking the occasional night class. By recognizing that this kind of commitment is what it will take to accomplish my goal, I can prepare myself accordingly. Right now might not be the optimum time to start, but if I want it bad enough, I will recognize when the timing is right, and I will know the right opportunity when it appears in my life.

How do you increase your commitment? While every situation and every person is unique, here are three specific methods that may prompt you to action.

1. Make a promise to someone you respect. Sometimes it is easier to keep the commitments we make to other people than the ones we make to ourselves. Because of our constant internal dialogue, we can easily dismiss what we tell ourselves as unimportant or just part of the "chatter" of our thinking. By downplaying the importance of our self-talk, we give ourselves a convenient excuse to postpone action, even though we know it will bring us long-term happiness and enjoyment. So pick someone who means a lot to you and confide in them that you are going to take action. Explain why this is important for you to do now, at this point in your life. Ask for help. Tell them that from this point forward, you are a different person. There is no turning back; however, you may need their support and encouragement to stay the course.

As a performer, this is the same approach I often take when attempting difficult stunts onstage. Since I was twelve years old, I've been a professional juggler, acrobat, and unicyclist. To this day I incorporate all those skills in my high-energy motivational programs. But in every presentation, I attempt to push the limits of what I can do physically. In one of my keynote presentations I begin my talk by describing the power of action, and I pose a "hypothetical" scenario. I ask the audience, "What if instead of talking about action, I started out today by demonstrating the power of action? Imagine if, after the introduction, I came running up the side steps and threw my body into a tumbling run, performing a round-off, back handspring, back tuck, landing here, ready to begin." Many are intrigued at this point, especially since I am usually wearing a business suit, but few anticipate the next move. To drive home the point and provide the visual and emotional amplification of the message, I perform the routine, exactly as described.

Of course, this makes for an effective opener. The audience is astonished, intrigued, and curious about what I'm going to do next. But the real point is that for me this takes a tremendous commitment (especially as I get older). Despite the fact that I've done it hundreds of times before, it is always a tense moment. The way I achieve the necessary level of commitment is to promise to perform it, onstage, in front of a lot of people. Then, after all, there is no turning back.

2. Invest time or money in your new endeavor. "I'd like to buy a guitar today," I told the salesman. He suggested that I try out several models, listen to the different tones, and select the one I liked the most. There was only one problem with this approach: I didn't know how to play one, not even the basic chords. But this was the day I decided to move my goal (learn to play a musical instrument) from level one to level two. In the end I had the salesman, who did know how to play, perform for me. He played the same song on five different models, and I selected my new instrument. I walked out of that store with a new level of commitment and an appointment to start lessons.

With this same approach, I upped my commitment to becoming a professional speaker by joining the National Speakers Association—before I had even attended the first meeting. At the time I was an entertainer with a good show and a desire to deliver a greater message. But when I met Shep Hyken, a terrific speaker and magician, he challenged me to follow through on my aspiration to make the transition from entertainer to speaker. Shep told me that NSA was the place to learn quickly. So I joined over the phone and showed up at my first meeting, already a member. It took a while before I realized that this was an unusual approach. Typically, people come to a few meetings to get a feel for the organization and meet people; then they contemplate the future, weigh the potential benefits, and finally decide whether to make the investment. Not me—I just joined. After doing so, I quickly assimilated into the organization, presented to the group, and was selected to represent our chapter at the national convention, all of this in the span of two months.

In college, my roommates, Jon and Eric, and I decided to take a scuba course during the summer session. The eight-week class was taught by Donovan Connely, a bear of a man with a big, bushy mustache. We had spent the first three weeks in the classroom learning the wide variety of ways in which one could meet one's end while practicing this sport, including drowning, aeroembolism, dangerous sea creatures, and the excruciating decompression sickness known a "the bends." Needless to say, we all looked forward to getting past this phase and into the water, where the fun part of the training would begin. The first day in the pool, however, was the infamous swim test. This involved treading water for fifteen minutes, swimming the width of the pool underwater, demonstrating several different swimming techniques, and, after all that, a freestyle endurance swim, traversing the pool twenty times. I failed the last trial and left, humbled and defeated. I would have one more attempt the following week. If I could not complete the test, I would be forced to drop the class and would miss the culmination of our training, the checkout dive in the Florida Keys. Both Jon and Eric had passed with flying colors, so I was faced with a decision: Would I increase my commitment or acquiesce to defeat? In response, I immediately went out and purchased all my scuba gear, including mask, snorkel, fins, weight belt, and a pair of swimming goggles. I spent each afternoon that week in the pool, building my strength and confidence. Because of this investment of money and time, and Jon and Eric's poolside cheerleading, I did succeed the next week (just barely) and went on to complete my certification.

3. Burn your boats. In 1519 the Spanish Conquistador Hernán Cortés led his men to newly discovered Mexico. This explorer had the wild ambition to conquer the powerful Aztec empire and claim the territory for Spain. Upon landing near the present-day site of Vera Cruz on April 21, he did something his men did not expect: Cortez ordered them to burn their ships. The soldiers were stunned but obedient. I can only imagine the emotions they experienced while watching their vessels go up in flames, destroying any possibility of an escape route. Needless to say, they found a new level of commitment. At that point, the only way to get back to Spain was to conquer the Aztecs! A little more than two years later, after numerous battles, setbacks, and losses, victory was finally complete when the emperor Cuauhtemoc surrendered, and the Aztec empire was no more.

How can you apply this same principle to step up your commitment? Simply put, burn your boats. Remove the escape route that will safely carry you back to where you were before. If where you are is unacceptable, what bold action can you take now that will force you to go forward?

When I started my speaking career, I had a comfortable business doing entertainment for conventions and trade shows. And everyone who hired me saw me in that light, as a comedy juggler, not a speaker. One day I realized I needed to take a bold action, and I decided to start refusing jobs for entertainment, announcing to the world that I was now a full-time professional speaker. Was this a risk? Absolutely. Performing juggling shows was how I made my living. But once I burned that boat, I became increasingly committed to succeeding as a speaker. And that bold action convinced those around me that I was serious about accomplishing my mission.

The Third Level of Commitment

What does the third level of commitment look like? Well, here are a few fun examples. The third level of commitment to:

> Deciding to get married is . . . saying "I do."
> Deciding to become a parent is . . . becoming pregnant.
> Taking a vacation is . . . boarding the airplane.
> Writing a book is . . . sending the manuscript to the publisher.
> Buying a house is . . . signing the documents at closing.
> Improving your speaking skills is . . . getting up in front of an audience.

If you wait until you remove all risk, you may never take action. I am not suggesting that you quit your job today and start a business without any kind of plan. Planning is critical, and that subject will be covered in depth in chapter four. I am suggesting that many people spend their lives preparing to take action, and because they never feel completely prepared, they never discover their true talents and capabilities. As you read this book, I would like you to make a commitment to implement the ideas you learn, and experience *success in action*. You may be wondering what I mean by that, so let's define it.

> ***Success in Action:* A proactive approach to life; a method for personal and professional growth that promotes attaining your goals by embodying them from the outset; learning by doing; leading and inspiring others with your actions.**

Success in Action is a way of being and doing that keeps you engaged and focused on what's important. It's an action orientation that gives you power to more effectively manage your internal and external life, enabling you to take control and take responsibility for your success as *you* define it. Such a mindset will affect not just you but all the people you touch. Remember, life is not what happens to you each day—it's what *you make it*.

It's not what you know but what you *do* with what you know that has the power to transform your life. Most people already have some idea of what they should do, and yet, for various reasons, they don't follow through. They fail to take action in a way that creates long-lasting success. I want to help you bridge the gap between what you know and what you do, empowering yourself to custom-build a life rich with achievement, rewards, and fulfillment.

By adopting this orientation, you will experience internal rewards: less stress and better health, as well as greater joy, meaning, and purpose in your life. Happily, this means you will also reap external rewards: achievements and accomplishments in your personal and professional life. Sound too good to be true? Read on! I truly believe that you can have it all, and that you deserve to be a *complete* success.

To some people, success is a reflection of how much they earn. To others, it's all about how much they are able to help other people. Some measure success by their social status; others, by maintaining a certain state of health or fitness.

The success I am talking about, though, is multidimensional. It is a state of being, a *complete* success, spanning the five most vital areas of life: your work, health, relationships, spiritual growth, and personal interests, all wrapped into one exquisite work of art called "your life." This means transcending the ordinary, finding

Your Life Pattern—
Illustration by Tony Brischler

balance, and achieving breakthroughs, not just in this or that area but right across the board. To do this, like an expert juggler, you have to look up and see the big picture.

Remember, life isn't just sitting there, posing quietly while you study it from all angles. It is fluid, constantly shifting and changing, all-encompassing. We cannot pursue happiness by focusing exclusively on one or two of the five spheres in the illustration on the previous page. Do that and they all come tumbling down. True satisfaction and life enjoyment can only come from making forward progress in *all* these areas. It's a question of balance, and so important that I've devoted the final chapter of this book exclusively to that subject.

If you feel as though you are pursuing a number of disjointed, unrelated objectives simultaneously, you will quickly find those objectives at odds with one another, and you'll become overwhelmed. The only way to find peace and contentment in your life is to see that all your goals are interrelated, all taking you to the same place. Think of your life as a pattern of simultaneous actions, with each of your spheres moving in mutually supportive harmony with the others.

I began my entrepreneurial career at the age of twelve, as a professional juggler. The practice and performance of juggling enabled me to start a business, pay for my college education, meet my wife, and travel to hundreds of interesting places. But more important, it taught me the mindset for handling many tasks simultaneously. The key to juggling is that you never look down at your hands. You must always look up. The idea is to synthesize all the objects in a way that enables success. Instead of focusing singly on each throw and each catch (a strategy that will bring instant failure), you expand your focus to see the pattern of how all the objects fit together.

When I first learned how to juggle three balls, I was ecstatic. I was so excited that almost immediately after achieving modest success, I tried juggling four, with no success whatsoever. The failure came from trying to juggle the four balls using the very same pattern I had learned for three. Balls repeatedly crashed into one another and caromed off in every direction. When I asked my mentor what I was doing wrong, he gave me some profound advice: "When you add the fourth ball, you need to learn a new pattern. The addition of one more ball changes everything."

Seeing the pattern—a breakthrough moment at eleven years old

When we add something new to our lives—a goal, responsibility, hobby, relationship, or whatever it may be—we are not just "piling it on" our present pattern. The addition of even one new element changes the entire design. When you take an idea from this book and implement it in your life, it will send out ripples that affect your relationships, work, health, spiritual growth, and personal interests. That is as it should be. I believe you have the capacity to grow in all these critical life areas simultaneously.

None of us will ever reach our ultimate potential, for the simple reason that human potential is infinite. But, you can make progress every day. The process of pursuing success in all areas of life will create both internal and external rewards. So let's get started. Are you ready to commit to a new level? Good, because you've just been cleared for takeoff!

Action Assignments

1. Consider a specific change you would like to implement in your life, or a result you would like to achieve. Identify one action you can take to move that ambition from the first level of commitment to the second level—then do it!

2. Now consider the third level of commitment, from which there will be no turning back. What action will get your wheels off the runway and engage your complete determination? What new levels of motivation do you think you will experience?

3. Which of the three strategies presented for increasing your commitment do you think will work best for you? Why? What would it look like if you used one or a combination of these techniques to give yourself a jump start toward your goal?

4. Do you believe that achieving *complete success* is possible? Is it desirable? Is this a goal worth pursuing?

HARNESS YOUR THOUGHT POWER

To thine own self be true.

—William Shakespeare

It is impossible to act in a manner inconsistent with your thinking.

—Dan Thurmon

A s we have already established, success in life is determined not by your circumstances but by your actions. But then, where do your actions come from? Every action is a result of a preceding thought. If you are able to manage your thinking in a constructive way, then you can manifest your desired actions and results with greater consistency and success. Not only that, but—and this is one of the most valuable secrets you will ever learn—it is actually *impossible* to act in a manner inconsistent with what you are thinking. That may at first sound like an outrageous claim, but if you examine and test the statement, you'll find it completely accurate—every time, in any situation. If you are trying to accomplish something while thinking contradictory thoughts, you may as well try to levitate by pulling upward on the chair you are sitting on. You are literally trying to pull off an impossible feat, setting yourself up for frustration and failure. Remarkably, the opposite is also true. If you flood your mind with images of your success, it becomes impossible to act as if you will fail. I'm not saying it's impossible to fail. Setbacks are, of course, a part of life and growth. But when you are acting *as if* you are already successful, your actions will support that reality, and you will enjoy a much greater likelihood of manifesting the results you desire.

This chapter is about using the unbelievable power of your thoughts to fuel your actions. The aim is twofold: First, I intend for you to validate yourself as the unique, awesome individual you are, fully able to hone, and to trust, your original thoughts. By honoring your own ideas and expressing yourself, you tap into your greatest asset and the reservoir of your personal power. Second, I want you to understand that you always have a choice between positive and negative thinking. By cultivating the habit of honoring your individuality while at the same time consistently choosing a positive focus, you will greatly enhance your odds of achieving what you want in life.

Think for Yourself

No one else on earth thinks exactly the way you do. You are an absolute original. This is evidenced not only by your appearance but also by your personality, your "take" on things, and the sum total of your life experience. Each of these aspects of you has infinite value because each is one of a kind. Not another soul has what you have, nor can he or she acquire it at any price. Your uniqueness is a tremendous treasure you already own, and its worth only increases with use.

Both my children, Eddie and Maggie, are bundles of action. They know themselves. They act like themselves every day. They constantly match their actions with their individuality. Like children all over the world, they have no problem being themselves.

Allen Funt, the originator of *Candid Camera*, loved to catch people being themselves. He particularly enjoyed learning from children. "Children are beautiful," he said. "They're so original, so independent.

They're everything you wish adults were. But adults are constantly hard-minded, conforming and subject to bowing to group pressure. They're moving away from individualism toward the herd."

To prove his point, Funt contrasts two clips from *Candid Camera* episodes. One clip shows a man in a department store walking *up* a *down* escalator. He is followed by another customer, who also walks up the down escalator. A few moments later a woman follows suit. Several more customers mindlessly do the same thing a short while later.

The second clip captures children's behavior. I'll let Allen Funt tell the story:

"A child walks up to a large, empty box. He inspects it carefully, decides it's a fortress. He gets into it and shoots away at an imaginary enemy. Another child strolls up to the box the previous child is vacating. She decides it's a house, gets into it and plays grown-up. A third child sees her antics and approaches the same box. But he decides it's a roller coaster and gleefully slides it down a nearby incline."

As these video clips show, too many adults fail to take advantage of opportunities to express their true nature. Children, though, have absolutely no difficulty being themselves. Expressing your own uniqueness and individuality is your birthright, and when you start giving yourself permission to cultivate your own personality, you begin again to experience the wonder that is you.

This striving for self-awareness and individuality is our natural calling. According to the ground-breaking Swiss psychologist Carl Jung, it is our journey toward individuation. Mother Teresa believed it was our God-given nature. Explorer and adventurer John Goddard called it our *"natural self."* For many people, the quest for self-knowledge becomes a lifelong search. A fortunate few "find themselves" early on in their quest for selfhood, while most get so preoccupied, they forget to look, letting life just pass them by. But this gnawing hunger to know ourselves is very much a part of who we are—it's *supposed* to be there.

Part of that self-discovery process begins with taking a look at ourselves: our strengths and weaknesses, beliefs and attitudes, perceptions and behaviors. Self-examination is not an easy process, but it is a necessary one if we want to live the full, creative life we are meant to live. Many of us fail to recognize our own incredible worth and spend years, or even a lifetime, searching for something we already possess—our own uniqueness.

Taking stock of ourselves is something we need to do on a regular basis. "Ninety percent of the world's woes," says Sydney Harris, "comes from people not knowing themselves, their abilities, their frailties and their virtues." Moreover, he says, "Most of us go through life as complete strangers to ourselves."

At some point in our lives we all have been tempted to be something or someone we're not. When Charlie Chaplin first started making films, the film director insisted that the young actor imitate a popular German comedian of the day. Unfortunately, Chaplin took his advice and spent years trying to be something he wasn't. Finally he decided to imitate himself, and became one of silent film's mega-stars. Robin Williams, Carl Lewis, Oprah Winfrey, and Michelle Kwan had similar experiences before they discovered themselves and became their own models.

When the renowned psychologist William James declared that the average person develops only ten percent of his or her latent mental abilities, he was speaking of the majority, the millions of people who have never truly found themselves. I can tell you from personal experience that the only way you will ever be successful is by being successfully *you* first. There's no one else quite like you. Never before, since the beginning of time, has there been someone of your stature, ability, and potential. And never again, throughout the ages to come, will there be another quite like you.

Think Positive

Take a closer look at the kinds of thoughts that cross your mind each day. Psychologists estimate that during the course of a day a typical person averages over 62,000 conceptualizations. That's a little over 2,583 thoughts per hour. I don't know how anyone can calculate such a stampede of thoughts, but the study does show that our mental operations are continuous.

Most people, though, don't think much about the *kinds* of thoughts that power their day. They don't fully appreciate the amount of internal dialogue that hums constantly through their brains. Unfortunately, most of the mental chatter is negative, because the majority of us grow up in negative environments. Our home, school, and religious environments are built on negative messages such as "No, you can't do that," "You shouldn't wear this," "You mustn't go there," or "You're not old enough." Our work environments reinforce that pessimism by hammering negative messages at us: "Don't rock the boat," and "No one has ever done that before," and "That will never work here." Add the influences of negative messages and depictions portrayed in our news media. Even our "entertainment" often includes violent story lines, frightening images, and sarcastic humor. With such a constant barrage of negativity, it's no wonder we fall into the trap of negative thinking. It takes a conscious effort and considerable discipline to command your mind to do otherwise.

While negative perspectives serve an important role in steering us away from danger, their misuse or overemphasis can limit our growth and happiness. Negative thinkers look for negative outcomes, create negative outcomes, and reinforce negative outcomes. If our constant parade of thoughts is mostly negative, our actions will follow suit. Until we learn to monitor and censor our negative thoughts, we will miss valuable opportunities at work, lose quality time with our family, and contaminate free time with negative expectations. "Argue for your limitations," says Richard Bach in his book *Illusions,* "and sure enough they're yours."

Take a few moments right now to answer the following questions:

- Which do I have more of: negative thoughts or positive thoughts?
- Are most of my negative thoughts about my talents and abilities? My work? My kids? The economy? The way I look?
- How often do I say, "I can't," or "I'm not good enough?"

If you found yourself admitting that you've had more than your share of negative thoughts, you're in good company. As they say, awareness of the problem is half the battle, and after reading this chapter you will be able to limit your negative thoughts about yourself and about others as well. Your thoughts are so powerful, they underwrite your success or failure.

The great Roman emperor and philosopher Marcus Aurelius summed it up in eight words that still hold true today: "Our life is what our thoughts make it." If we think happy thoughts, chances are, we'll find happiness. If we think positive thoughts, we'll see things from a positive perspective. If we doubt our abilities, we'll get plenty of opportunities to reinforce that perception, too. You are not, to paraphrase Norman Vincent Peale, "what you think you are, but what you *think*—you *are!*"

Let's take a closer look at the power of our thoughts, especially of repetitious thinking. I am convinced that our peace of mind, our ability to achieve, and the joy we get out of living depend not so much on what we are, where we are, or what we have done, but on what we think about during each day. For those of you who may think this borders on "Pollyanna" thinking, I believe you'll change your mind when you read the fascinating research about the grooves of success—or failure—caused by the sheer wattage of our thought power.

Grooves of Success

> *People will do anything, no matter how absurd, in order to avoid facing their own souls. They will practice yoga . . . observe a strict regimen of diet, learn theosophy by heart, or mechanically repeat mystic texts . . . all because they cannot get on with themselves and have not the slightest faith that anything useful could ever come out of their own souls.*
>
> —Carl Jung

No matter how intelligent, attractive, wealthy, or talented you are, if you do not feel good about yourself or think well of yourself, you will find it difficult, in Jung's words, to "get on with yourself." Thinking positively about yourself is critical to your success and is the only way you will ever achieve success in action.

Regardless of how you define success, what you think leaves a powerful impression on your consciousness. When certain thoughts, attitudes, and beliefs are repeated often enough, they can literally change the way you see the world. Your success in life is determined not by the circumstances in which you find yourself but by your actions, which in turn result from your thinking. I'm going to share some extraordinary research that has revolutionized our understanding of the relationship between what we think and what we become. The studies have been replicated hundreds of times all over the world and have proved to be reliable and definitive.

The landmark study was conducted at the University of Pennsylvania by physicist David Bohm, who proved conclusively that thoughts that are repeated often enough and strongly enough, with emotional weight, leave *grooves* in our gray matter. Sounds incredible, doesn't it? Here's how he describes the process:

> *When experiments are conducted using radioactive tracers to see what happens in the brain itself, every idea, every feeling creates a radical redistribution of the blood in the brain. Once you bring blood into a certain pathway all the time, you grow more cells in the affected area, and less cells somewhere else. With repeated strong, intense thoughts, the brain's synapses get very fixed, and create grooves in the brain's neuropathways.*

Bohm's study proves that we can change the very physiology of our brains by focusing our thoughts in a concentrated direction. We quite literally have the power to program *grooves of success* in our brains. We can make it happen just by thinking about it. And we can prevent it from happening just as convincingly.

Our thoughts have an almost unbelievable effect on our physical powers, too. The renowned British psychiatrist J. A. Hadfield reports a striking illustration of the power of the mind over the body in experiments based on mental suggestion. He asked his subjects to test the effects of mental suggestion on their physical strength, which was measured by gripping a dynamometer. He tested their strength under three sets of conditions:

1. Under normal waking conditions, their average grip measured 101 pounds.
2. After he hypnotized them and told them that they were very weak, the average grip was less than 30 pounds.

3. He hypnotized the subjects again and told them they were very strong, filling their minds with positive thoughts of their Herculean strength. The average grip was now 144 pounds—the subjects' physical strength had increased by nearly half.

Hypnotic "grooves," it appears, work just as effectively as repetitive grooves. Thought power becomes physical power when we honor both thought and action. Years ago I read a thought-provoking book that had a profound effect on my life. It is titled *Illusions*, by Richard Bach. In it he said, "You are led through your lifetime by the inner learning creature, the playful spiritual being that is your real self . . . All learning is finding out what you already know. Doing is demonstrating that you know it . . . you're always free to change your mind and choose a different future, or a different past."

If Bach is right, and I believe he is, we are the architects of our future. Our thoughts drive our actions, and our actions determine our future.

It is interesting to note that while thoughts create action, actions create thoughts as well. You can prove it to yourself right now. Put a big, broad grin on your face. Now let your grin curtsy into a playful smile. Extend your smile into uproarious laughter. Go ahead, do it—no one's going to lock you up. Even if you have to force it, it is important that you allow yourself a good belly laugh.

It is absolutely, positively physically impossible to remain blue, bored, or depressed while you are *acting out* the symptoms of being ridiculously happy and contented. Your actions—smiles, grins, and then laughter—changed your thoughts and feelings and created a positive environment filled with the sights and sounds of happiness. I don't know how you felt immediately before your "laughter fit," but I'll bet you feel a little more relaxed and happier now. If you were in earshot of others, you probably caused some curiosity and smiles around you as well. And that's another thing: Our actions also shape the environment of others. You'll read more about that in the next chapter.

Although this laughter exercise was contrived, your body didn't know the difference. The physiological effects of your "self-inflicted" laughter produced the same therapeutic benefits that would have occurred if you had enjoyed a good laugh under less contrived circumstances.

Endocrinologists have measured the effects of laughter on our immune system. Laughter is connected to our neurology and elevates the immune system. Norman Cousins' best-selling book *Anatomy of An Illness* certainly opened many people's eyes to the notion that "people who laugh, last." William Fry Jr., MD, who has researched the physiology of laughter for over forty years, lends support to Cousins' belief that laughter is like "internal jogging." Laughter enhances respiration and circulation, oxygenates the blood, suppresses the stress-related hormones in the brain, and activates the immune system.

So laugh it up! It's one of the best health insurance policies you can have. Fortify your health and energize your day by lifting the corners of your mouth frequently. You'll increase your health quotient by a few decibels with a hearty laugh. Practice laughing at the minor irritations that come your way, at some of the things people say, at the delays caused by inclement weather or slow traffic signals, at the petty differences between people's viewpoints, and especially at yourself. Actress Ethel Barrymore said, "You grow up the day you have your first real laugh at yourself."

Let's take a quick "laugh meter" test. How often do you laugh? How many times during the course of a normal day are you able to rear your head back and enjoy a lengthy belly laugh? Wherever you fell on the "laugh meter," make an effort to double it in the next thirty days. I highly recommend that you begin a campaign to create "laughter grooves" along your daily path. Laughter is one of the chief ingredients of *success in action,* and it's contagious. I hope you'll catch it.

Suspend Your Disbelief

Right about now I can almost sense some of you beginning to doubt the practicality of this advice. Even in the midst of a chapter about positive thinking, the negative thoughts creep in to sabotage your transformation. They sound like this:

- "Nobody can be positive all the time."
- "I just can't do it—it's too silly."
- "The world is such a negative place. Does he expect me just to ignore it?"

- "Part of my originality *is* my negative thinking and sarcasm. People *expect* it from me."

All of us have negative thoughts that invade our minds. That is completely normal, and there is nothing pathological or "wrong" with it. What is destructive, though, is allowing these thoughts to take up permanent residence or go unrecognized. When we experience a negative result, we can usually trace it back to a negative thought. At that point, the solution is not to do battle with the negative representation or seek to destroy it and banish it from our thinking. That's a bit like telling yourself, "Don't think about a white elephant." I suggest a gentler, more effective method for dealing with the demons of negativity: Suspend your disbelief.

Recall a movie that you thoroughly enjoyed. This film had you *completely* captivated. You sat down and gave yourself absolutely to the story line, images, characters, and all the implausible events that took place. In the theatrical world, this is called the audience's "suspension of disbelief." It is a decision, whether conscious or unconscious, to surrender to the experience and go with it, adopting the mindset, "What if this really happened?" This is a technique you can use to defuse negativity in your own life. Instead of combating your fears or self-doubt, grappling and struggling (mostly unsuccessfully) to overcome them, just suspend your disbelief temporarily, and circumvent the negativity with what-ifs:

- "What if I could be more positive more often?"
- "What if I could learn this new skill?"
- "What if the world were a positive place?"
- "What if my true nature were to be more positive and helpful to others?"

For the past two years, I have dedicated several days each month to work as a trainer for Cirque du Soleil's youth outreach program in Atlanta. Perhaps you have experienced the magic of this one-of-a-kind theatrical experience. Cirque du Soleil's performances combine circus with theater, high-tech lighting, elaborate stages, ingenious story lines, and enchanting, innovative music. In 2004, The founder of this troupe,

Guy Laliberte, became one of the world's newest billionaires because of the tremendous success of his productions. What you may not know is that Cirque du Soleil is a company with a high moral conscience, and that it dedicates a significant part of its resources and profits to helping others, particularly "at risk" youth. The founders of Cirque were themselves street kids. They rose from very humble beginnings, and they never forgot their roots. The program is called Cirque du Monde, which is French for "Circus of the World." Cirque du Monde programs span the globe, including Brazil, Canada, Germany, Great Britain, the United States, and even Mongolia. As one of the Atlanta trainers, I have the opportunity to work with teenagers who have been abused, neglected, or otherwise damaged by negative circumstances. We teach them circus skills, including juggling, trapeze, unicycling, clowning, and gymnastics. But what we really teach is self-confidence and trust. It is amazing, rewarding work.

Recently at a Cirque du Monde session, I was working with a fifteen-year-old boy who excelled at many of the skills. Yet for some reason, he had not learned to juggle. Let's call him "Chance." I approached Chance and said, "How about learning to juggle today?"

"Nah, that's okay," he replied, seemingly uninterested. But I heard more in his answer than mere indifference.

"Why not, Chance?" I asked.

"I can't do it."

"Not with that attitude, you can't!" His honest acknowledgment of his self-doubt gave me the perfect intro. I explained that it is impossible to act in a manner inconsistent with your thinking.

"If you've tried it in the past while you were telling yourself you couldn't, you were trying something impossible. Now, if you would like to learn, I know I can teach you, but first you have to change your thinking. What if you could learn to juggle today? Do you think that's possible?"

He agreed that it was, in fact, possible, so I asked him to suspend his disbelief for a while and just focus on the possibility of learning today. Within minutes, Chance was juggling. His transformation and excitement were heartwarming, but the real payoff would not come for three more weeks.

At the end of each ten-week session, we stage a performance for the counselors, supporters, and other students at the facility. Chance had not only mastered the juggling, but had learned to perform it while standing atop a rolling globe. He stole the show. Afterward, the trainers and students were watching a videotape of the performance as they shared in the celebration. When Chance's routine came up, he watched with pride, then turned to another student and said, "You see that right there? That is a perfect example of why you should never tell yourself you can't do something. I was so sure I couldn't juggle, but Mr. Dan said I could, and he changed my mind about it."

He had become the teacher and encourager. He was passing the message on to another. I was speechless and extremely gratified, praying that the message would help him overcome other challenges down the road.

You Can If You Think You Can

> *All achievement is largely the product of steadily*
> *raising one's levels of aspiration and expectation.*
> —Jack Nicklaus

I have built my life's work on the premise that although beliefs, values, attitudes, and good intentions all are important ingredients to anyone's success, it is the actions we take that ultimately determine our success or failure. You can have all the money, talent, good looks, and education in the world, but unless you use them by taking wise and prudent actions, you will never accomplish the goals you have set for yourself. You don't have to look hard for examples that prove this truth—just pick up a newspaper or turn on the TV.

This is probably not the first book you've read on success, goals, happiness, and achievement. Your local bookstore has rows and rows of titles on the subject. However, if you've read this far, I believe you're searching for that missing ingredient, that magic elixir, that will help make your dreams come true. If that is your reason for choosing this book, I believe with all my heart that you will be able to appreciate what I am about to say: The only thing—the *only* thing—that stands between you and the success you want is *you*. So get out of your own way! Take that all-important step, and you're truly on your way.

This philosophy is characterized by one of my favorite people, the explorer John Goddard. His story is so extraordinary that I've included a brief sketch of his exploits in chapter four, *Ready, Set, Goals!* The chapter is on—you guessed it—goal setting. I've been so impressed with John's accomplishments and his famous goals list that I've written a similar list for myself. I can attribute my private pilot's license certification, musical abilities, skydiving and scuba diving experiences, business pursuits (including writing this book), acting and dance training, travel, adventure, hiking, and mountain biking interests to his influence. I have been able to accomplish many of the goals I commit to and write down, but the list keeps growing all the time.

One of my greatest delights in life is to help people see that their success is determined by actions, not circumstances. And when their actions are fueled by "can do" thinking, the chances for success skyrocket. People with a can-do mindset think and speak positively. They use action words to describe their goals, their circumstances, and themselves:

> *I can* meet any challenge with poise and confidence.
> *I can* find the perfect career and excel in it.
> *I can* be successful at anything I want to do.

Joel Weldon, one of the most respected seminar leaders in the National Speakers Association, has been a prophet of the can-do philosophy for many years. His unique business card is a heavy eight-ounce can with a label that reads, "Success Comes in Cans, Not Cannots." He says, "Success is harnessing your heart to a task you love. It is zeroing in on your goals and becoming absorbed by your work. It is putting your shoulder to the wheel of achievement . . . success comes in cans, not *cannots.*"

A good place to start is by taking a quick look at the four "I cans" below. Take a few minutes to complete each sentence with the emphasis on what you can accomplish. Keep your statements positive, and gear them to what you most want to make happen in your life. Write them down in the space below, on a separate sheet of paper, or in a journal or notebook. Don't wait, though. Do it right now, before reading on.

I can _____

I can _____

I can _____

I can _____

After you've completed these statements, keep them where you can refer to them from time to time. Monitor your progress. Prove to yourself that success comes in "cans."

Althea Gibson, a top American tennis star in the 1950s, wrote a book entitled, *I Always Wanted to Be Somebody*. She describes her view of success and her love for tennis:

> *I always wanted to be somebody. I guess that's why I kept running away from home when I was a kid even though I took some terrible whippings for it. It's why I took to tennis right away and kept working at it. I was the wildest tomboy you ever saw . . . and I was determined that I was going to be somebody.*

Althea's drive, determination, and confidence are defining characteristics for people who believe they can "make it happen." Tiger Woods believed he could be the best golfer in the world. Bill Gates thought he could create a technology empire. Fred Smith believed he could create overnight parcel post delivery. Howard Head wanted to revolutionize the two industries he loved most—skiing and tennis—so he invented the first metal ski and the most successful oversize tennis racket in history. Oprah Winfrey thought she could rule the talk show ratings. Ted Turner envisioned a twenty-four-hour media and news empire. And test pilot Michael Melvill believed he could pilot the first privately funded vehicle into outer space. How about you? If you suspend your disbelief for just a moment, what do you think you can accomplish?

Become Your Own Talent Scout

*When I stand before God at the end of my life, I hope
I won't have a single bit of talent left and will say,
"God, I used everything you gave me."*
—Erma Bombeck

Everyone has special talents, skills, and abilities. One person may have a real knack for public speaking, while someone else may be a whiz in math or science. One has extraordinary "people skills;" another has a fine singing voice. There will always be some people who can outjump, outclimb, outsell, outsave, outrun, or outthink others. The important thing is to discover your own talents and develop them to the best of your ability. Be your own talent scout—sign up for what you do best!

Some of us have special talents but discount them or take them for granted. I have found in my own life that it is most rewarding and personally satisfying to recognize, accept, and develop the talents and skills I have naturally, as well as the ones I acquire. Doing something well, whether it's writing or babysitting, painting a masterpiece or a garage door, takes patience, persistence, and hard work. In his book *No Ordinary Moments*, Dan Millman said that "natural talent is overrated—the successful professionals I know in the fields of athletics, acting, law, medicine and business attribute their success more to hard work than to natural talent."

I believe that raw talent coupled with hard work and responsible action is an unbeatable combination. You can have all the talent in the world, but you've got to apply it, or it's the same as not having it. Sometimes becoming your own motivator, your own talent scout, is the result of a major life challenge. The obstacles we encounter, the disabilities we incur, and the disappointments we suffer cause us to discover talents and abilities we never knew existed.

Michelangelo carved his famous statue *David* from an imperfect block of marble. Other sculptors, at one time or another, had begun work on the massive block and then abandoned it when they discovered that it had a serious flaw. A deep gash in one side had made the stone unacceptable to sculptors for decades. Michelangelo, however, saw something in the marble that no one else had seen. He accepted the block, flaws and all, and created a masterpiece.

Bing Crosby exposed his big ears without apology. Barbra Streisand refused to have surgery on her nose. Mel Tillis began singing to hide his stutter. Actor James Earl Jones has always been painfully shy, as well as a stutterer. In a *Los Angeles Times* article, responding to an interviewer's question about his stuttering, he described how people overcome apparent disabilities through sheer willpower:

> *My voice is a gift that often doesn't work. I still have difficulty getting thoughts out, so my goal is to say something with clarity. I left the church at the age of 14 because I couldn't do Sunday School recitation without the kids laughing . . . but I persevered . . . I wasn't going to let speaking be a disability . . . The great Olympic runner, Wilma Rudolph, had serious leg problems, (dancer) Gwen Verdon had rickets as a child. Demosthenes put pebbles in his mouth and became a great orator. If you acknowledge a weakness and overcome it, it can define your life.*

James Earl Jones could just as easily have decided to define himself as a stutterer and accept the speech impediment as a permanent vocal fixture. Millions of people enjoy his deep, rich voice today because he chose to be his own talent scout and transform his awkward speech into an enviable asset.

All the people mentioned above began where they were. They took the hand life dealt them and turned disappointments—even disabilities—into talents. A twelve-year-old immigrant named Harry Lind also turned his disability into a talent, and in the process revolutionized vaudeville.

Harry Lind was born in Jamestown, New York, in 1879. His mother was a Swedish immigrant who ran a boarding house for other immigrants. To help support his family, Harry worked long hours in a furniture factory.

He walked to work every day, took the freight elevator down to the factory floor, and worked sixteen-hour shifts. Harry was getting good at building fine furniture, and he knew that this would be his lifelong career. Then change entered his world, in dramatic fashion. One morning, when he was twelve, he started a typical day that would soon turn tragic. When he began his descent to work on the freight elevator, the cable above him suddenly snapped, plunging him to the basement floor. In those days the elevators had no ceiling, so there was nothing to protect young Harry from the plummeting cable. The coiled metal struck him on the head and shoulders, almost killing him.

Partially paralyzed from the waist up, the youngster was told by well-meaning doctors that he would never regain the use of his arms. Undaunted by their devastating diagnosis, Harry decided he would prove the medical authorities wrong. On one of his office visits several weeks later, Harry surprised the doctors by slightly moving both arms.

The enthusiastic but tentative doctors decided to reward Harry's courage, and gave him an Indian Club (a wooden pin) and asked him to hold it tightly. He was unable to grip it at all on his first attempts, but several weeks later, he could grasp it and turn the club in a small circle. Each day he would make an exhausting effort to expand his range of motion, widening the circular path of the club, little by little. He worked with both hands, eventually regaining control of his forearms and shoulders. Finally, Harry was able to rotate the club and toss it from hand to hand without dropping it. He added a second club, then a third one.

The rest, as they say, is history. Harry made his professional juggling debut in 1900, and later teamed with another juggler, Frank Gregory, to perform in vaudeville productions. Both lads were good enough to be booked into New York's prestigious Tony Pastor's Club. Harry soon gained a reputation as one of the most talented of all club swingers. In addition to his phenomenal success as a world-class juggler, Harry became the leading manufacturer of juggling clubs and was one of the eight cofounders of the International Jugglers Association. Harry's juggling career was a return on the effort he invested in that first Indian club: the gift of his strength, physical ability, and self-confidence. He refused to allow what could have been a lifelong disability to define who he was. I have undying respect and admiration for Harry Lind.

I incorporate both juggling and gymnastics into my speaking presentations as metaphors to encourage each member in my audience to take purposeful, coordinated, and determined actions in order to achieve the success he or she wants in life. My acrobatics and juggling generate visual impact during my performances, escalating the level of enthusiasm and excitement so that my audiences can make the connection between thoughts, words, and action. As I tell the story of Harry Lind, I teach that often our greatest gifts, those that help us develop thoroughly original personalities, arise from adversity.

Life-threatening injuries spurred Harry Lind to turn tragedy into triumph. Fortunately, most of us discover our unique talents under less traumatic circumstances. We may get clues in the form of compliments from family, friends, and colleagues, or awards from organizations and employers, praising us for our specific expertise or talents. I believe the lesson for all of us is that while some of our unique talents may spring from adversity, most of what differentiates us comes from our normal, everyday attempts to develop our God-given abilities.

It is how we think about these talents that powers our day. A talent is nothing more than actualized potential, pointed in the right direction, at the right time, with the right thoughts. When the right thoughts turn into the right actions, we create the traction that propels us toward our goals. A quick look in the mirror tells us where we've been, but an alert look ahead, fortified by our positive thoughts and unique abilities, will help us to embody *success in action.*

Action Assignments

1. Express your individuality by changing one thing about the way you look. Reconsider something you've thought about for a while but never took action on. Make it a positive improvement. You may want to cut your hair, change hair color, let it grow, or create a new style. Maybe it's time to change the eyewear, grow a beard, shave the beard, get a complete makeover. It could be a change in your style of clothing, jewelry and accessories, footwear, or even eye color (through the miracle of tinted contact lenses). Change something about your physical appearance that helps you feel more comfortable and congruent with who you are.

2. Take another look at the four "I can" statements you completed a short while ago. Will you combine desire with action? Will you accomplish or improve on all four of your "I cans"? I believe you can if you put all of *you* into what you do. Establish your own record of successes. To gauge your progress, start a journal or keep your wins in a notebook. Reward yourself for each success, and begin to see everything you do as *success in action*.

3. Write a powerful positive statement (ten words or less) that you could use to create "grooves of success" in your gray matter. Your affirmation can be a statement about your health, finances, happiness, relationships, talents, future, etc. The more concise, the better. Post your affirmation in a conspicuous place so you can readily see it for the next thirty days. Memorize it. Repeat it aloud or to yourself as often as your time and commitment allow. Remember, physicist David Bohm's study proved that we can literally change the physiology of our brains by focusing our thoughts in a concentrated direction over time.

4. Think of a time in your past when you faced a serious, life-changing challenge. It could have been a health issue, a job-related difficulty, a family crisis, financial troubles, property loss. What special skills, talents, and interests did you discover you possessed as a result of having gone through the traumatic event? Which newly found skill or talent has helped you the most? What interests have you, like Harry Lind, permanently adopted and built into your lifestyle? Which of your old strengths are still there? What weaknesses have you overcome? In what ways are you a better person as a result of that life-changing event?

IGNITE YOUR INCREDIBLE INFLUENCE

Each one of us has a circle of influence. Within this sphere so many souls and minds are involved; with our rise, they rise; with our fall, they fall . . . The size of our sphere corresponds to the size of the sympathy of our heart. As our heart grows our sphere grows . . . Everything in our environment is . . . affected by our thoughts . . . We can repel those in our . . . sphere of influence by our coldness or attract them by our sympathy and . . . goodness.

—Hazrat Inayat Khan

You never know who's in your audience.

—Dan Thurmon

Many people do not realize the awesome power of their influence. We can literally change people's lives by what we say to them or about them and by how we behave toward them. Scott Adams, creator of the extraordinarily popular *Dilbert* comic strip, tells this story about his beginnings as a professional cartoonist:

You don't have to be a "person of influence" to be influential. In fact, the most influential people in my life are probably not even aware of the things they've taught me.

When I was attempting to become a syndicated cartoonist, I sent my portfolio to one cartoon editor after another—and received one rejection after another. One editor even called to suggest that I take art classes. Then Sarah Gillespie, an editor at United Media and one of the real experts in the field, called to offer me a contract.

At first I didn't believe her. I asked if I'd have to change my style, get a partner or learn how to draw. But she believed that I was already good enough to be a nationally syndicated cartoonist.

Her confidence in me completely changed my frame of reference: it altered how I thought about my own abilities. This may sound bizarre, but the minute I got off the phone with her, I could draw better.

Scott Adams' story illustrates the power that positive expectations can have, not only on our self-confidence and self-esteem, but on our careers. He believed in Sarah Gillespie's glowing assessment of his art ability. By a single well-placed compliment, the power of her influence transformed a struggling artist into a successful syndicated cartoonist.

The power of our influence can affect people either positively or negatively. "There are two ways of exerting one's influence," said the great American educator and writer Booker T. Washington. "One is pushing down, the other is pulling up." The focus of this chapter is to introduce the positive aspects of influence that invite people to take life-affirming, soul-enriching actions to improve their lives. Of course, negative influence plays a part in shaping our lives as well, and we are also influenced by genetics and environment; but right now let's look at the influences created by positive human interactions. Here's how I define positive influence:

Positive Influence: **Having a positive, powerful, and persuasive influence means you are able to touch the hearts and minds of others and move them to take responsible, life-enriching actions that improve their lives and the lives of those around them.**

In every generation there are a few gifted individuals who capture the hearts and minds of millions of people. Their presence is magical. The power of their influence affects the collective consciousness of everyone on earth. They earn undying admiration and unswerving allegiance as they create an extraordinary effect on others and shape the events of their time. Although the power of their influence is incredible, they are not the only people in the world with influence.

Let's revisit Scott Adams' insight above: "You don't have to be a person of influence to be influential. In fact, the most influential people in my life are probably not even aware of the things they've taught me."

We often fail to recognize the amount of influence we can have on another human being. And the consequences of our influence can last forever. Often the amount of influence we have on people is directly proportional to the level of passion and enthusiasm we bring to the situation—the greater our passion and enthusiasm, the more powerful the influence. Influence is based on the language of emotion, and it is emotion, not logic, that drives human behavior. People who can harness other people's emotional energy through their influence become powerful lightning rods, transforming individuals, communities, and even nations. Let's have a look at some of these positive "influence peddlers."

Positive "Influence Peddlers"

> *The influence of each human being on others is a kind of immortality.*
>
> —John Quincy Adams

Making people laugh is one of Lisa "Pinky" Aiello's favorite things to do—but their laughter is a joyful reaction she never hears. Pinky was born completely deaf. Her deafness is genetic, although she has hearing parents. Aiello specializes in juggling, unicycling, and clowning and also teaches American Sign Language. In 2002, she and her partner, Paul Dymoke of Maryland, another clown who is deaf, won first place in the group competition at the Clown Convention in Las Vegas—in the hearing clown world.

Aiello's role model was Charlie Chaplin. Attracted to the silent screen, she watched every one of his movies, especially his facial expressions and body language, and learned how to use her gestures to express her feelings on stage as well as off. She performs for hearing as well as hearing-impaired audiences, but wants to do more performances at schools for the deaf because she believes deaf children need role models. She tells deaf children they can do anything and be anything they want if they take action and believe in themselves.

Another positive "influence peddler" is a young man who has revolutionized the world of golf. He is the only golfer to win three U.S. Amateur Championships in succession. He won the Junior Amateur tournament and, at twenty-one, was the youngest professional golfer to win the Masters Golf Tournament. In his first six years on the PGA tour, Tiger Woods won forty professional tournaments and eight of golf's major tour events.

Tiger swung his first golf club, a sawed-off three iron, when he was eleven months old. By his own jubilant admission, his parents were his devoted influence peddlers. Tiger's father, Earl, shepherded him through every phase of his golf development. Just before bedtime every night, Earl used to sit on Tiger's bed and tell the youngster how successful he was going to be at life and at golf. Earl also told his son that he would be able to help many people in his life. Tiger's mother, Kultida, used to get up early and drive him to golf tournaments all over California. She kept score for him and encouraged him to do his best with every golf shot, no matter what hazard he had hit the ball into.

Tiger never forgot his parents' instructions and exemplifies a life of positive influence. He even organized the Tiger Woods Foundation to promote both golf and non-sports-related activities for disadvantaged children.

NBA star Michael Jordan says that Tiger "will succeed and expand across all racial barriers . . . I admire him . . . for establishing higher ground, for raising the bar . . . in using his immense influence to help others . . . I really do believe he was put here for a bigger reason than just to play golf. He's not a god, of course, but I do believe that he was sent by One."

Millions of us, I'm sure, agree with "Air" Jordan's assessment. Both these world-class athletes have influenced untold millions of people the world over. But I also believe that anyone with a passion for what he or she does can influence a lot of people. The ripple effect of our actions can go far beyond our reach—we never know how far our influence travels. That's why it's so important to follow the Golden Rule, a rule that's been around for two millennia: *Do unto others as you would have them do unto you.*

In his classic book *How to Win Friends and Influence People,* Dale Carnegie quotes American industrialist and steel-industry multimillionaire, Charles Schwab. He tells the reader Schwab's words "ought to be cast in eternal bronze and hung in every home and school, every shop and office in the country—words that will transform your life and mine if we will only live them."

These words that Carnegie felt could be so influential in transforming lives are akin to the Golden Rule: "The way to develop the best in someone is by appreciation and encouragement . . . I have yet to find anyone, however great or exalted, who did not do better work and put forth greater effort under a spirit of approval than they would ever do under a spirit of criticism."

Interest and appreciation can take many forms and can come at any time, from anyone. For Tiger Woods, it came early in life. For others it comes later in life, when age, circumstances, and willpower come together in just the right way.

One of my favorite stories about the power of influence and how it can literally change someone's life concerns Idaho businessman Don Bennett, the first amputee to climb to the summit of Mt. Rainer. He made the trip to the 14,410 foot summit on one leg and two crutches.

During a particularly difficult portion of the climb, Bennett and the other climbers had to cross a steep and treacherous ice field. In order to get safely across the ice, the climbers had to put crampons on their boots to keep from slipping and falling down the ice slope. The trek was not so easy for Bennett because he only had the benefit of one crampon on his one boot. Although his crutches gave him some stability, they frequently punched through the surface and got stuck.

After several frustrating attempts to hobble across the unforgiving ice field, he decided to fall facedown onto the ice and inch his way across the slick surface. He pulled himself as far forward as possible, stood up, lowered himself again to stretch his body to a prone position, inched forward again, stood up, and repeated the caterpillar-like process.

Bennett's daughter was also a member of the team. She stayed by his side during the whole laborious process, coaching her father and encouraging him to pull harder. After four grueling hours, her father began to falter. She knelt beside him, urging him forward, telling him what a wonderful father he was.

He did not want to disappoint his daughter, the team, or himself. Finally, with his daughter's encouragement and the team's support, Bennett conquered both the ice field and the summit. His inner resolve and the team's active support helped him achieve what many had felt was impossible.

Don Bennett was influenced by his daughter's love and admiration for his courage and determination. Her influence was based on their relationship.

Drawn by her confidence in his ability, he defined himself not by his disability, but by his strength of character. She expected her father to succeed and refused to let him fall short.

Before we explore how you can use the power of your influence to motivate and inspire others, let's take a closer look at how expectations can shape people's environment and transform doubters into doers, and victims into victors.

Self-Fulfilling Prophecy

In Greek mythology there is a story about Pygmalion, king of Cyprus, who was also a great sculptor. One day he carved a statue of a beautiful young woman, entirely from his imagination. No woman had modeled her; no woman could compare. The young king fell in love with his own creation and was so smitten that he spent all his time gazing at her and thinking of her.

He wished she were a real flesh-and-blood woman, but alas, she was crafted of ivory. Lovesick, Pygmalion summoned Aphrodite, the goddess of beauty, love, and fertility. He pleaded with her to bring his beautiful statue to life. Although she was reluctant at first, Aphrodite finally relented and gave the statue life.

Basing his drama on this classic tale, playwright George Bernard Shaw wrote *Pygmalion* for the theater. You may remember it as the delightfully spun musical *My Fair Lady.* In the stage version, Professor Henry Higgins teaches phonetics and meets the perfect person on whom to test his skills: an ill-spoken Cockney flower girl named Eliza Doolittle.

Higgins believes that by the force of his immense skill and will, he can transform the poor flower girl into a striking lady. Like the king of Cyprus, he is successful, and he manages to accomplish the first-ever "extreme makeover." Not only that, Eliza begins to believe in herself. She becomes the lady that her dress and demeanor make her appear to be.

Psychologists, sociologists, and behavioral scientists have long known about the benefits of expectancy and conditioning. Robert K. Merton, a sociology professor at Columbia University, was the researcher who coined the phrase "self-fulfilling prophecy." He theorized that when an influential person expects someone to behave differently or along prescribed lines, that person's behavior will tend to meet those expectations.

Harvard psychologist Robert Rosenthal expanded Merton's notion of the self-fulfilling prophecy and called it the "Pygmalion Effect," after the mythical King of Cyprus. His research team proved that people tend to live up—or down—to our expectations of them. The researchers also discovered that when people learn they are capable of performing according to expectations, they begin to develop a self-expectation that reinforces their newfound competencies. The more they meet expectations, whether positive or negative, the more self-reinforcing those expectations become.

Although we can't turn an ivory statue into a real person, we can, through the power of our influence, transform people's static view of themselves so they can discover and then honor the talents and abilities they didn't know they possessed. We can be facilitators in helping people achieve their dreams. They still need to take the necessary steps toward making their dreams more real today than yesterday, but we can help them appreciate themselves enough to take those critical first steps. In our "Henry Higgins" role we can help them dream, expand their thinking, and broaden their perspective of what is possible to achieve in life.

Notice, the word *if* appears in the center of the word *life. L-i-f-e.* The center of the word represents our iffy existence. "Iffiness" underscores our everyday thoughts, feelings, and actions: "*If* I do this," or "*If* that happens," or "*If* only I had done this instead of that, gone here instead of there, stopped then instead of now . . . " Life is full of *ifs*—or at least half of life is. The iffy part of life may be filled with uncertainties and doubt, but the other half of life brings us certainties, stability, and direction.

What if you were to spend the next few minutes "iffing" yourself? I'm serious! What *if* you could learn more about the power of your own influence? What *if* you realized how influential you really are? What *if* I told you that you could change the direction of someone else's life just by saying the right thing at the right time? What *if* you discovered that more people are affected by what you do than you ever realized? What *if* you could help someone move beyond his or her self-doubts long enough to accomplish something really significant and life-affirming? What *if* someone told you what a difference you've made in his or her life? What *if* you had the answers to all the above questions?

Take the next few moments to do just that! Answer each *if* question by completing the following sentence: "I will . . . " Spend some time with this exercise. It will enlighten you more than you can imagine. Become your own positive influence peddler for a few moments.

Once you've satisfied yourself with the answers to these important life questions, you are ready to take the next step: discovering your preferred style for influencing the behavior of others.

Influential Empowerment

> *There are people whose feelings and well-being are within your influence. You will never escape that fact.*
> —Hugh Prather

Finding out that you have helped another person in a significant way is truly a cherished memory. When people come up to the front of the room after I have finished a keynote address and thank me, through misty eyes, for validating and encouraging them, it is an enormously gratifying experience—one that stays with me long after the banquet hall has cleared. When people tell me I've made a difference in their lives, I feel both excited and humbled. Delivering speeches and seminars for a living is a huge responsibility because what I say and how I deliver my message affects thousands of lives each month.

I decided early on in my speaking career that I would strive to make a positive impact on all my public and personal audiences. We all make an impact by what we say, and even more of an impact by what we do. And we make the greatest impact by who we are. I try to live my life and do my job in such a way that these three areas of influence support one another, like the legs on a stool. And I demonstrate my commitment and my principles by my actions, incorporating juggling, acrobatics, and physical challenges that test my abilities and punctuate my message. I call this "Speaking with Visual Impact™."

Because of the limited time I am able to spend with my audiences, my job is to maximize the impact of each encounter. I want to influence them in such a way that every person will want to take immediate action toward goals they would have deemed unreachable before they experienced my presentation. That's a tall order. I was fortunate to learn valuable skills as a performer delivering thousands of shows in every conceivable environment for more than twenty years. This experience taught me how to influence people in group settings, how to develop a persuasive message, and how to spontaneously create and improvise new content. But the most valuable lesson may be this: You never know who is in your audience.

You Never Know Who's in your Audience

In the spring of 1994, I was hired to perform at Callaway Gardens, the largest botanical garden in the state of Georgia. Thousands of people come every year to enjoy the Spring Celebration and behold the glorious profusion of azaleas in full bloom, and my job was to entertain the crowds as they strolled outside the Butterfly Center.

I had just finished a very successful show. I was covered in sweat, and the performance adrenaline was still pumping through my body. What a thrill it is to do what I love and get the immediate and spontaneous appreciation of a grateful audience. They applauded, cheered, and then walked away. That is, everyone walked away except one man, who took action.

As I was putting away my six-foot unicycle and fire torches, I noticed an older gentleman approaching. He introduced himself as Merck Smith. Interesting name, I thought. He told me he was once a juggler. As a younger man he had taught himself to juggle balls and even decided he wanted to learn clubs, but he was out of luck because he couldn't find them anywhere. Merck's luck changed in 1941, when he went to war. During World War II he was a cartographer, making maps to enable American pilots to find their enemy targets. He was stationed in England, then Africa, then Italy. It was there, in 1944, that his troop was visited by a USO tour, a group of entertainers and celebrities who brought the soldiers a little taste of home and lifted their morale with a wonderful show.

There was a juggler in the show, whose act Merck especially enjoyed. Afterward, he approached this entertainer just as he approached me so many years later. They began to talk. Hearing that Merck wanted to learn to juggle clubs, the performer told him about a man who might be able to help. "He's a top-notch juggler, but also a woodworker. He makes his own clubs for himself and for others as well. If you were to write him a letter and explain your situation, I'm sure he would make you some for a very fair price."

Merck was ecstatic at the chance to have real, professional props, and he gladly took down the man's address, as well as his name: Harry Lind—the immigrant boy who had overcome a debilitating injury to become a world-famous juggler.

Merck was not short on self-expectations. He ordered five clubs. He told me his thought process was, "I'll certainly learn three. And if I enjoy it, I'll probably learn four. And, whatever happened, I didn't want to run out of clubs."

When he got home from the war the following year, the clubs were waiting for him. He taught himself how to juggle three clubs very well, and before long he was doing a respectable job with four. Then, as time went on, other things in Merck's life took a higher priority, such as his job and his family. The clubs went back in the original cardboard box and sat on a shelf in his garage, where, by the time I met him, they had been for forty-nine years.

"I still have them," he told me. "I always thought that maybe, one day, I would run into a juggler who could use them. If you would like to have them, I am more than happy to just give them to you."

I was flabbergasted. Here in front of me was a complete stranger, offering me a set of clubs made by Harry Lind himself, one of the greatest legends of the juggling world. I didn't know how I could ever possibly repay him for such a generous gift—but don't worry, I accepted. I was at his house the next day!

We took the cardboard box down from the garage shelf, where it had been for so many years, and walked into the sunlight. When Merck opened the box, the sun hit the clubs, and they were beautiful: simple but elegant, each one handcrafted from basswood, perfectly balanced, and covered in thin canvas. In those days vaudeville jugglers would paint their props, but these clubs were never painted; the once-white fabric was now yellow with age.

I grabbed three, thinking, *Harry Lind made these, and certainly he had to juggle them, just to make sure they felt right. Today I am going to juggle them, too.* I moved over onto the grass, just in case. And when I let go of the clubs, I realized their true beauty. Not only did they feel fantastic, like driving a high-performance automobile, but they also "rang true." Because the bell of the club is hollowed out to give it balance, the tone of the wood sings with each catch, making a beautiful "ping." Different juggling patterns created different rhythms, almost as if I were playing music in the air. I finished with a high throw, without a drop. Merck handed me the fourth club.

I smiled my appreciation, took a deep breath, and tossed them sequentially into the air. I remember saying to myself, *I'm juggling a vintage set of Harry Lind clubs.* Just as with three, they were falling perfectly, this time making a four-club rhythm. I even threw one behind my back and finished clean—no drops. Merck's jubilant expression confirmed his delight at seeing his clubs in action. Then, simultaneously, he and I glanced into the box and eyed the last remaining club.

Have you ever been in a situation where, even though you knew you were about to try something you didn't really know how to do, you felt that if you jumped right in, you could trick yourself into getting it right? That's exactly how I felt when I picked up the fifth club. My motivation to succeed was enormous because of the nature of the gift and the legend behind it. I had to get it right. In what seemed like slow motion, all the clubs formed a perfect pattern of double flips above my head, and I sustained it for about twelve catches. It seemed like forever. That one moment is what later enabled me to internalize the skill for keeps. I suppose, sometimes in life we really do fake it until we make it.

I thanked Merck Smith profusely for about the hundredth time before I left. When I got home, I took the clubs out of the case and held them but didn't juggle them. I was so excited, I didn't know what to do with them. I decided that such a monumental gift should be preserved, displayed. So I hung them on the wall. They had their own special rack, and each club slid neatly into place.

People who came to my house would ask, "What are those?" and I would proudly tell the story of Harry Lind and Merck Smith. They were a great conversation piece. But the more I told the story, the less meaningful it became. When I walked by the club display on the wall, instead of feeling satisfaction, I felt a restlessness, a persistent nagging. Then I thought back to what Merck said the first time I met him at Callaway Gardens: "I always thought maybe one day I would run into a juggler who could use them."

"Use them!" I said aloud. "They weren't ever intended to be wall decorations."

I knew what I had to do. If you're ahead of me, that's okay, because it means you understand the relationship between taking care of something valuable and being willing to risk letting go of it at the same time. I had juggled all five clubs at Merck's that day. It was something he had envisioned. He wanted to see his clubs in action. It was knowing they would be used for a good purpose that brightened that afternoon for him. This was what they were created for; Harry Lind would have liked that. The sounds made from the tossing and the catching are part of the essence of the clubs. Without the "air time," the clubs never fulfill their purpose. Although they risk being chipped or broken from use, they are not meant for wall displays—they are engineered for flight.

So the clubs are not on my wall. I carry them in a case to each of my seminars. As I tell this story from the stage, I close it by taking out the clubs turned on the lathe of Harry Lind and juggling them as a tribute to expert craftsmanship, and as a metaphor for our power to influence others. Harry Lind made them to be juggled. Merck Smith gave them to be juggled. He had waited almost fifty years to give them to the right juggler, and he picked me! And each time I tell the Merck Smith story, they *are* juggled.

Every time I juggle those exquisite clubs, I risk damaging them. It only takes one drop, one errant toss, one mishap. But the risk is worth it. It teases out my best. I become one with the clubs, the human extension of their purpose, part of their essence and worth. Now, I would never intentionally put those clubs at risk, but when we reach out to influence others, there is also a perceived risk. We are all given gifts. Some we are born with; I believe those are gifts from God. Others we acquire in the course of a lifetime. What I learned from Merck Smith is this: For your gifts to appreciate in value, it is never enough merely to *appreciate* them. Don't hang them on the wall! You must *use* them, and in the spirit they were intended. You must pass the gift along to inspire and influence those around you.

I do not take the nature and degree of my influence lightly. Everything I do, on and off the stage, has an impact, and I want that impact to be positively stimulating. My interest in wanting to influence people in the right way led me to research the power of influence. I discovered that there are seven generally accepted types or styles of influence. Most studies have used the "social power and influence" research of J. R. P. French and B. Raven as the basis for a description of the typical types of influence. Although I've changed the

Merck attended a presentation in 1998 and watched his clubs and his story take flight.

names of the various types for clarity's sake, the research they are based on is sound.

Before I describe each of the influence styles, I want you to complete the Influence Profile below. After you complete the profile, you will find a description for each influence style, including your own. Don't spoil it for yourself by reading ahead. Complete the self-assessment first, then read about your own influence style.

Influence Profile

Listed below are twenty-one pairs of statements, which explain how you view your relationships with people on a day-to-day basis. Consider your attitudes, responsibilities, and personality as you assign point values to each of the statements below. Allocate a total of three points for *each set of two* statements. Base your point allotments on your assessment of how much each statement applies to your ability to influence others. Divide the three points for *each set of two* statements as follows:

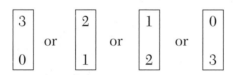

1. ____ A. I can punish or penalize people who do not cooperate with me.

   ____ B. People know I have close connections with very influential people.

---

2. ____ E. Because of who I am, I am in a position and have the authority to delegate whatever I don't want to do myself.

   ____ F. People simply like me for who I am and enjoy doing things for me.

---

3. ____ C. People respect my skills, talents, knowledge, and work experience.

   ____ D. I either have or can obtain immediate access to information that is important to others.

---

4. ____ G. I can reward and support people who cooperate with me.

   ____ A. I can punish and penalize people who do not support me.

---

5. ____ B. People know I have close connections with very influential people.

   ____ C. People respect my skills, talents, knowledge, and work experience.

---

6. ____ D. I either have or can obtain immediate access to information that is important to others.

   ____ E. Because of who I am, I am in a position and have the authority to delegate whatever I don't want to do myself.

---

7. ____ F. People simply like me for who I am and enjoy doing things for me.

   ____ G. I can reward and support people who cooperate with me.

---

8. ____ A. I can punish and penalize people who do not support me.

   ____ C. People respect my skills, talents, knowledge, and work experience.

---

9. ____ B. People know I have close connections with very influential people.

   ____ D. I either have or can obtain immediate access to information that is important to others.

---

10. ____ C. People respect my skills, talents, knowledge, and work experience.

     ____ E. Because of who I am, I am in a position and have the authority to delegate whatever I don't want to do myself.

---

11. ____ D. I either have or can obtain immediate access to information that is important to others.

     ____ A. I can punish or penalize people who do not support me.

---

12. ____ E. Because of who I am, I am in a position and have the authority to delegate whatever I don't want to do myself.

     ____ B. People know I have close connections with very influential people.

---

13. ____ F. People simply like me for who I am and enjoy doing things for me.

     ____ C. People respect my skills, talents, knowledge, and work experience.

---

14. ____ G. I can reward and support people who cooperate with me.

     ____ B. People know I have close connections with very influential people.

---

15. ____ A. I can punish or penalize people who do not support me.

     ____ E. Because of who I am, I am in a position and have the authority to delegate whatever I don't want to do myself.

---

16. ____ B. People know I have close connections with very influential people.

____ F. People simply like me for who I am and enjoy doing things for me.

17. ____ C. People respect my skills, talents, knowledge, and work experience.

____ G. I can reward and support people who cooperate with me.

18. ____ D. I either have or can obtain immediately access to information that is important to others.

____ F. People simply like me for who I am and enjoy doing things for me.

19. ____ E. Because of who I am, I am in a position and have the authority to delegate whatever I don't want to do myself.

____ G. I can reward and support people who cooperate with me.

20. ____ F. People simply like me for who I am and enjoy doing things for me.

____ A. I can punish or penalize people who do not support me.

21. ____ G. I can reward and support people who cooperate with me.

____ D. I either have or can obtain immediate access to information that is important to others.

Influence Profile Scoring Sheet

Go through each of the two statement sets in the Influence Profile and add all the scores associated with each of the A, B, C, D, E, F, and G statements. Start in the A Statements and tally those scores; go to the B statements; then total the C statements, and so on, until you have point totals for each letter. Transfer those totals to the Statement Totals below.

To check your addition, your total score for all sets combined should equal 63.

Statement ( ) +	( ) +	( ) +	( ) +	( ) +	( ) +	( )	= 63	
Totals A	B	C	D	E	F	G		

Transfer these totals to the Influence Matrix below by shading each row (horizontally) in relation to the total score for that type of influence. (You may want to use a different-colored marker for each style.) This will provide you with a visual representation of your style of influence, from your dominant style to your least preferred style.

Your Influence Matrix

Total	0	5	10	15	18
A. Despotic					
B. Synergistic					
C. Omnipotent					
D. Encyclopedic					
E. Status					
F. Charismatic					
G. Philanthropic					

© Motivation Works Inc.

Influence Style Descriptions

You can easily find your dominant influence style preference based on your score above. Although most people tend to use one or two influence styles more than the others, each of us uses each of these styles at one time or another. This is a general assessment and simply indicates your tendency to prefer one style over another in exercising the power of your influence.

Despotic Influence: This type of influence is a highly coercive style, based on tyrannical control, force, and fear. Scoring high in this style is seen as forcing compliance and obedience to your wishes. People who prefer this style enjoy punishing those who fail to take their advice, by withholding opportunities and information, giving reprimands, inflicting intentional embarrassment, excluding "offenders" from inner-circle activities, and censoring compliments and praise. With this style there is no chance of ever gaining real commitment or trust from those on the receiving end of intentional punishment and abuse, verbal or otherwise. It should come as no surprise that this is the least preferred style of dealing with people on a day-to-day basis. People need encouragement, not coercion.

Synergistic Influence: *Synergism* is an apt term for this highly collaborative style. It is based on the concept "You scratch my back, I'll scratch yours." Scoring high in synergistic influence forces those affected by this type of influence to comply if they want to gain your favor and avoid the wrath of your influential connections. People who use this style get others to do things because they can promise access to and alliances with important people. Synergists are usually phenomenal networkers and coalition builders, who use those connections to influence less-connected friends and associates. People of character who use this style in its more positive applications can be access providers for many deserving, hardworking people who need an "in" to jump-start their dreams.

Omnipotent Influence: The strengths of this style are its credibility and competence components, since it is based on the provider's uncommon expertise, experience, and knowledge in a given area. Scoring high in this style is viewed as having the expertise and technical competence to enlighten, guide, and direct the activities of less-qualified and less-knowledgeable people. Omnipotent influence is credible influence because the people seeking it know that the provider has the wherewithal to steer them clear of the hazards and pitfalls associated with their goal.

Encyclopedic Influence: This influence style is based solely on the provider's possession of or direct access to information that is perceived as valuable and expedient by others. Scoring high in encyclopedic influence means your expertise lies in helping people gain access to time-critical data, records, and files that will improve their chances of success. Those who have encyclopedic influence have information power—and in the "information age" that means powerful influence.

Status Influence: Sometimes called "pecking order" influence, this style is based on an individual's actual position in an organization, community, association, family, club, church, and so on. Such a position gives the influence provider a sort of chain-of-command status or "slot" in the hierarchy. Scoring high in status influence means that those who work with you relative to your position in the organization feel they must defer to your authority and clout. People seeking your guidance and advice depend on your power of position to help them achieve their goals.

Charismatic Influence: This type of influence is based on the provider's personal magnetism, charisma, and dynamic personality. Scoring high in charismatic influence means you are generally respected and admired by people. Your dynamic, magnetic personality itself compels people to seek your advice and counsel just because you're who you are. People want to be around you, gain your favor, "touch your garment." People are automatically drawn to you and generally believe anything you say. If the negative side of charismatic influence, its narcissistic side, is controlled or, even better, eliminated, this style can do much to lift people's self-esteem and sense of self-worth.

Philanthropic Influence: This style is based on the provider's ability to dispense both tangible and intangible rewards. Scoring high in this style suggests that the philanthropist has the "Midas touch" when it comes to helping people realize their dreams. The rewards can be tangible, such as seed money, equipment, materials, human resources, and transportation; or intangible, such as praise and verbal recognition.

Now that you know what your influence profile looks like, rank your influence styles from the most used (dominant) to the least used. Which one is your second most preferred (backup) style? Which one did you score the lowest in? When you seek help and advice, which of the styles would you go to first to get the help you need? Under what circumstances would you seek help from someone who has a despotic influence profile? How can you use your influence style to help someone this week?

You may want to ask your friends, family, or colleagues to take the Influence Profile. It should generate lively discussions, don't you think?

The important thing about an assessment like this is that it helps you learn more about yourself. Hopefully, you'll use it wisely so you can be a positive role model and change agent, one who helps people take a step closer to their dreams. When you communicate your concern and interest in someone else's success through your particular style of influence, the people you help will admire your passion and authenticity. The raw energy and enthusiasm that you project will help people climb their respective summits to find their own unique vision of success.

When you ignite your incredible influence, be sure to appreciate both the nature and timing of the help you give people. You never know who's in your audience.

Action Assignments

1. I shared the story about the Harry Lind clubs that Merck Smith gave me. At first I hung the vintage clubs on the wall, but then I decided to use them in my presentations because such exquisite clubs were not meant for display—they were designed for "air time." Think about some material object in your possession that you have "safeguarded" to such an extent that it is not being used for the purpose for which it was designed. Consider rescuing it from its particular "prison" and *use* it as it was intended to be used. Enjoy it, for heaven's sake! Volunteer it for special occasions, or draft it into daily use.

2. Remember Scott Adams' story, in which he said he could draw better the moment he got off the phone with Sara Gillespie, his positive encourager? Think of a time in your life when you had a similar experience, when your performance was improved simply because someone told you that you were good. Now list the names of three people you can encourage in a similar fashion, and then take action to ignite your incredible influence.

3. Help someone "grow forward." Honor the tutelage of your own mentor by coaching someone who is deserving of your time. It doesn't have to be employment related. You may want to mentor someone who shares your interests or someone who has the passion, talent, and desire but needs the guidance you can provide. Find a mentee, or open yourself to the possibility and let one find you.

4. Assess the power of your influence. Think back over your life and see if you can find a common thread in the power of your influence. Ask yourself: What have people always come to me for? Has it been for advice, counseling, access to others, loans, spiritual help, entertainment? How have people seen me? As an intellectual, comedian, prophet, instigator, cheerleader, pragmatist, innovator,

gourmet cook, peacemaker, risk taker? Determine where you believe you have been most effective, consistent, sought after, creative, helpful. Sum up the power of your influence in one word.

4

READY, SET, GOALS

From early childhood I had always dreamed of becoming an explorer. Somehow I had acquired the impression that an explorer was someone who lived in the jungle with natives and lots of wild animals, and I couldn't imagine anything better than that! Unlike other little boys, most of whom changed their minds about what they want to be several times as they grew older, I never wavered from this ambition.
—John Goddard

The author of that statement is most known for his amazing "life list" of accomplishments. At the age of fifteen John Goddard listed 127 goals he wished to experience or achieve in his lifetime. The list is impressive and audacious, but the results have been truly amazing. With his permission, I would like to share his original 127 goals and subsequent accomplishments, each identified by a check mark for completion.

Explore:
1. ✓ Nile River
2. ✓ Amazon River
3. ✓ Congo River
4. ✓ Colorado River
5. ✓ Yangtze River, China
6.   Niger River
7.   Orinoco River, Venezuela
8. ✓ Rio Coco, Nicaragua
9. ✓ The Congo
10. ✓ New Guinea
11. ✓ Brazil
12. ✓ Borneo
13. ✓ The Sudan (nearly buried alive in a sandstorm)

Study Tribal Cultures in:
14. ✓ Australia
15. ✓ Kenya
16. ✓ The Philippines
17. ✓ Tanganyika (now Tanzania)
18. ✓ Ethiopia
19. ✓ Nigeria
20. ✓ Alaska

Climb:
21.   Mount Everest
22.   Mount Aconcagua, Argentina
23.   Mount McKinley
24. ✓ Mount Huascarán, Peru
25. ✓ Mount Kilimanjaro
26. ✓ Mount Ararat, Turkey
27. ✓ Mount Kenya
28.   Mount Cook, New Zealand
29. ✓ Mount Popocatepetl, Mexico
30. ✓ The Matterhorn
31. ✓ Mount Rainier
32. ✓ Mount Fujiyama
33. ✓ Mount Vesuvius
34. ✓ Mount Bromo, Java
35. ✓ Grand Teton

36. ✓ Mount Baldy, California
37. ✓ Carry out careers in medicine and exploration
38.   Visit every country in the world (visited 122 at this writing).
39. ✓ Study Navajo and Hopi cultures
40. ✓ Learn to fly a plane (have flown forty different aircraft)
41. ✓ Ride horse in Rose Parade

Photograph:
42. ✓ Iguazú Falls, Brazil-Argentina border
43. ✓ Victoria Falls
44. ✓ Sutherland Falls, New Zealand
45. ✓ Yosemite Falls
46. ✓ Niagara Falls
47. ✓ Retrace the travels of Marco Polo and Alexander the Great

Explore underwater:
48. ✓ Coral reefs of Florida
49. ✓ Great Barrier Reef, Australia
50. ✓ Red Sea
51. ✓ Fiji Islands
52. ✓ The Bahamas
53. ✓ Explore Okefenokee Swamp and the Everglades

Visit:
54.   North and South Poles
55. ✓ Great Wall of China
56. ✓ Panama and Suez Canals
57. ✓ Easter Island
58. ✓ The Galapagos Islands
59. ✓ Vatican City (saw the Pope)

60. ✓ The Taj Mahal
61. ✓ The Eiffel Tower
62. ✓ The Blue Grotto
63. ✓ The Tower of London
64. ✓ The Leaning Tower of Pisa
65. ✓ The Sacred Well of Chichén-Itzá, Mexico
66. ✓ Climb Ayers Rock in Australia
67.   Follow River Jordan from Sea of Galilee to Dead Sea

Swim in:
68. ✓ Lake Victoria
69. ✓ Lake Superior
70. ✓ Lake Tanganyika
71. ✓ Lake Titicaca
72. ✓ Lake Nicaragua

Accomplish:
73. ✓ Become an Eagle Scout
74. ✓ Dive in a submarine
75. ✓ Land on and take off from an aircraft carrier
76. ✓ Fly in a blimp, hot air balloon, and glider
77. ✓ Ride an elephant, camel, ostrich, and bronco
78. ✓ Skin-dive to forty feet and hold breath two and a half minutes underwater
79. ✓ Catch a ten-pound lobster and a ten-inch abalone
80. ✓ Play flute and violin
81. ✓ Type fifty words a minute
82. ✓ Make a parachute jump
83. ✓ Learn water and snow skiing
84. ✓ Go on a church mission
85.   Follow the John Muir Trail
86. ✓ Study native medicines and bring back useful ones

87. ✓ Bag camera trophies of elephant, lion, rhino, cheetah, cape buffalo, and whale
88. ✓ Learn to fence
89. ✓ Learn jujitsu
90. ✓ Teach a college course
91. ✓ Watch a cremation ceremony in Bali
92. ✓ Explore depths of the sea
93.   Appear in a Tarzan movie
94.   Own a horse, chimpanzee, cheetah, ocelot, and coyote
95.   Become a ham radio operator
96. ✓ Build own telescope
97. ✓ Write a book on the Nile expedition
98. ✓ Publish an article in *National Geographic* magazine
99. ✓ High-jump five feet
100. ✓ Broad-jump fifteen feet
101. ✓ Run a mile in five minutes
102. ✓ Weigh 175 pounds stripped (still does)
103. ✓ Perform 200 sit-ups and 20 pull-ups
104. ✓ Learn French, Spanish, and Arabic
105.   Study dragon lizards on Komodo Island
106. ✓ Visit birthplace of Grandfather Sorenson in Denmark
107. ✓ Visit birthplace of Grandfather Goddard in England
108. ✓ Ship aboard a freighter as a seaman
109.   Read the entire Encyclopedia Britannica (have read extensive parts in

each of the 24 volumes)

110. ✓ Read the Bible from cover to cover

111. ✓ Read the works of Shakespeare, Plato, Aristotle, Dickens, Thoreau, Poe, Rousseau, Bacon, Hemingway, Twain, Burroughs, Conrad, Talmage, Tolstoy, Longfellow, Keats, Whittier, and Emerson (not every work of each)

112. ✓ Become familiar with the compositions of Bach, Beethoven, Debussy, Ibert, Mendelssohn, Lalo, Rimsky-Korsakov, Respighi, Liszt, Rachmaninoff, Stravinsky, Toch, Tchaikovsky, Verdi

113. ✓ Become proficient in the use of a plane, motor-cycle, tractor, surfboard, rifle, pistol, canoe, micro-scope, football, basketball, bow and arrow, lariat, and boomerang

114. ✓ Compose music

115. ✓ Play "Clair de Lune" on the piano

116. ✓ Watch fire-walking ceremony (in Bali and Surinam)

117. ✓ Milk a poisonous snake

118. ✓ Light a match with a .22 rifle

119. ✓ Visit a movie studio

120. ✓ Climb Great Pyramid of Cheops (Egypt)

121. ✓ Become a member of the Explorers' Club and the Adventurers' Club

122. ✓ Learn to play polo

123. ✓ Travel through the Grand Canyon on foot and by boat

124. ✓ Circumnavigate the globe (four times)

125.   Visit the moon

126. ✓ Marry and have children (two sons, four daughters)

127. ✓ Live to see the twenty-first century

Now that you have read this incredible list, consider your goals. I am not suggesting that we all set our objectives as high as John Goddard's. But I will say that if he was successful in achieving all those life aspirations with his resources of time, energy, and money (and by the way, he was completely self-financed, working to earn or raise the money for each of his adventures), then isn't it possible that you can accomplish far more than you presently imagine?

Committing to specific goals is an act of faith and courage. It is also a requirement in order for you to experience success in action. Furthermore, when you establish compelling goals, you engage a mysterious force that magnetically attracts the people and experiences necessary for you to accomplish your objectives. Unfortunately, the opposite is also true. If you neglect making conscious choices about what you want your life to become, you will experience an ambiguous existence, enduring whatever happens to you or becoming a part of someone else's plan for your life. In short, *if you fail to plan, you are planning to fail!* I believe that Napoleon Hill was the first to offer people that advice, and it's as true now as it was back in 1937. Despite truckloads of literature on the subject, most people have never learned how to set effective personal and professional goals. Few have made goal-setting a regular part of their lives. Some people even have a pinch of psychological resistance to getting their goals down in writing.

Goal-setting is one of those things, like regular exercise and healthy eating, that almost everyone pays eloquent lip service to, but that few actually do. For far too many people, the main form of exercise they get is running back and forth from the TV to the refrigerator during commercials. Most people treat goal-setting the same way. They think about goals; they know that goals are good for them—they may even have jotted a few goals down from time to time. Unfortunately, that's the extent of most people's goal-setting experience.

"Without a goal it is difficult to concentrate and avoid distractions," says creativity researcher Mihaly Csikszentmihalhyi. "For example, a mountain climber sets as his or her goal to reach the summit not simply because he or she has some deep desire only to achieve it, but because the goal makes the experience of climbing possible. If it were not for the summit, the climb would become pointless ambling that leaves one restless and apathetic."

Csikszentmihalhyi is right, of course. Without a clear conception of where we are going, we would do a lot of "pointless ambling." We would, as the saying goes, confuse activity with accomplishment. During my seminars I like to demonstrate visually the importance of setting clearly defined goals. I begin by juggling several clubs at a low level, and then take the pattern higher into the air. Then I tell the audience, "If you want to move to a new level of success and performance, here is the key: Do not look at your hands!" At that moment, I look down at my hands and attempt to catch the plummeting objects. Of course, the clubs come crashing to the floor.

The point of the demonstration is this: If you want to take your performance to higher and higher levels, the secret to effective juggling is that you must keep looking up. You must keep your focus fixed upon the point in space where you want the throws to go. Of course, the catches are important, but in order to make all the catches and still see what is coming next, you must stay focused on your goal. I then juggle the clubs again, pushing them higher and higher toward the ceiling. Never once do I look down at my hands. I stay focused on the targets— the goals for my throws—and the catches happen spontaneously.

When you develop the ability to remain focused on your target, even in the midst of confusion, then you begin to see the pattern that is created when all your goals relate to one another. Others begin to see what you see. Your vision becomes contagious, and people will be attracted and willing to help you achieve what you most desire.

Goals help us concentrate and focus on what we want to achieve, and they help block out annoying distractions. Purposeful action through conscientious goal-setting is the one thing all successful people have in common. Take a look around you right now. What do you see? Are you at home or at your office? Are you sitting in a chair, on the sofa or floor, or are you curled up in bed near your reading lamp? Are you surrounded by modern technology: a telephone, computer, fax machine, electric pencil sharpener, laser printer, cell phone? Are you using a pen or colored highlighter to mark meaningful passages or make notes in the margins of this book? Do you see furniture, photos, a coffee cup or a soda can?

All those manufactured items started out as ideas in someone's mind before they became material objects. They are the technological outcomes of someone's creativity, resourcefulness, and desire to create something new or improve on an existing design by modifying its shape, size, or purpose. Those thoughts became desires, and the desires became goals. Goal setting becomes a self-fulfilling process, one characterized by concentration, focus, and direction.

Improve Your AIM

The greater danger for most of us lies not in setting our aim too high and falling short, but in setting our aim too low and achieving our mark.

—Michelangelo

Squinting through life has it drawbacks. If you can't see where you're going and are unsure of your direction, you're liable to end up someplace you hadn't planned on being, or giving up just a few paces short of your goal without knowing it. The often-told story of swimmer Florence Chadwick illustrates this point very well. The following is adapted from an article by Joel Weldon entitled "Keep Your Goals in Sight."

> *She was the first woman to swim the English Channel in both directions, and now at age 34 her goal was to become the first woman to swim from Catalina Island to the California coast. On that Fourth of July morning, the channel was like an ice bath and the fog was so dense she had difficulty seeing her support boats. Fortunately she had trained in the cold Atlantic Ocean and was in peak condition, so she was prepared to face the unforgiving waves and chilling temperature.*
>
> *Her support team hovered in boats nearby and gave her hot soup and tea from thermoses. They greased her body to help protect her from the frigid waters. Her mother and the trainers offered her encouragement. Sentries were posted to keep the ever-present sharks at bay.*
>
> *Against the ice-cold grip of the sea, she struggled on, hour after hour, while millions watched on national TV. All her planning and training, however, hadn't fully prepared her for the treacherous combination of fog and sea. Sixteen hours into her swim, she began to cramp. Her muscles screamed in pain with every stroke she took. Finally, with only half a mile to go, she asked to be pulled out.*
>
> *Still thawing her frozen body several hours later, she told reporters, "Look, I'm not excusing myself, but I lost sight of my goal. If I could have seen land, I might have made it . . . I'm not sure I ever had it firmly in mind."*

It was not fatigue, the threat of sharks, or even the icy chill of the channel that defeated her. It was the fog, which prevented her from seeing the shore. The message is clear: We may not encounter as physically demanding a trial as Florence Chadwick's, but the same thing that defeated her—losing sight of the goal—can defeat us. We can have all the talent, opportunity, time, and support we need to accomplish something really significant, but if we're unable or unwilling to set clearly established goals, we'll succumb, as Florence did, to the "fog" of poorly defined objectives.

By the way, there's more to Florence Chadwick's story. Two months later she attempted to conquer the channel again. This time, despite the ever-present fog, she swam with determination, faith, and focus, and became the first woman to swim the Catalina Channel, eclipsing the men's record by a little more than two hours.

Florence Chadwick improved her *aim* by keeping her eyes on the ultimate goal. Taking AIM, an acronym for "Actions Intelligently Managed," is the entire process of goal-setting in a nutshell.

Taking AIM

A— Actions: expressing your intentions and level of commitment.

I— Intelligently: taking the right actions thoughtfully and intentionally, keeping the desired outcomes in sight.

M—Managed: effectively using the right resources at the right time to ensure your goal-getting success.

Though this may sound obvious, the first step in taking aim is to know what you're aiming at. Intelligently managing your actions requires a conscious awareness of the world around you, because you must constantly assess information as being relevant or irrelevant to your objective. A selection process is quietly at work here. Conscious awareness is itself a result of selection. You are constantly filtering out data from your environment, allowing some information in and keeping the less critical "noise" out. Put another way, your conscious mind selects particular aspects of your environment to focus on and simply ignores the rest.

Let's experiment: Step over to the nearest window. Take a five-second look outside, then return to your seat. During the next ninety seconds, describe in writing everything you saw.

Now scoot back over to the window again and refresh your memory. Look at the scene before you. Did you describe everything? Chances are, you didn't. I set you up, of course, because it's impossible for anyone, in such a short time span, to catch all the information available to the senses.

The reason you weren't able to describe everything your conscious-ness "collected" was that your perceptual filters only selected things that made the biggest impression on your subconscious. According to researchers Berelson and Steiner, perception is the complex process by which "people select, organize, and interpret sensory stimulation into a meaningful and coherent picture of the world."

In less sophisticated language, we can think of perception as the process of making some kind of sense out of experience by filtering out what makes little or no sense to us.

In information theory terms, the eye can handle about five million bits of information per second, but we can only reasonably interpret and understand approximately five hundred bits per second. Without these perceptual filters, we couldn't improve our AIM. The same goes for goal-setting. Without written, clearly distinguishable goals, our actions cannot be intelligently managed. Our AIM would be poor, and so would the prospects of our being able to come anywhere close to *success in action.*

From Wish-Crafter to Goal-Crafter

> *The future does not belong to those who are content with today, or apathetic . . . timid and fearful in the face of bold projects and new ideas. It belongs to those who can blend passion, reason and commitment into written action.*
>
> —Robert F. Kennedy

Until goals are written, they're nothing more than *wish-craft*. A goal is a measurable, written statement of definite steps toward the realization of a wish, dream, vision, or desire. Capturing goals on paper gets them one step closer to fulfillment. Goal-setting, as the saying goes, is goal-*getting*. And there's plenty of research to support the idea of capturing goals as written statements.

There are many formulas floating around for achieving goals, but they all have four things in common: Effective goals are specific, linear, action-oriented, and measurable. Before we discuss these four attributes, it's time for you to turn *wish-craft* into *"goal-craft."*

As I mentioned earlier, the goal-crafter I admire more than anyone else is the explorer John Goddard. He has pursued each of his stated goals with such fearlessness and intensity that he has been honored by presidents, kings and queens, tribal chiefs, and peers all over the world. He belongs to the Adventurers' Club of Los Angeles (youngest member ever admitted), the Savage Club of London, the Royal Geographic Society, the French Explorers Society (the only American member), the Archaeological Society, and the Mach II Club.

He has been bitten by a rattlesnake, charged by a rogue elephant, and trapped in quicksand. He has survived multiple plane crashes, been caught in earthquakes, and almost drowned. And at age 80, he is still goal-driven. He keeps adding to his goals list and uses the same four-step goal-attainment formula I present in this book.

If you're ready to turn your *wish-craft* into *goal-craft,* grab a pen and paper or your computer keyboard, and title the first page *My Life Goals* or *My Goals List,* or come up with a title of your own. Now list as many goals as you can imagine. When you fill up the first page, start another, then another. The point is to brainstorm as many goals as you can. Don't worry about how you're going to achieve a particular goal or when you might accomplish it. Generate as long a list as possible. Devote some time to this exercise.

Keep your goal statements brief at this point. We're going to work with your goals list in chapter five, *Perfect Your Timing*. For now, though, the important thing is to get as many goals as possible on paper. Plan to spend at least an uninterrupted half hour right now to generate your goals list. Later, as you think of a few more goals, take a break and then add them to your list. Keep a pen and pad nearby for the next couple of days so you can capture any "incoming" ideas as they arrive.

The reason this step is so important is that you have transformed *wish-craft* into the initial stages of *goal-craft*. Writing goals down is a self-organizing principle. If you really want to be successful—at anything—recording your intentions forms one of the cornerstones of your life script. Written goals become the blueprint for your "core" movements. They give direction and content to your progress. They help determine which sensory data from the environment you pay attention to and which will be overlooked—remember the perceptual-filters exercise a few pages ago.

Setting definite life goals changes our awareness by triggering our perceptual filter system to be on the lookout for experiences and circumstances that relate to these goals. You've seen this principle in operation many times. This is why, for example, the minute you purchase a new car, you begin to see the same car everywhere you go. Those other cars were already part of your visual environment, but you hardly noticed them or may have missed them entirely. Once you became interested in that particular car, your consciousness was geared to seek information and input (much like the search command technology in your computer) and bring them into your conscious awareness.

The more you deliberately look for something, the more you will notice it. By capturing your goals in writing, you help to ensure that the information and resources you need to accomplish that goal will "pop" into your conscious awareness. I've heard story after story from people in my audiences attesting to the unfailing nature of this "search command" principle, and I have found it to be true in my own experience.

The interesting thing about this "search command" perceptual mechanism is that it has always been available—and active—all our lives. It has been associated with our health, safety, and well-being since birth. We may have been "drifting" when it comes to understanding our higher purpose or fully developing our talents and skills, but our self-preservation instincts have been operating all along to protect and sustain us. Psychologists call this concept "conditioning."

This instinctive conditioning is always present. Its job is to help us become aware of opportunities to supply ourselves with food, shelter, and clothing. But we are a "higher order of being," as Thoreau reminds us. Setting goals takes us to a higher level of conditioning. Goals enable us to use our inborn conditioning powers to reach beyond our basic needs and attain our decided aspirations. Our circuits are wired for success; all we have to do is train them in the right direction. It is completely up to us to make it happen.

Goal Power Is Go Power

> *I know of no more encouraging fact than the unquestionable ability of people to elevate their lives by conscious, calculated endeavors.*
>
> —Henry David Thoreau

In 1969, England and France began discussing how nice it would be to link the two countries with a tunnel. (The concept was initially proposed in the eighteenth century). By the spring of 1980, the two countries began laying the groundwork for the colossal undertaking. In 1994, nearly two and a half centuries after the idea was first conceived, a thirty-one-mile-long tunnel beneath the English Channel was opened to the public. The two neighbors had finally gotten serious about their mutual goal.

Linking England and France by subterranean rail, the Channel Tunnel, or Chunnel, as it is affectionately called, is, as of this writing, the largest privately financed underwater project in human history. This massive engineering feat cost $13.7 billion and took seven years to complete. In addition to carrying 8.5 million metric tons of freight each year, the Chunnel affords millions of people the opportunity to take a three-hour nonstop rail trip between London and Paris.

The same goal-setting formula that built the Chunnel can make it possible for you to build your future. In principle the mechanics are the same. Both the British and the French started by deciding what they wanted. This is the first level of commitment. Then they moved to the second level when they began to take action, formulating a plan, obtaining materials and equipment, and breaking the large goal down into smaller steps. As investors were secured, promises made, ground broken, and construction went into full stride, the team reached the third level of commitment, and there was no turning back from completion.

You have made great strides in deciding what you want and getting the list of goals you've generated down on paper. Congratulations! Your next step is to take action, and it all starts with a plan. Let's get started using your goals list, and apply the SLAM formula to each of your goals:

The Goal SLAM Formula

Effective goals are Specific. The more specific the better. For years I have encouraged my audiences to set thoroughly clear and concise goals. The size and scope of each goal will partly determine how long it takes to complete it, but what matters most is that you articulate each goal in language that captures its importance and essence. If your goal is not specific, it is merely an intention and thus cannot be acted upon.

For example, "I want to climb a mountain" is an intention. "I want to climb the north face of Mt. Everest with the team that sets out on May 25" is a specific goal statement. "I want to learn to juggle" is an intention. "I will juggle three balls for fifty consecutive catches without dropping, by August 5" is a specific goal statement.

When you shift your thinking from wishful thinking to specific written goal statements, you are well on your way toward goal fulfillment. Pablo Picasso once said, "From the sky, from the earth, from a scrap of paper, from a passing shape, from a spider's web . . . we must pick out what is good for us." When you make your goals specific, you literally "pick out what is good" and turn possibilities into probabilities.

Effective goals are Linear. Every goal should have calendar dates attached to it: a start date, a completion date, and milestones in between. A timeline for each goal is critical for keeping you on track by identifying bottlenecks, ensuring continuity, and monitoring the pace of accomplishment. You may be familiar with Horace's famous quote "Carpe diem" (seize the day), made famous in the movie *The Dead Poets Society*, starring Robin Williams. Both the ancient Roman poet and Williams' character are telling us that all we have is right now. By taking timely actions, we can "seize the day" and take calculated steps toward each goal's achievement.

Most people underestimate the amount of time it will take to achieve their goals. Estimating time frames can be tricky—just ask anyone who has taken on a "simple" home improvement project. A good rule to follow when setting timelines is to add contingency time (perhaps an additional twenty to twenty-five percent) to cover unforeseen events or requirements. You can always adjust your time frame to keep things on track.

Timelines will vary depending on the goal. For simplicity's sake, I generally divide my goals into three types: short-range, medium-range, and long-range goals.

1.   The timeline for short-range goals is from one day to six months.
2.   Medium-range goals go from six months to a year.
3.   Long-range goals go from one to five years and beyond.

Effective goals are Achievable. Be realistic. If you have bad knees, maybe running a sub-three-hour marathon is not a reasonable goal. Or if you have never cooked a meal, don't expect to win an internationally sponsored gourmet cooking contest. If you have never parred a golf course, it just isn't realistic to expect a spot on the professional golf tour. One of the most common mistakes people make in goal-setting is to start out with unrealistic goals. And keep in mind that what is child's play for one person is mere wishful thinking for someone else. While many people set goals that are completely out of reach, others settle for mediocrity—goals so easily achieved that they fail to hold one's interest. Both kinds will likely go unrealized. The ideal goal is one that is achievable, yet wild and compelling enough to get you excited and keep you moving forward.

There is a believability quotient at play in all this. Successful goal-crafters believe they can accomplish what they have envisioned. They are mentally, emotionally, and physically ready to meet the challenges entailed in realizing their goals. They know that goal power is go power.

Effective goals are Measurable. You won't see progress unless you can tell how much progress you've made. Remember the Florence Chadwick story earlier in this chapter? She had quite literally lost sight of her goal and had no clear idea of how far she had come toward it. Effective goal-crafters are milestone-conscious and outcome-focused. They quantify their achievements by keeping score and measuring results. For example, if your goal is to lose weight, how much weight must you lose to meet your goal? You can't know how you're doing if all you have is an intention to lose weight, rather than a measurable goal. The missing ingredients are specificity, linear requirements, achievability, and measurability. A properly stated weight-loss goal statement would read: By September 5, I will have lost fifteen pounds. This goal statement meets the SLAM criteria for an effective goal statement.

Take another look at your list of goals. Now separate your goals into the following categories: Health, Relationships, Work, Spiritual Growth, and Personal Interests. By this time you may have thought of a few more goals, and you should add them to the appropriate lifestyle compartments. Make sure there are goals for each category. Once you have compartmentalized your goals, turn to the Goal Profile on the next page. You may want to reproduce it and enlarge it to an 8½ x 11 inch format to give yourself plenty of room. Better still, for an electronic copy of this and other resources, go to www.danthurmon.com. Make enough copies so you have one Goal Profile for each goal. You may want to review the SLAM goal-setting formula, as well as the sample Goal Profile on the following page, before you begin.

GOAL PROFILE

Goal Statement:	Today's Date:
Overall Benefit:	Lifestyle Area:

Possible Obstacles:	Resources/Support/Solutions:

Milestone Schedule

Incremental Goal	Action Steps	Start Date	Finish Date	Investment (Money/Time)	Reward Received
1.					
2.					
3.					
4.					
5.					
6.					
7.					
8.					
9.					
10.					
11.					

Overall Target Completion Date:

Positive Affirmation(s):

Signed:

Witnessed:

GOAL PROFILE

Goal Statement: To weigh 160 lbs. by July 4		Today's Date:
Overall Benefit: To increase self-esteem and improve body image		Lifestyle Area: Health

Possible Obstacles:	Resources/Support/Solutions:
27 lbs. excess weight	Join Weight Watchers
Not used to exercising	Exercise: Start with 10 minutes low-impact aerobics, twice a week
Love food too much	Eat smaller portions, reward myself occasionally with dessert
Work 6 days a week	Reach agreement with supervisor
Love to play computer games	Play after exercise, cut out snacks, try other activities
Lower back pain	Go to Chiropractor
Spouse is terrific cook	Enlist her confidence and support

Milestone Schedule

Incremental Goal	Action Steps	Start Date	Finish Date	Investment (Money/Time)	Reward Received
1. Drop 5 lbs to 182	Eat smaller portions, walk 1 mile course around neighborhood	Jan 4	Feb 25	1 hour	X
2. Drop 5 lbs to 177	Eat smaller portions, cut out snacks, exercise 10 minutes, walk around block	Mar 1	Mar 25	1 hour	X
3. Drop 4 lbs to 173	Bicycle 20 min., exercise 15 min.	Mar 26	Apr 15	90 min $400 for bike	X
4. Drop 4 lbs to 169	Reward myself with dessert. Aerobics 30 min. Hike 30 min.	Apr 17	Apr 30	2 Hours	X
5. Drop 3 lbs to 166	Bicycle 40 min. Hike 45 min.	May 1	May 25	2 hours	X
6. Drop 3 lbs to 163	Swim 30 min., bicycle 60 min.	May 26	June 15	2 hours	X
7. Drop 2 lbs to 161	Continue eating smaller portions, Hike 1 hour	June 16	June 30	1 hour	X
8. Drop 1 lb to 160	Bicycle 1 hour. reward myself with dessert.	July 1	July 4	90 min.	X
9. Maintain 160 for 3 mo.		July 5			
10.					
11.					

Overall Target Completion Date: July 4

Positive Affirmation(s): I enjoy my perfect weight of 160 lbs.; Nothing tastes as good as health feels.

Signed: **Goal-crafter**

Witnessed: **I Am Somebody**

You Never Know Who's in Your Audience—Part Two

*Really believe in your heart of hearts that your
fundamental purpose, the reason for your being, is to
enlarge the lives of others. Your life will be enlarged
also.*

—Pete Thigpen

On March 22, 2002, I was at the Nashville airport, having just completed a presentation for Southern Motor Carriers. It went beautifully, and I was still charged with performance energy as I prepared to head home. During my program, I had shared the story of John Goddard's amazing life list of accomplishments with my audience. As usual, this hit home and helped set the tone for my message: that we all can achieve more in life if we commit to compelling, exciting goals.

I was through the security checkpoint and trying to get a quick bite to eat before my flight when my cell phone rang. I glanced at the caller ID, which displayed, "Private." I answered, "Hi, this is Dan," and the voice on the other end—one I had never heard before—said, "Hello, Dan. This is John Goddard." My pause was longer than normal as I processed this information.

"John Goddard?"

"Yes, Dan. I hear good things about you."

Six months earlier I had delivered a program for the National Association of Student Councils in Charlotte, North Carolina. The auditorium was filled with 500 high school students, who were gathered to learn leadership skills and set goals for their lives. I had decided this would be a perfect situation to share the story of John Goddard's amazing life. After the presentation, one of the students approached me and introduced herself as Reneé. She thanked me for the program and especially for talking about John Goddard.

"You see," she explained, John Goddard is my great-uncle."

Once again, this illustrates one of my favorite mottos: You never know who's in your audience.

Reneé and I corresponded by e-mail several times after that initial meeting. In one of my notes, I shared with her that it was one of my life goals to meet her great-uncle. Reneé then decided to take action, and because she did, Dr. John Goddard was now calling me on my cell phone.

"I just returned home from a lecture tour and received the most wonderful letter from my niece, Reneé. She told me about you and was quite impressed. Tell me, Dan, how do you use my story in your presentation?"

I explained that I used his story to illustrate the power of setting goals for one's life.

"I think the problem is that most people don't set their goals high enough," he said. Then he asked, "What do you think?"

It seemed strange that *he* was asking *me* what I thought. Let's just say I was a little intimidated. "Well, Dr. Goddard, I think that is true. And I also think that people don't understand the power of writing down their goals."

"Of course," he said. "It all starts there. When you write them down, you make them real. And by the way, please call me John. Let me ask you, Dan, how many goals do you think I have accomplished by now?"

He was testing me. Putting me on the spot. Fortunately, I knew the answer because I had researched his life—he had accomplished 108 of his 127 goals. But I decided to guess slightly lower to flatter him. I said, "Well, John, if you could have accomplished a hundred of your hundred twenty-seven goals, what an amazing life you would have led. How many have you done?"

Then John Goddard said something I will never forget. In a sharp tone he said, "Dan, I wrote *that* list when I was fifteen years old. Surely you don't think that is all that I have aspired to do."

I nearly dropped the phone. Then he explained that his life list now contained 600 goals. And at this point he has achieved 520. Implied in this statement was a question to me: How are *you* doing?

At the conclusion of our conversation, John asked me to fax my bio so that he could learn more about me and what I do. He said, "I've never met a man I couldn't learn from."

Now, I was more than a little bit intimidated. But when I returned home, I faxed the information. I also sent him a video of my presentation. He called me immediately and was very supportive and encouraging. He said that he was extremely impressed and that my programs were unique, creative, and exciting. Then he paid a compliment beyond all others when he said, "You know, Dan, I think that you and I are kindred spirits."

We exchanged more phone calls and letters. He sent me his book entitled *The Survivor: 24 Spine-Chilling Adventures on the Edge of Death*. It's a collection of stories, all of them recounting the times he almost died while in pursuit of his goals. It's a very exciting read and includes stories of dodging hippos in the Nile and Congo Rivers, nearly drowning in rapids, climbing ropeless down a treacherous cliff, and making a forced crash landing in a small aircraft.

On May 16, 2002, I was able to check another goal off my list when I met John Goddard. My friend Philip Solomon and I met him at his California home. We talked about life, and he showed us his many treasures from his world travels. As I gazed in awe at the models and photos of the many high-performance aircraft John has piloted, my admiration grew by the minute. Each piece of art, tool, weapon, or photo he showed us unveiled another amazing story. I got the sense we could talk for days and not scratch the surface of the tales he could share. Then we went to lunch at his favorite Mexican restaurant and talked some more. John Goddard even picked up the check.

Passing clubs with Mike Vondruska around John Goddard
in front of the Pyramids of Giza (November, 2004)

Our friendship has grown since that first meeting. Twice I've joined John and his wife, Carol, on their annual "friends and family hike." In November of 2004, I accompanied them on a ten-day adventure exploring the wonders of Egypt. And John Goddard has even played a major part in the completion of this book, contributing the foreword and offering a steady supply of encouragement. I promised him that I would finish it—and that one action increased my commitment tenfold. That you hold this volume in your hands right now is a testament to his influence.

It has been said, if you want to be great, surround yourself with great people. In my estimation there are none greater than John Goddard. He is truly a model for achievement in life. He is a perpetual student of nature and people, ever curious and inquisitive. Most striking, though, is his humility. For all his accomplishments, he is still very approachable and has a remarkable ability to make other people feel special and important.

Action Assignments

1. Recall one experience when you took particularly good AIM and *intelligently managed* your *actions* to achieve a goal. This should be a memory that brings back positive feelings of accomplishment. Then remember a situation where your AIM was off and your results were less than desirable. Which experience taught you a more valuable life lesson? How has that experience changed you? What lesson did you learn? In what ways have you applied what you learned to other aspects of your life?

2. How many of the Goal Profiles did you complete? How many will you implement as a result of having read this chapter? Select a dozen Goal Profiles to jump-start your success. Let's call them your "golden dozen." Now let's travel through time and project yourself five years into the future. At that time, how successful will you feel if you have accomplished every one of those goals? How will you feel if you haven't taken action?

3. How do you feel about the statement *If you fail to plan, you're planning to fail*? Take a few moments to ponder this question, because your future depends on your thoughtful answer.

4. If you had an opportunity to meet John Goddard, what would you ask him? What would you most want to know? If you were to promise him something, what would you promise?

5

PERFECT YOUR TIMING

*By learning to use our small windows of time with velocity,
we are able to use our big windows of time much more
effectively.*

—Julia Cameron

There's no present like the time.

—Dan Thurmon

What if a representative from your bank were to call and tell you that a new account has been opened in your name? Here's the deal: This unique account is designed for withdrawals only. Every morning, bright and early, a deposit of $86,400 is made into your account by an unseen benefactor. The only catch is this: At the end of each day, any money left in the account will be removed, and you will be denied access to it again. But the good news is that the next morning and every morning thereafter, another $86,400 gets deposited like clockwork.

You're probably asking yourself, "Where's that bank been all my life?" Right? If there were such a bank, and if those dollars were really getting deposited each day, what would you do? If you're like most people, you'd make sure you spent every dime, so none of it would go back to the bank! You'd pay bills, pay off your mortgage, keep your family well clothed and well fed, go shopping (big-time), take the vacation you've always wanted, decide whether to retire from work, donate to your favorite charity, give money to friends, buy a new car, invest some, blow some. If you had interests similar to mine, you might buy a new mountain bike, a set of golf clubs, or an airplane. One thing is for sure: You wouldn't leave it in the bank.

The good news is that you really do have this account. But before you leave on a transatlantic shopping spree, I'd better explain one more thing. The daily deposits are not monetary but temporal. You don't receive $86,400; you get 86,400 seconds—60 seconds a minute, 60 minutes an hour, 24 hours a day, which comes out to 86,400 seconds every 24 hours.

Are you still interested in drawing from that account? I hope so, because you'll need to spend it wisely in order to achieve the goals you listed in chapter four. You have an opportunity to use each minute, every hour, to your advantage. It'll take work and focus, so you'll need to keep your priorities in place if you want to enjoy *success in action*.

Every one of us, regardless of our status, pedigree, affluence, or influence, receives only 86,400 seconds in a day to spend or lose. Yet some people manage to accomplish so much more in that same time allotment than others do. The purpose of this chapter is to help you maximize your investment by learning some essential techniques to leverage this precious resource to your benefit.

Time Flies

> *Time is life. It is irreversible and unreplaceable. To waste your time is to waste your life, but to master your time is to master your life and make the most of it.*
> —Alan Lakein

What is your belief about time? How much can you get done in a day? In an hour? A fleeting minute? A second? The following people took those questions to heart:

- Peter Rosendahl set a unicycle sprint record of 12.11 seconds (29.72 kmh, or 18.47 mph) for 100 meters from a standing start in Las Vegas, Nevada, on March 25, 1994.

- Fred Rompelberg rode a bicycle 167.043 miles per hour (268.831 kmh) at Bonneville Salt Flats, Utah, on October 3, 1995. He has been cycling professionally for thirty years and has held eleven world cycling records.

- Babu Chhiri Sherpa completed the fastest ascent of Mt. Everest from a base camp at 17,551 feet to the summit in 16 hours 56 minutes on May 21, 2000.

- Will Howard of Marietta, Georgia, joggled (jogged while juggling) one mile in 4 minutes, 42.36 seconds on February 1, 2003. I was there in the crowd to cheer him on!

- Dustin Phillips of Topeka, Kansas, drank 91 percent of a 14-ounce bottle of tomato ketchup through a quarter-inch straw in a world record time of 33 seconds on September 23, 1999.

- Seandale Price from Chicago rapped 683 syllables in 54.501 seconds on the set of *Guinness World Records: Primetime* in Los Angeles on June 24, 1998.

- Michel Dupont and Claude Hetru flew an Air France Concorde jet 22,858.8 miles in 31 hours, 27 minutes, 49 seconds to establish the fastest aerial circumnavigation of the world. They left JFK Airport in New York and flew eastbound to Toulouse, Dubai, Bangkok, Guam, Honolulu, and Acapulco on August 15 and 16, 1995.

Those are incredible feats! So incredible, in fact, that each of these people is in the *Guinness Book of World Records*. They set a goal and got there faster than anyone else. In order to accomplish their goals, they did whatever they had to do and avoided anything they didn't need to do. They learned how to set their priorities and manage their time so they could make each moment count.

Time is a perishable resource—the seconds really do fly by. People who are accustomed to *success in action* know how to multiply their minutes to save hours. In the words of John F. Kennedy, they "use time as a tool, not as a crutch."

To effectively manage our time, we must master two simultaneous disciplines: First, we must learn how to manage the time we have and stay in control of our schedule. Second, we must strive to expand each moment toward its infinite potential. In this way you can drastically accelerate your learning, making quantum leaps in your abilities and success. By "warping" time, you can also learn to create original experiences that engage people in a way that causes them to lose their perception of time, thereby deepening your interaction with them. But before you can become a master of the moment, you must first learn to focus your efforts with precision. What is true for masterful juggling is also true for your life. When it appears as though you are doing many different things all at the same time, what you are actually doing is just one thing at a time really, really fast. In other words, when you are at your best, your actions happen quickly and in the proper sequence.

First Things First

> *Successful people know they need to get many things done—and done effectively. Therefore, they concentrate their time and energy on doing one thing at a time—and on doing first things first.*
>
> —Peter Drucker

What are you doing with your time? How often have you asked yourself, "Where did this week (or month, or year) go?" How did you spend all that time? The French Concorde pilots, Michel Dupont and

Claude Hetru, used a little over thirty-one hours to circumnavigate the globe. The following exercise will help you see how you spend your time in any given week. Again, this is an opportunity for you to commit completely and take an action for a short period of time in order to enhance your use of *all* your future time. I'm not asking you to account for every minute; however, the more accurate you are in accounting for your time, the more valuable this personal inventory will be. You will be taking a giant step toward understanding how you spend your day. Do you engage in activity or accomplishment? Are you idle or active? Goal directed or distracted?

For simplicity's sake, think in terms of quarter hours, half hours, and hours as you compute the time you spend on your daily and weekly activities. Your Daily Activities Inventory (DAI) is based on twenty-four hours, and your Weekly Activities Inventory (WAI) is based on one-hundred sixty-eight hours. Complete the Daily Activities Inventory first and transfer the time spent on each activity to the Weekly Activities Inventory.

You may enlarge and reproduce each of these inventories or visit www.danthurmon.com for an electronic version. I suggest that you track your activities for at least four weeks. That should give you a pretty good idea of how you're spending your time. I have left space for additional activities in each area so you can customize the activity pool to meet your specific lifestyle.

M T W T F S S   DAILY ACTIVITIES INVENTORY
Circle one

Complete the estimated time column first. Estimate how long you think it takes to complete each activity before you begin tracking the time. Then track each day's activities and record the actual time in the middle column (Actual Time), and compute the difference (Variance).

Work-Related Activities	Estimated Time	Actual Time	Variance
1. Commuting to and from work			
2. Reading and responding to email and other correspondence (in-box stuff)			
3. Meetings			
4. Telephone, teleconference calls			
5. Handling written correspondence			
6. Job travel during work hours			
7. Customer contact			
8. Training and development			
9. Handling emergencies and other snafus			
10.			
11.			
12.			
Totals			

Family Activities	Estimated Time	Actual Time	Variance
13. Family get-togethers indoors			
14. Mealtime			
15. Helping with homework			
16. Extra curricular school activities			
17. Housekeeping/laundry			
18. Yard and lawn work			
19. Grocery shopping			
20. Errands			
21. Doctor visits			

	Estimated Time	Actual Time	Variance
22. Family outings, recreation, spectator sports			
23. Religious/community involvements			
24. Paying bills			
25. Automobile cleaning and maintenance			
26. House maintenance and repair			
27. Visits/phone calls with family and relatives			
28. TV, listening to music			
29. Video games, board games			
30.			
31.			
32.			
Totals			

Personal Activities	Estimated Time	Actual Time	Variance
33. Grooming			
34. Sleeping			
35. Eating snacks			
36. Hobbies, self-development			
37. Rest and relaxation, quiet time, centering			
38. Fitness, physical recreation			
39. TV, radio and music listening, video games			
40. Leisure reading, letter writing			
41. Parties and socializing			
42.			
43.			
44.			
45.			
Totals			
Daily Totals	24	24	0

Weekly Activities Inventory

Activity	M	T	W	T	F	S	S	Weekly Total
1.								
2.								
3.								
4.								
5.								
6.								
7.								
8.								
9.								
10.								
11.								
12.								
13.								
14.								
15.								
16.								
17.								
18.								
19.								
20.								
21.								
22.								
23.								

Weekly Activities Inventory

Activity	M	T	W	T	F	S	S	Weekly Total
24.								
25.								
26.								
27.								
28.								
29.								
30.								
31.								
32.								
33.								
34.								
35.								
36.								
37.								
38.								
39.								
40.								
41.								
42.								
43.								
44.								
45.								
46.								

As you may have gathered by now, the way you spend your days is the way you spend your life. When I first did this exercise, it was a mandatory assignment in a management class I needed for graduation from the University of Georgia. At first it seemed tedious and difficult, but it became more natural after just a few days. After tracking my time for a full month, I was amazed at the amount of time I spent on routine, mundane, time-wasting activities. Some routine activities— brushing teeth, combing hair, eating breakfast, paying bills, sleeping— require a certain amount of time. Self-care, grooming, eating, and financial responsibilities will have to remain part of our lifestyle habits.

Other time-consuming activities, however, we can modify or elimi- nate, such as driving to work, watching TV, yard work, housekeeping, phone conversations and e-mail correspondence, idle time, and so on. Managing the time associated with these activities is not only within our control, it is part of our goal-crafting responsibility. In the last chapter you generated a goals list in five life areas. You listed many goals that you believe will help you become more successful and fulfilled, both personally and professionally.

The purpose of this chapter is to help you establish priorities for your activities so you feel fulfilled, productive, and in control. My work has taken me all across America and abroad. I've presented to many different types of people and organizations, including corporate boards and CEOs, sales leaders, managers, health-care professionals, schools, financial institutions, secretaries, and homemakers. Through this wide variety of contacts, I have repeatedly heard one overriding criticism of time-management systems: traditional methods don't work because they ignore a basic reality about life itself—that we live with and around other people. Therefore, we are never entirely free of our responsi- bilities to others. We do not live in a social vacuum. We have obligations to other people, which affect the amount of time we can devote to our personal and professional interests.

Most of us are not in a position to isolate ourselves from others. We enjoy friendships and love our families too much to cocoon ourselves away so we can pursue our goals at all costs. The techniques I present in this chapter have this connectedness with others in mind. Rather than impose one rigid set of priority-setting rules that are supposed to fit everyone, I've designed this chapter to give you a wide variety of techniques, so you can manage multiple priorities. You will notice a definite lack of dictatorial "shoulds" and "musts" and "have tos." I believe we are all on a path of self-expression and responsibility. Richard Bach puts it this way: "All the events of our lives are there because we have drawn them there. What we choose to do with them is up to us." When it comes to enjoying the things we really want to do in life, we can "draw them there" by learning how to set priorities for what's important.

No one knows your responsibilities, needs, pressures, and problems as well as you. That's why you are in the best position to decide which priority-setting techniques will work best for you—you have the best vantage point. Learning how to set priorities is not a "once only" get-organized project. It's an ongoing skill for imposing order and sanity on your day.

What you value is reflected in how you use your time. Another way of putting it is, what you spend time doing is what you value doing. When you've used all 86,400 seconds, your day is gone. What you've done, or haven't done, is history. So let's make history together.

Let's Have the Time of Our Lives

> *The secret to writing musical scores is knowing what not to put in writing.*
>
> —James Taylor

People often ask how I manage to juggle all the things I do in my life without going crazy. Between presenting speeches and seminars, meeting with corporate clients, running a complex business, collaborating with my office staff, nurturing my marriage with my beautiful wife, Sheilia, raising my children, Eddie and Maggie, rehearsing with the band at church, teaching students at Cirque du Monde, and traveling for pleasure, things can get pretty intense. It all comes down to choice—where will you invest your time and energy to get the greatest value? And because life is unpredictable, we need a method of setting priorities that leaves room for emergencies and other things that "come up."

I believe that when we are using our time and energy well, we can have the time of our lives. Having a well-organized world, one based on managing multiple priorities, is much more than knowing where to find your car keys or organizing your TV viewing time. It is about keeping and improving the deeper connection between the various aspects of you and the multifarious parts of your busy life. When you enter each day with a purposeful sense of coordinating your time, energies, and conscious choices, those 86,400 seconds become charged with positive possibilities.

The rationale I use is based on a time-tested model, which I call the Action Priority Model. I ask myself the following two questions whenever I need to set priorities:

- How important is it?
- How urgent is it?

There's a great saying among pilots: "When in doubt, fly the plane." With all the activity that makes up flying—communications, navigation, looking for traffic, monitoring instruments, and so on—flying can be overwhelming. So, the most important task is to make sure the plane stays in the sky. Fly the plane. This is also true for our lives. It's easy to get overwhelmed with activity. At such moments, it is crucial that we develop the skill to evaluate quickly what matters most—what we need to do to keep our plane in the air and moving toward our goals.

The following Action Priority Model may be useful in evaluating your activities.

ACTION PRIORITY MODEL

Level of Importance

	Low	High
Sense of Urgency — High	High Urgency, Low Importance *Demands your attention, but doesn't really matter*	High Urgency, High Importance *Needs to be taken care of immediately*
Sense of Urgency — Low	Low Urgency, Low Importance *Serves as a distraction or escape*	Low Urgency, High Importance *Accelerates your growth—the key to your success*

©Motivation Works, Inc.

If something falls in the lower left quadrant (Low Urgency, Low Importance), it is probably a distraction or escape for you. You must learn to skip these tasks or minimize the time you spend with trivial activities. Sometimes an escape is necessary and enjoyable, but recognize these are low-priority items.

If something falls in the upper left quadrant (High Urgency, Low Importance), it is generally something that someone *else* deems important, but it is not essential to your well-being or success. Often, we engage in these tasks (e-mails and phone calls, for example) in order to feel productive and significant. But, in truth, we are wasting our energy and time on tasks that do not matter.

Anything that falls in the upper right quadrant (High Urgency, High Importance) usually needs to be addressed right away. This could be a family emergency, a deadline at work, or an unexpected issue with your health. Busy, productive people pride themselves on their ability to handle such emergencies, taking control of important, urgent situations. And, sometimes such tasks are unavoidable, but many times they could have been prevented. Truly successful people learn to do the things that are important *before* they become urgent emergencies.

It is the tasks in the lower right quadrant (Low Urgency, High Importance) that often determine our long-term results. We must recognize that even though important tasks may not demand our immediate attention, they are the key to accomplishment. Such tasks may include your morning workout, the daily disciplines of study or practice, or communication with individuals who have an important place in your life, personally or professionally. At first glance, these actions don't appear to be urgent, since life goes on whether you take care of them or not. But from the perspective of your goals and values, they take on an increased sense of urgency as you recognize that what you do today will have amplified consequences down the road.

I don't always handle my priorities according to this model, but this method of understanding the different types of activities we encounter has been most valuable as a tool to leverage the value of my choices and my time. When it comes to managing multiple priorities, every day is a learning experience. "Perhaps the most valuable result of all education," said Thomas Huxley, "is the ability to make yourself do the things you ought to do, when you ought to do them, whether you like it or not."

I strive to do just that. Knowing what needs to be done is the key to developing a flexible to-do system so you can assign an up-to-date priority to each task, activity, goal, opportunity, problem, and distraction.

Although this model may seem fairly simplistic, it is a good priority barometer. When I am faced with a number of things to do, I decide which ones are truly important and I determine whether the "urgency" is real, imposed, or imagined. Then I can make an informed judgment about how to spend my valuable time. One of the chief benefits about being a serious goal-crafter is that it forces me to set priorities *in favor of my goals*. The kind of force I'm referring to here is discipline. I'm always thinking about the goals I have set for myself, and the priorities associated with those goals.

One of my favorite stories on disciplined thinking about priorities comes from Dr. Louis Tartaglia's book *Thirsting for God: Spiritual Lessons of Mother Teresa*, which he cowrote with Father Angelo Scolozzi. In it Dr. Tartaglia describes one of Mother Teresa's Vatican visits:

> *Mother Teresa was a warm and compassionate spiritual messenger with a single-minded message. She lived to minister to the poorest of the poor, and she never deviated from it. Even when she visited the Pope at the Vatican, her attention was focused on the poor.*
>
> *At one point she forgot why she was there, and Father Angelo, who had accompanied her, asked how she could possibly forget the purpose of such a visit. Mother Teresa told him, "I was looking at all of those rooms. Some weren't being used. I was thinking how many beds we could put in there for the poor, and how many of the poor we could take care of."*

Mother Teresa never took her eyes off her goal. Her every impulse was honoring the priorities she had set for herself and for her mission. More important than her visit with the Pope was her sense of urgency to fill those beds and rooms with the poor. For Mother Teresa, that priority came first.

Father Angelo relates that Mother Teresa's "distraction" became a call to action and, ultimately, a beautiful expression of love.

> *I believe it was this distraction that originated the request of a house in the Vatican. which now is a reality for the street people of Vatican City. It was built by [Pope John Paul II] as a gift to Mother, and the name of the house is Gift of Mary.*

Mother Teresa placed the things she considered urgent and important at the top of her list of things to do. She also was able to prevent the merely urgent from crowding out the truly important, by planning ahead so she could limit the onset of what many people see as emergencies. In Mother Teresa's own words,

> *We are committed to feed Christ who is hungry, committed to clothe Christ who is naked, committed to take in Christ who has no home—and to do all this with a smile on our face and bursting with joy . . . But the important thing is not to try to do everything . . . I don't have time to do everything . . . only those things pleasing to Christ.*

Because she couldn't do everything, Mother Teresa did what mattered most. By living her life with unwavering devotion to a single focus, she changed the world for the better and provided love, hope, and inspiration to millions of people.

Warping Time

It isn't so much the years of our lives as it is the collective moments that define us. How we enjoy and utilize the precious now is the key to our destiny. When you think back on your life, it's the moments that you remember. When you are completely present in the moment, whatever you are doing, you can create the very real experience of slowing down the passage of time. In his book *About Time*, Paul Davies ties time to the person experiencing time:

> *Einstein's theory of relativity introduced into physics*
> *a notion of time that is intrinsically flexible. Although*
> *it did not quite restore the mystical ideas of time as*
> *essentially personal and subjective, it did tie the*
> *experience of time firmly to the individual observer.*
> *No longer could one talk of the time—only my time*
> *and your time, depending on how we are moving. To*
> *use the catch phrase: Time is relative.*

Time is relative in the way we experience it. The five minutes you spend filling your gas tank are quite different from the five minutes spent in a passionate embrace with the person you love. The experience of watching a two-hour presentation on the history of tax law would be far different for me than two hours spent at a favorite movie. One thing my wife can't comprehend is how I can spend four or five hours playing one round of golf. To me that time passes quickly, because I love the game and the companionship that comes along with it. On the other hand, Sheilia thoroughly enjoys "memory booking." She will gleefully spend hours cutting photos, arranging them with borders, backgrounds, captions, and keepsakes from our experiences. While I enjoy looking at the books once they are completed, the process would bore me to tears. Time is relative, and when we understand this, the practical application has the power to transform our life experiences in three specific ways.

First, we can alter the way *we* experience time by our conscious level of participation in the world around us. When we are not enjoying our circumstances, we can change our orientation or refocus our efforts to make the time pass more quickly. Soldiers pass miles by singing cadences together in unison. Families pass the hours on cross-country road trips by playing car games such as "find the out-of-state plates." I love the solitude of yard work because it allows me the time to engage in creative thinking and problem solving. In a corporate environment, trips to the water cooler to associate with others make the time pass more quickly. So does the process of immersing yourself in your work to a deeper, more stimulating level. Even if the job is tedious, your approach to the job can be one of fascination.

The second use of the "time is relative" mindset has less to do with how *you* experience the world than with the experiences you create for *others*. My good friend the master magician Howie Marmer and I have had long conversations about this subject. Howie is an expert in creating moments of amazement that alter his audiences' perception of both time and reality. As performers we have studied the art of quickly connecting with people by using humor, skill, surprise, and interaction in order to elicit a desired response. That desired response may be applause, laughter, closing a negotiation, or persuading someone to embrace an idea or at least to suspend their disbelief. To have the greatest impact with an audience, however large or small, you must be successful at enabling them to lose track of time. To do this, you must deliver something beyond what they expect to experience. When this happens, the person will likely make the unconscious or conscious decision to go along with the show and will, by this decision, become connected to the performer at a deeper level. When this happens, seconds can have the impact of hours and, in many cases, create memories that last a lifetime. Or the reverse experience can be true. When I am at my best while speaking in front of audiences, my ninety-minute program seems to go by in no time, both for me and for my audiences. I have had complete strangers come up after the program and comment how the time just seemed to fly right by, as if it had only been a few minutes. Those are the experiences I live for. I know that in those moments, the audience is completely engaged and more open to receiving the message I deliver.

The third aspect of warping time relates to the time frame of our learning processes. I alluded to this in chapter three when I described the sensation of "tricking yourself" into accomplishing something the first time you try it. This phenomenon, widely experienced, is often referred to as "beginner's luck." Jugglers have that experience frequently, which is why it is so much fun to experiment with new tricks. Many times when learning a new juggling trick, I will "accidentally" get it right on the first try, only to spend the remainder of my practice session trying to repeat the success.

Learning is a process with many components: Developing skills, acquiring information, and repetition are some of the elements we tend to focus on. Just as important, though, is our giving ourselves *permission* to get it right. Whatever our learning process entails, it is essentially a confidence-building process. We must convince ourselves that we can learn the skill and move to a new level of competence and trust. This undertaking, like time itself, is relative. I believe that we can accelerate the process of learning to levels beyond our normal experience, as illustrated by the following true story.

Learning at the Speed of Freefall

Have you ever had a day that altered your life forever? Maybe it was your wedding day, your graduation, or the birth of your child. Do you want another day like that? Well, it doesn't have to involve another wedding, more education, or childbirth. You can create such a day with one simple action—a phone call. Look up "Skydiving" in the phone book and make an appointment to jump from an airplane. Your perspective on life and time will never be the same again.

The wonderful thing about modern skydiving is the popularity of the "tandem jump." With this method, the student is literally attached to the teacher. The harness you wear locks tightly into the harness of

R.G. helps me suit up for the big jump.

the tandem instructor, as if you were carrying him on your back. The benefits are outstanding. First is the mindset. Now someone who has never jumped before can participate with the knowledge that he or she is with an experienced professional, trained to handle even the most incompetent student. The comforting thought is, *I'm pretty sure that the instructor doesn't want to die either, so I'm probably safe.*

The other advantage to tandem jumps is the learning curve. Instead of a six-hour class to teach you how to jump solo from 3,500 feet, in about forty-five minutes you are ready to jump from as high as the plane will take you. And instead of opening your parachute as you leave the airplane, you can immediately experience the ultimate sensation of freefall.

On the day that my friend Philip and I went to the Freefall Ranch in Warm Springs, Georgia, it was a banner day for skydivers. There was a special plane making a guest appearance at the airport: a rare Helio Stallion. This meant that we would be jumping from 14,000 feet instead of the usual 10,500. This altitude would afford us a full sixty seconds of freefall before we would open our parachutes! That meant I would achieve two of my life goals in one day with one jump: (number four) "Take a skydive," and (number thirty-five) "Freefall for one minute."

The adventure began on a beautiful spring day with a ninety-minute drive from Atlanta to Warm Springs. We encouraged each other the whole way there, doing our best to keep up our nerve. The excitement we felt was like an electrical current running through us. It was nine a.m. when my big brown van pulled into the parking lot, and the place was just starting to come alive.

We signed the most ridiculous waiver you have ever seen, surrendering our rights to sue should we be maimed or killed. (All standard stuff, I assure you—it helps if you don't even read it. Just take action: sign it, move forward.)

Stunning action photos adorned the walls of the "training room": captured images of freefall moments, taken of previous students as well as expert skydivers. We gazed in wonder, knowing that before this day was over, we would be the ones in those photos.

I met my instructor, known simply as R. G. "It stands for 'Real Good,'" he told me. That was reassuring, and I hoped it was true. The entire atmosphere of the Freefall Ranch was upbeat and fun. After watching a short video to learn the basics of freefall, we then received some more personalized instruction.

We learned the procedures for exiting from the airplane by practicing on a mock-up outside. It was made of plywood and two-by-fours, but it allowed us to rehearse the procedure for getting clear of the plane in the most efficient manner. We became acquainted with the equipment we would be using, and found some jumpsuits that fit us. The plan was that we would pull our own rip cords at 5,000 feet after performing several freefall maneuvers, such as right and left turns and "tracking," which involves streaking across the sky horizontally, like James Bond.

"This is an altimeter," R. G. told me. "You wear it on your wrist like a watch, and it tells you how close we are to the ground. If this sucker gets to three thousand feet and we're still hauling bobo toward Mother Earth, reach back and smack me. If that doesn't work, pull this to activate the reserve chute." How much of this was an act? I wasn't sure, but he did have my attention.

The plane was ready, and we huddled inside with six other jumpers, ten of us in all. We wore our jumpsuits, harnesses, leather helmets, and goggles. Everyone but Philip and me was an experienced jumper. They all looked completely relaxed—even bored—about the trip to jump altitude. There were no seats and certainly no seat belts. Those conveniences had been removed to make room for skydivers. Each had paid twenty dollars for a lift ticket to 14,000 feet. Philip and I had paid a good deal more for instruction and rentals, but price was not an issue at this moment.

The takeoff seemed sluggish with the weight of a full load, but soon enough we were up and climbing, making ascending circles in the sky to gain altitude. Although it was actually less than ten minutes, the ride seemed to take forever. Our perception of time was altered by the intensity and anticipation. During that time, several of the veteran skydivers actually napped. Others sat silently while mentally rehearsing their aerobatic routines. Philip and I were just taking it all in, trying to stay cool. Overheating from nervousness, my goggles fogged completely. This concerned me, and I thought it was important. But when I pointed it out to R. G., he just smiled and said, "You don't need to worry about *that.*" His comment left me wondering just what I *was* supposed to be worrying about.

Finally, the pilot swung around and shouted, "Jump run! Here we go!" My altimeter told me we were at 14,000 feet. My heart racing, I knew it would be just moments before we left the security of this "perfectly good airplane."

The spotter looked below, preparing to call the jump. His job was to judge the appropriate time to jump, taking into account location, wind speed, and direction. His ability to properly call the jump would determine whether we would be able to land near our desired target, the grassy field next to the runway.

"GO! GO! GO!!" he shouted. The door flew open, sending a rush of cold air through the plane. Instantly, my goggles were free of fog, and I understood why R. G. had dismissed my earlier concern. In the blink of an eye, all six veteran skydivers had disappeared out the door, leaving only Philip, me, and our two instructors. Everything we did had to happen fast, or we would be too far from the airport when we exited. It was decided earlier that I would jump first. So R. G. immediately attached four very strong clips to my harness. I confirmed each one, checking to see that they were secure. Those four clips were the only thing connecting me to him—an important link considering that he was the one wearing the parachute.

Harnessed together and on our knees, we shuffled toward the door. The aircraft cabin was loud and windy. There was still time to back out, but that was not really an option. I wanted this experience too much to quit now. "Ready"—we rocked forward—"Set"—we rocked backward—"GO!!" We were gone. As we fell into space, we entered the third level of commitment. Our momentum carried us into a double forward somersault before R. G. shouted, "Arch!" We arched our bodies so that we could become stable and properly oriented, falling belly-first. The acceleration felt as if we were on a supercharged motorcycle. There is no "stomach flutter," like what you experience on a roller coaster—just wild, thrilling acceleration.

I checked my altimeter, just as we had rehearsed. This would be the first of three such checks. We were at 13,000 feet, and the dial spun backward like a flashback scene in a bad sixties science fiction movie. R. G. began to shout a series of in-flight commands.

"Right turn!" We altered our position ever so slightly, bending sideways at the waist for a moment, and then straightened back out. That action spun us 360 degrees. "Left turn!" It felt as if we were flying now as we spun our bodies in the opposite direction.

"Now track!" I straightened my legs and torso and moved my arms behind me, striking an aerodynamic position. This changed the sensation from falling straight down to flying forward—which we were. I found out later that we were adjusting our course to get closer to the airport. We then came out of our track, back into our arched position. I checked my altimeter for the second time; it read 7,000 feet. The remaining seconds went by quickly, and then R. G. waved his hands in front of my face. I checked again to confirm that we were at 5,000 feet. It was time to pull the rip cord. I only had a few seconds to do this, or R. G. would do it for me. I reached, grabbed, and extended my arm completely, freeing the parachute. This was the moment of truth.

In an instant, the sound created by the wind racing through my helmet went from loud to perfectly quiet. But the silence was broken as I let out an involuntary "Yahooooooo!" Our descent had slowed dramatically, and we hung there in midair, under a beautiful multicolored canopy. A few seconds later, I heard another voice and another loud whoop. Philip was there just above me! We both glided toward the ground, performing turns and spins and steering toward our desired landing spot. As the ground rose up to meet us, we pulled down on our steering cables to stall the chute, creating a well-timed moment of lift and a perfect stand-up landing!

In "real time," the experience went by very quickly. It was so intense that when I was back on the ground, my initial reaction was, "What happened?" The skydiving experience had overwhelmed me. I knew that I had enjoyed it, but it took about two weeks to think back and remember everything that had happened during the jump. As I would remember each moment more clearly, the entire experience slowed down in my mind.

But the most amazing learning experience didn't take place until my second skydive, which was months later. During that jump, I noticed that my level of awareness and understanding was remarkably different—it was much clearer and better. During the maneuvers, I could really feel and control the turns and use my body as an instrument for flight. I was taking in the experience instead of having the experience overwhelm me. Time seemed to pass much more slowly, even though this jump was from a mere 10,500 feet, limiting us to only 45 seconds of freefall.

Think of this: My first jump involved only one minute of freefall. Sixty seconds. And I only did it once. Still, after only one minute of practice, my skills and awareness had increased exponentially. How could that be?

This was an example of accelerated learning, a real-life time warp experience. The phenomenon could occur because the experience of skydiving is so intense and engages every one of the senses, bringing together body, mind, and spirit. While falling through the sky at 120 miles per hour, you are so completely involved in what is happening that the learning takes place at an increased rate of speed. You are extremely vested in the outcome, it being a matter of life and death. Due to all these factors, you become marvelously capable of learning quickly.

My fourth skydive was with my wife, Sheilia. We had been dating for about a month, and I took her to the Freefall Ranch as a surprise for her birthday. I didn't tell her where we were going or what we'd be doing until we were about two miles away. Pulling the car over to the edge of the road, I revealed the secret. To my delight, she was very excited and eager to participate. I told her about the accelerated learning process and encouraged her to really enjoy the experience, slow it down, and stay focused on the moment. She did just that. In fact, Sheilia was able to learn even more quickly than I had and felt tremendous confidence after only one jump.

I have had five jumps to date. No matter how much time passes between them, I find that during each jump I am dramatically more comfortable and proficient. My instructors have let me have full control of the jump and perform flips and other more advanced maneuvers.

So the question that occurred to me is this: Can we accelerate the learning process in other aspects of life? Why not? If we use some of the principles that work for skydiving, then we are able to "warp" time and thereby shorten our learning curve.

In life we often undertake learning curves in order to develop new skills. With skydiving, it's not a learning curve so much as a learning cliff. You are learning at the speed of freefall! In this environment you will be stimulated to a level that forces you to transcend your limits and beliefs. Learning at the speed of freefall is a real and repeatable phenomenon. You can learn job skills, life skills, languages, physical abilities, and new technologies much more quickly if you build these six key principles into your learning process:

1. Learn by doing.
2. Commit completely.
3. Engage all your senses.
4. Increase the intensity.
5. Make it important.
6. Practice mentally—review and examine what you know on a regular basis.

And any time you feel in need of an attitude adjustment or a change of perspective, there is one action you can take that will bring you immediate results: skydiving. Do it. Trust me; you'll never regret that you did. In the meantime, when you encounter life's turbulence and can't find the ground, strap on a "priority parachute" and jump!

Seven Powerful Priority Parachutes

The following techniques—I call them "priority parachutes"—will help you manage important priorities and minimize distractions. Self-discipline is the key. As a practical matter, discipline simply means mastering distractions, disappointments, and setbacks. When you allow your attention to drift, that is, when you lose sight of your priorities, you can remind yourself that you are the one—the only one—who has the final say over the distractions and obstacles you face. Any one of these "parachutes" can give you a safe landing. I recommend trying all of them to pick the right match for your particular lifestyle and goal schedule.

1. Get the big picture. Your time, energy, and attention need direction. The hunting strategy of the American bald eagle gives us an excellent metaphor for setting priorities. This great bird flies high above the treetops, spreading its enormous wings, gliding and circling with ease. However, despite its calm and stealth, there is a steady concentration, an intense focus, as the bird selects its prey. An unsuspecting fish, hundreds of meters away, has no idea it is the focus of attention. Biding its time until just the right moment, the eagle begins its rocketlike swoop toward the target. The timing must be right, because the eagle will not strike where it first saw the fish. It must anticipate where its prey will be at the point of the strike.

The eagle started with the big picture and then found its prey. Its high flight represents your lofty position as you consider which of the dozens of goals you need to concentrate on first, and which ones you need to swoop down on later.

This method of getting the big picture has always been useful for me as a performer. During my early performing years, I would feel very nervous before showtime—almost paralyzed with fear. I felt enormous pressure to get it right and do a good job. Then I developed the habit of "zooming out." I simply would imagine myself from an outside perspective, ready to go onstage. Then I would zoom out again, imagining an exterior view of the theater or building I was performing in. Then, zooming farther out, I would see the building far below, then farther, until the image in my mind was one of the earth itself, spinning smoothly in space. With this perspective, my problem—having jitters before the show—seemed insignificant. And my priorities became increasingly clear: Relax, be present, focus on the audience, and have fun. To this day I still feel a tingling rush of anticipation before each of my performances.

2. Think 80-20. This priorities parachute is based on one of the most tried-and-true management theories in the past fifty years. The 80-20 principle was formulated by Italian economist Vilfredo Pareto. Pareto's Law states that only about 20 percent of the causes bring 80 percent of the results—of anything. Put another way, 80 percent of our budget is spent on 20 percent of our bills; we generally wear 20 percent of our clothing 80 percent of the time; 80 percent of the sales come from 20 percent of the sales force. Pareto calls 20 percent the vital few, and 80 percent the trivial many.

Applying the Pareto principle to setting goal priorities helps you identify the vital ingredients necessary to achieve the results you want.

The vital few tasks (contacts, activities, objectives) are the things you want to do first so you can make the most progress in the least time. Separate the trivial from the important, the profitable from the marginal, the expedient from the principled, the wants from the needs.

3. Schedule unstructured downtime. Some goal setters look at a loaded calendar as a badge of importance. For them, a heavily annotated calendar says, "Look how important I am, how in demand I am, how successful I must be." Some people become activity fanatics and end up hydroplaning through life. A busy life quickly turns into a chaotic one, testing our stamina and our sanity, and creating a lopsided set of priorities and values. This downtime parachute cautions priority fanatics to slow down and allow time for peace, quiet, and renewal in their overloaded calendars.

In his book *Solitude*, British psychologist Anthony Storr concludes:

> *It appears . . . that some development of the capacity to be alone is necessary if the brain is to function at its best and if the individual is to fulfill his/her highest potential. Human beings easily become alienated from their deepest needs and feelings. Learning, thinking, innovating, and maintaining contact with one's inner world are all inflated by solitude.*

Scheduling unstructured downtime is a critical priority in itself. Rest and relaxation are necessary for the psyche to replenish itself and the body to renew itself. Managing priorities takes energy and stamina. A quiet walk is as valuable as a goal objective met. Without time-outs, goal getting can lead to burnout.

4. If you have priorities of equal value, start with those you find less fun. This tactic helps guarantee that you won't keep putting less desirable priorities off or avoiding them altogether. Ask yourself how you can change disagreeable priorities to make them more satisfying. Once the unpleasant priorities are taken care of, everything else will seem easier.

5. Keep your priorities list close at hand. Carry a priorities notebook (PDA, scratchpad, binder, laptop) with you when you travel. Use your waiting time to review your priorities and accomplish worthwhile objectives.

6. Learn how to say "no." Don't allow people to buttonhole you into long-drawn-out activities or projects that get in the way of your meeting your goals. As tactfully and diplomatically as you can, say "no."

7. Ask people who are priority champions. Learn from people who can set and then meet priorities on a routine basis. Find out what works and what doesn't. Ask for their advice and feedback on your priority-setting plans. Apply the techniques that work for you. One of the best ways to improve your own priority management abilities is to learn from the experience of others.

Action Assignments

1. Pretend you have just set a world record and it has been recognized in the *Guinness Book of World Records*. What record would you have set? Describe how you set the record. Were you the lone record holder, or did you set the record with someone else? Where did you set the record? Be specific. Is there another record you would like to set? Describe it. How would achieving that record make you feel? Can you see yourself receiving recognition for the award?

2. As quoted earlier in this chapter, Richard Bach said, "All the events of our lives are there because we have drawn them there." What have you drawn into your life this past week that will prevent you from accomplishing your goals?

3. What will you do with the next 86,400 seconds, starting now?

6

IF THE BALL IS IN YOUR HAND, THROW IT!

Life is a checkerboard, and the player opposite you is time. If you hesitate before moving, or neglect to move promptly, your markers will be wiped off the board by time. You are playing against a partner who will not tolerate indecision.

—Napoleon Hill

Are you a fan of the snooze button? Many people absolutely love to set their morning wake up call earlier than they need to rise, just so they can experience the satisfaction of the snooze and buy themselves a few more minutes of rest. I don't get it. Why not just set the alarm for the time you actually want to wake up and then, when the alarm sounds, go ahead and get out of bed? Are those extra few minutes really that enjoyable or restful? Maybe they are and, after all, it's a harmless routine. So snooze away.

But life has a snooze button as well. And, the effects of pushing this button are not harmless. In fact, they can be devastating. The snooze button I am referring to are the four words "one of these days." We use them to relieve ourselves of responsibility or change. The short-term effect of saying "one of these days" is the same as the snooze button on your alarm clock. We gain a temporary respite from our obligations.

What is the most important change you need to make? What are you intending to do "one of these days?" Upon reading that question, I am certain that an answer came to mind. We know what we need to do. We think about what we need to do. We intend to do it . . . one of these days.

When it comes to making positive changes in life, one thing is clear: It's your move. Your thoughts power your choices. Your choices power your actions. Your actions power your life. Procrastination, too, is a choice: the choice not to act. People have many reasons for procrastinating, and we'll address these later in this chapter. Many excuses are valid and even useful because they make us feel comfortable, safe, and justified. But, the only way to take charge of your life is to take responsibility for your present circumstances, good and bad, and initiate changes. It's up to you, and the time to take action is now.

When I teach juggling, I always encounter students who make the first two throws, then simply get stuck, unwilling to let go and release that third ball into the air. So I tell them, "If the ball's in your hand, throw it!" This simple and fun statement has such real meaning to me about life in general that it has become a personal mantra. It means this: When you encounter an opportunity or experience an insight, that moment is charged with energy, and the opportunity or insight is there in your life for a reason. *This* is the moment to act. Take the next step. Make the next positive "throw." Harness the momentum of life and move it forward.

For years I have taught this concept to audiences. If the ball's in your hand, throw it! When I say that, though, it usually gets a good laugh, because some misinterpret my statement. One possible meaning, the one that some managers are accustomed to, is "If the ball is in *my* hand, I'm going to throw it—as quickly as possible—to someone *else*!" While it is true that delegating responsibilities is key to our productivity, some people "throw the ball" to relieve themselves of the burden of decision. This is not the intended message.

Life can quickly become overwhelming if we try to keep track of everything at once. Successful jugglers, however, know the secret to effectively managing many things at once. As we saw in chapter five, when we appear to be doing many different things all at the same time, what we are actually doing is just one thing at a time, quickly and in the proper sequence. The expert juggler executes just one throw at a time: the one in the hand. This is, after all, the only thing we do have control of—making the best throw we can to keep the pattern moving smoothly. People think that juggling is about making great catches, but it isn't. Juggling is about making perfect throws. If you make a perfect throw, then the catch happens naturally, and you experience the thrill of spontaneous success.

To accomplish more in life and maintain our momentum, we can create a lifestyle of action. The best time to handle life's challenges is to deal with them as they arise. I am not saying that everything you face can be handled immediately—or that it even should be, for that matter. What I am saying is that in many cases we choose inaction for the wrong reasons. For example, let's say you are at home one evening and happen to think about an old friend you haven't talked to in years. Your inner voice says, "You know, I really should get in touch with that person to say hello and see how he's doing." Guess what? The ball's in your hand—throw it. Pick up the phone and make the call. Or you can ignore the inner voice, resolve to contact that person again one of these days, and perhaps you will let months or years pass before making the call. As time passes, old contacts become much more difficult to find, and the mental hurdle of making the effort to reach them will appear more daunting than ever before. That is why this chapter is all about putting an end to putting it off.

When we put off projects, changes, and improvements for our lives, it may be because we think these actions will be difficult. But with the passage of time, and the knowledge of tasks left undone, our perception changes. Often we turn relatively small, simple things into *huge* obstacles, and we burden ourselves with guilt and other negative thoughts simply because we didn't handle the task when it was at hand.

None of us knows how much time we have left. That's why it is so crucial for each of us to seize every minute of every day, to do the things we need to do to gain a sense of satisfaction and fulfillment. We can choose to put an end to putting it off, or put it off until the end catches up to us. The choice is ours.

Webster's defines *procrastinate* as "to put off intentionally and habitually." According to that definition, I believe it is safe to say that all of us, at one time or another, have intentionally and habitually put off doing something that needed doing. Even those of us who maintain a healthy bias toward action allow procrastination to creep up in a variety of ways.

Procrastination Quiz

1. Do you set high standards for yourself?
2. Do you sometimes take on more tasks than time or resources permit?
3. Do you tend to be self-critical when you are dissatisfied with your performance?
4. Are you the kind of busy person who finds it difficult to say "no"?
5. Do you frequently find yourself overworked?
6. Do you tend to be a perfectionist?
7. Do you pay particular attention to details and insist on checking everything before you take the next step?
8. Have people ever called you a pack rat because you seldom throw things away?
9. Are you constantly irritated by unfinished business and unsolved problems?
10. Have you ever been accused of causing bottlenecks because you need additional information or resources?
11. Do you like to think things out clearly before you sign off on changes?

If you answered "yes" to three or more of these questions, you are a card-carrying member of the International Procrastinators' Club. Congratulations. "But wait," you say, "many of those items listed are really positive qualities. It's good to be careful and set high standards. It's normal to want to know all the available information before making a commitment." In certain cases, that is true. But if you are completely honest with yourself, I am sure you can recall a time when you used one or more of these tactics to forestall a decision that you were actually quite ready to make. We pay a price for procrastination. Let's take a quick look at the downside of delay.

The Price We Pay for Procrastination

> *You decide you'll wait for your pitch. Then the ball starts toward the plate, you think about your stance and you debate whether you should swing. And then you realize the ball that just whizzed past you for a called strike was your pitch.*
>
> —*Bobby Mercer*

Procrastination is the universal time killer, and when it kills time, it blocks opportunities. Dale Carnegie wrote, "One of the most tragic things I know about human nature is that all of us tend to put off living. We are all dreaming of some magical rose garden over the horizon, instead of enjoying the roses that are blooming outside our windows today."

Anyone who practices wish-craft without taking action loses the incredible potential of the present. People sacrifice today for what might happen tomorrow. They retreat from the real world and convince themselves that anticipation and denial are safer than today's reality. Procrastinators want to live in a perfect world, one free from responsibilities, decisions, and consequences. Here are the most common costs associated with procrastination.

An unfulfilled, unenriched life. "Life," said Samuel Johnson, "affords no higher pleasure than that of surmounting difficulties, passing from one step of success to another, forming new wishes and seeing them gratified." Procrastinators seem to miss this important insight. They downplay their accomplishments or put them off entirely. They block their own fulfillment through their apathy and dissatisfaction. Each day remains empty because they put nothing substantial into it. The soulless vacuum they create adds to their diminished self-worth. This loss of soul is a terrible price to pay for choosing inaction over action.

An undercurrent of unrest and panic. Panic strikes procrastinators who are confronted with life issues that make them feel uncomfortable or inadequately equipped to resolve those issues. This embedded current immobilizes chronic procrastinators, who see themselves as incapable of making even the simplest decisions. Some veteran procrastinators spend their lives feeling a sense of panic and unrest about their jobs, their relationships, their finances, and their future. They flounder like fish caught in a net, never quite knowing what to do or how they got where they are. They are frightened of life and the responsibilities it brings.

A recurrent state of boredom. Boredom is the human equivalent of inertia. It is an emotional reaction to the uncertainties of life itself. Procrastinators find themselves carried by the currents of life, pushed along by circumstances that they believe to be outside their ability to handle. Soren Kierkegaard captured the essence of boredom in his elaboration of "Summa summarum: I do not care at all":

> *I do not care for anything. I do not care to ride, for*
> *the exercise is too violent; I do not care to walk,*
> *walking is too strenuous; I do not care to lie down, for*
> *I should either have to remain lying, and I do not care*
> *to do that, or I should have to get up again, and I do*
> *not care to do that either.*

A resignation to merely coping. Procrastinators who pay this price are used to adjusting to the status quo. They conform to the wishes and actions of others, even if it means giving up a part of themselves. They see everything as a struggle and, by their negative thinking, attract similar and recurring situations that confirm their plight. These types of procrastinators use a reactionary strategy to "cope" with their roles in the world. Instead of seeing their active roles in causing or contributing to their dilemmas, they see themselves as victims of influences beyond their control.

A systematic waste of the present. Procrastinators, as a whole, bankrupt the present. If they would focus on the moments of opportunity, they would sense an eternal connection with the present. They would realize that the present moment is the only moment they will ever have. Unfortunately, when they lose their sense of the present, they lose any sense of the future. Author Brian Seaward sums it up nicely in his book *The Art of Calm: Relaxation Through the Five Senses.* He says, "The bottom line is to live in the present moment. We tend to live in the past with guilt and the future with worry. Although it is important to plan for the future, too many people [procrastinators] miss the present moment."

Procrastinators who waste the present waste themselves. "The same stream of life," says Rabindranath Tagore, "that runs through the world runs through [your] veins night and day and dances in rhythmic measure. It is the same life that shoots in joy through the dust of the earth into the numberless blades of grass and breaks into tumultuous waves of flowers." This kind of vibrancy is all around us, but most of the time procrastinators miss it because they don't allow themselves to enjoy the thousands of joyful moments that come their way each day.

Habitual pangs of guilt. Because they leave so much undone, procrastinators force themselves to live with guilt. They rationalize not taking the very actions that can alleviate or even prevent the feelings of guilt in the first place. Guilt remains an ever-present emotional weight because procrastinators settle for inaction and postponement.

Unserviceable goals. Many ardent procrastinators, like goal-crafters, have goals. Unfortunately, procrastinators are goal-setters but not goal-getters. Consequently, their goals are only wishes, which turn to vapor the moment the procrastinators realize they have a commitment on the loose. For them, goal-setting is a perfunctory process that sounds good but has little chance of being implemented.

A parade of unsolved problems. Experienced procrastinators see time as the healer of all problems, so they routinely hit life's snooze button, resolving to take action "one of these days." Unfortunately for them, and for the people close to them, time doesn't resolve all problems, and only intensifies some of life's problems. Fail to fix a leak in your bicycle tire, and you'll end up buying a new tire. Fail to put lunch meat in the refrigerator, and you'll have spoiled meat and a stinky kitchen. Forget to program the VCR or DVR for the TV show you want to watch later, and you'll find yourself looking for something else to do. Put off taking your medicine, and it could lead to serious health complications. Allowing unsolved problems to linger keeps procrastinators mired in difficulties instead of mobilized by solutions.

Chronic fatigue. Engineering purposeful delay and paving the way for postponement are tiresome and laborious activities. They can be excruciating ways to spend time and energy. It's no wonder that procrastinators, who are masters at delay and postponement, are so habitually tired. Putting off until tomorrow what can be done today is a monumental undertaking. Remembering all the things you're not going to do takes considerable energy. Chronic fatigue drowns the spirit in a sea of listlessness, hopelessness, and lifelessness. What an awful price to pay for choosing delay instead of deliverance.

A trunkful of lost opportunities. Procrastinators lose innumerable chances to accomplish worthwhile goals. With each unfulfilled goal, they forfeit the opportunities that come with it. Sooner or later, fewer opportunities come along, and even when the occasional lucky break does arrive, procrastinators generally miss it because they are no longer able to recognize it. After a while, opportunities dry up, leaving the procrastinator with a barren future.

Why We Procrastinate

> *Procrastinators are masters at rationalization and are usually aware that they are sabotaging their own happiness.*
>
> —Linda Sapadin

With so many people paying such a high price for procrastination, it is only natural to ask, "What makes people procrastinate?" Why would anyone knowingly want to lose important opportunities that can bring enrichment, empowerment, and success? What would possess a person to postpone lifesaving medical treatment? Of course, there are many reasons to delay, postpone, or avoid important responsibilities. Although this list is by no means complete, most people procrastinate for the following reasons:

To get someone else to do it. Procrastinators are inveterate delegators. They spend their time and energy manipulating support and are masters at manufacturing situations where their success depends on someone else.

To avoid responsibility. Since being responsible means fulfilling obligations, procrastinators avoid it like the plague. Typically, they complain that they are just too busy to take on something new. They say that they are already overwhelmed with activity.

To gain sympathy. "See how hard this is for me?" and "See, I knew I couldn't do it" are the battle cries for hard-core procrastinators, who see themselves as tired warriors who have done their best despite the odds stacked against them.

To get sidetracked into doing something else. For most of us, interruptions are annoying, but procrastinators pray for them. Procrastinators see interruptions as opportunities to veer off course. Heaven forbid that they should complete a job.

To save them from unpleasant and overly demanding work. Most of us would rather spend our time doing something we enjoy. Unpleasant tasks are, well, unpleasant, and no one enjoys doing them. What separates procrastinators from the rest of us is that they go to great lengths to avoid getting anywhere near an unpleasant chore.

To avoid embarrassment. Since procrastinators spend their lives avoiding responsibility, they have gotten very good at doing tasks that siphon off their opportunities for accomplishment. Unfortunately, they have usually neglected developing foundational skills along the way. Anything that tests their abilities mortifies them, because real involvement on their part might expose their underdeveloped skills. Sadly, their fear of embarrassment is nurtured much more readily than their willingness to overcome skill deficiencies.

To hide their short attention span. Procrastinators usually are so accustomed to aborted projects, simple tasks, and short work schedules that their stamina and attention span are quickly vaporized by the demands placed on them. Long-term assignments and large projects are simply too overwhelming for their self-defeating lifestyles.

To avoid change. Chronic procrastinators would rather stay uninspired, unproductive, unchallenged, untested, and underpaid than take a chance on rocking the boat. They are architects of the status quo and guardians of routine. Change means renewal, renewal means growth, growth means risk, and risk means stepping out of their fortified cocoons.

To disguise their lack of confidence. Lack of self-confidence drives procrastinators deeper into self-denial. Self-confidence is foreign to them since they avoid opportunities to develop it. Lack of confidence and lowered self-esteem go together, and these prevent procrastinators from becoming capable, productive human beings.

To conceal their disinterest. Procrastinators rarely say "no" to an idea. To do so would mean they have expressed decisiveness, and that goes against their nature. Instead of verbalizing their disinterest or disagreement, they pretend to go along with an idea and then fail to take action in support of it. You see, procrastination is itself a way of saying "no" to something new.

To secretly gain control. Procrastinators feel powerless to control their future. Some react by trying to gain control over trivial matters. For example, in the middle of an important face-to-face meeting, they will answer their cell phone whenever it rings. Unrelated, unimportant calls short-circuit productivity. The procrastinator displays "power" by making others wait for the unwelcome interruptions to conclude. Ironically, the person who practices this tactic will explain that he or she is being more productive by being "hands-on" and "always accessible." This is obviously not the case. In reality, this kind of tactic only offers the procrastinator a false sense of control.

Procrastination Prevention

You can't steal second base and keep one foot on first.
—Frederick B. Wilson

So far in this chapter we have identified reasons why people tend to procrastinate, and the price they pay for that procrastination. Now we're going to take a look at how to manage—and hopefully prevent— much of the unhealthy procrastination that limits our ability to put *success in action*. The rest of this chapter is packed with procrastination prevention ideas that can deflect delay tactics and inspire action.

Create a procrastination profile. Answer the following questions: When do I procrastinate? Why do I choose to procrastinate? Which tasks, activities, jobs, and relationships spark my procrastination habit? When do I procrastinate the most? Do I procrastinate more often when I start something or when I'm finishing? What early warning signals can I become more aware of to help me ward off procrastination? What price am I no longer willing to pay to feed my procrastination habit? How do I feel when I procrastinate? How do I want to feel?

Switch from "I'm gonna" to "I am." Instead of saying, "I'm gonna lose that extra fifteen pounds," say, "I am loosing fifteen pounds by eating less at each meal." Instead of saying, "I'm gonna learn to speak Spanish someday," say "I am learning to speak Spanish. I am listening to study tapes and memorizing three new words a day." Procrastinators are recognized by their gonnas, doers by their ams.

Switch from "have to" to "need to," "want to," or even "get to." Remove the phrase "have to" from your vocabulary. When you tell yourself or someone else that you have to do something, whatever it is, you are shirking responsibility. If you say, for example, "I have to go to work today," you are saying that it is a necessity and is out of your control. Someone else is mandating that you be there, and you have no choice in the matter. This is simply not true. You always have a choice. You don't "have to" go to work. Now, if it is important to you that you keep your job, earn a paycheck, and provide for yourself and your family, then going to work is an opportunity to fulfill all those needs. So instead you can say, "I need to go to work today." This small shift of vocabulary has enormous impact, because it transforms your statement from one of negative obligation to one of empowering potential. Considering that in the economic downturn of the past several years thousands of people have lost their jobs, you might even say, "I want to go to work today," or "I get to go to work today." Lots of people don't get to go to work. Try this with all the to-dos on your daily list. Banish the small, enslaving "have to" phrase from your vocabulary, and shed the illusion that anyone but you commands your actions.

Recognize that a life of delay, inaction, and postponement invites mediocrity and failure. Inertia causes stagnation and decay. If you're coasting, you're going downhill, so the time comes to stop the downward trend even if it means making an about-face. "Knowing is not enough," says Goethe, "we must apply action. Willing is not enough, we must do."

Identify moments of truth. The moments of truth I'm referring to are the moments immediately before procrastinators decide to postpone, delay, or avoid action. At that moment, procrastinators have a chance to summon the energy and the courage to take responsible action. It is in that moment of pivotal choice that something either gets done or gets sidetracked. Procrastinators, like the rest of us, draw moments of truth that demand decisiveness. If the ball is in your hand, throw it! With each positive throw, no matter how large or small, you gain power and control over your destiny.

Use self-talk to motivate yourself to take action. Learn to use positive statements that clearly state what you want to achieve in your life, starting with your goals. These self-talk statements (affirmations) can be highly effective if they are kept positive and short, stated in the present tense, and repeated during the day, both before and after you've started a task. For example, as you enter one of the moments of truth we have just talked about, say something like "I am accomplishing this task with speed, care, comfort, and joy," or "I welcome change as an ally," or "I am a product of success in action." Affirmations can be powerful action triggers. "Your word," said Florence Scovel Shinn, an expert in self-talk technology, "is your want." If repeated often enough, affirmations can help create the "grooves of success" I mentioned earlier. That makes affirmations a powerful anti-procrastination tool.

CLUB procrastination as often as you can. To use one of the classic pieces of equipment in juggling as an acronym, CLUB is just the thing for preventing procrastination, and throwing a club, like throwing a ball, is a perfect metaphor for these decisive actions.

C: Commit to taking one action step at a time. Look upward, focus with positive intention on your target, and commit to the desired results. Prepare yourself mentally and physically to let go and take action.

L: Launch your throw or initiative with your commitment. Make the best first throw you can. Then monitor the progress and make adjustments.

U: Use your talents. Identify what you are already good at, and build momentum and confidence using your strengths. Use your talents of observation to hone your existing skills and knowledge base.

B: Believe in your ability to handle responsibility and conquer fear. Believe also that you can learn new things to expand your evolving pattern of success.

Get into a witness protection program. The kind of protection I'm referring to is of your own choosing. Let a few close friends know about your anti-procrastination campaign and ask them to witness your progress. Tell them what your goals are and when you expect to achieve certain things, and invite their active support, even if it means them giving you a push once in a while. Remember Florence Chadwick and Don Bennett—they had their respective witness protection programs in place when they met their challenges, and so can you.

Identify the "Y factor." The first time my juggling partner, Philip, and I ever passed machetes around a volunteer from our audience, we discovered the astonishing power of the "Y factor." As we eyed each other and our brave assistant (who was clueless that he was part of a premiere performance), we each had the same thought: "We've never done this before. These things are really sharp." They were, as we had just purchased them from an Army-Navy surplus store and hadn't had the chance to dull them. I wondered, "Is this really a good idea, or should we procrastinate this trick until next show?" I glanced to Philip for support, but his expression mirrored my thoughts. Suddenly, it felt important to huddle up and renew our commitment. We paused the performance, leaving our volunteer onstage as we quickly regrouped. The audience thought this was part of the act, but it was actually a moment of truth. The question we asked each other was simple: "Why are we doing this again?" You see, when I refer to the Y factor, Y equals Why? And so we proceeded to answer the question, "Why should we follow through with the routine?" We found several reasons:

- **Because** the payoff was exciting. We wanted to top our previous performances and please the audience.

- **Because** we were ready. We had practiced machete juggling without the volunteer, and we had passed other objects around hundreds of other people in other performances. Surely all that prior experience was useful.

- **Because** we trusted each other and each other's abilities.

- **Because** it was showtime, and there was no turning back. Having promised the trick to the audience, we had reached the third level of commitment.

After our quick powwow, we followed through without dropping any knives or wounding our volunteer. The audience cheered, thinking that this was a routine we had performed countless other times. We knew, however, that this was a personal and professional victory, because we had used the power of the Y factor to manage our emotions and perform to new levels of achievement.

Using this example as a guide, ask yourself the Y-factor question: Why is it important that you follow through? What are the payoffs for the goal, task, project, or life challenge you are facing today? Why is now the time to take action? Why are you, right now, ready for the performance of your life?

Employ your night vision. Plan the next day's activities the night before. Get your proverbial ducks in a row. Planning ahead allows you to start your day with momentum before the parade of interruptions begins. Planning ahead also gives you a sense of achievement and confidence because you already know you are heading in the right direction.

Post your own billboard. This simple but effective strategy is worth its weight in flying lessons. On a three-by-five card, in large lettering, write SUCCESS IN ACTION. Stick the card on your wall or mirror, or tape it on the refrigerator or the dashboard of your car or truck. This technique may sound silly, but it works. It will become a billboard of success once you internalize the mindset. The message will remind you that if you put all of you into what you do, you will become *success in action*.

Ask yourself the all-important question. During the course of each day, stop what you are doing and ask yourself, Am I making the best use of my time right now? If the answer is "yes", continue with what you are doing. If you answered "no," stop what you are doing immediately. Don't extend the task a second longer. Seize each moment so you don't spend any of those 86,400 seconds on nonproductive pursuits.

Pay attention to your peak periods. Don't schedule difficult tasks for the times during the day when you know your energy level is at its lowest. Pay attention to your biorhythms. Fatigue can put a damper on anyone's plans. For me, mornings have always been my most productive time periods. I truly enjoy getting up early and having that "magic time" all to myself. This is usually the best time for me to write, work out, and create new programs.

Interrupt interruptions. Although we rarely have days in which we are not interrupted, sidetracked, or bushwhacked by unscheduled time robbers, there are things we can do to minimize their effects. For example, set an "end" at the onset of the interruption. When someone says, "Have you got a minute?" say as tactfully as you can, "I can spare half a minute. Will that be enough, or should we schedule another time?" That tactic usually handcuffs the interrupter and keeps you from falling into one of the most subtle procrastination traps.

Turn elephants into mice. Reduce overwhelming tasks into large tasks, and large tasks into smaller ones. Henry Ford once remarked, "Nothing is particularly difficult if you divide it into smaller jobs." Jugglers understand this extremely well. No matter how many objects are involved in a particular trick, they must throw just one object at a time (the one in hand). Individual throws combine to create the "pattern." With practice, we see this pattern clearly, as it is the synthesis of all the objects. The same strategy applies to juggling our priorities. The best way to handle monumental tasks is to divide them into "bite-sized pieces" so you can make the first throw. Over time, you will understand how all the objects, or objectives of your life, coordinate to create your ideal pattern.

Replace the familiar with the unfamiliar once in a while. Force yourself out of ruts and routines. Get up fifteen minutes earlier, or later. Drive a different route to work. Change your hairstyle or hair color. Brush your teeth and comb your hair with your nondominant hand. Eat lunch at a different restaurant. Wear clothing that a friend would know is not typically what you'd wear. Speak when you are usually silent; remain silent when you'd normally speak. Juggle beanbags instead of watching TV (or try the synthesis of those two actions: juggling while watching). Read a book instead of going to a movie. Do something different that deepens your understanding and appreciation of yourself and others. Replace procrastination with action, and live the life you are meant to live.

Play "truth or consequences." Ask yourself, "What's making me reluctant to do this?" Is it going to be difficult? Would you rather be doing something else? Is it going to test your competence, stamina, resolve? Is it something someone else can or should do instead? Do you doubt your ability? What is the truth about your reluctance? If you are tempted to do something else instead of the task at hand, ask yourself whether your procrastination is worth the consequences.

Don't be so hard on yourself. Many procrastinators are their own worst enemies. Don't turn your mistakes into life sentences, but rather see each experience as a learning opportunity, and apply the lessons you've learned. "Keep away from people who belittle your ambitions," said Mark Twain. "Small people always do that, but the really great make you feel that you, too, can become great." And to belittle your own ambitions makes even less sense. Remember, your success is determined not by your circumstances but by your actions, and your actions are a direct result of your thinking. So don't be so hard on yourself.

Make the best of rest. "Work smart and play smart" is the slogan for this procrastination buster. Many people find it difficult to enjoy a few cubic feet of peace and quiet. Procrastinators, in particular, burn huge amounts of energy worrying about what they're not going to do. In his spy thriller *The Bourne Identity*, Robert Ludlum makes the profound statement that "rest itself is a weapon." Fatigue is counter-productive to success in action, so learn to make the best of rest. You may gain an extraordinary benefit if you learn a meditation technique and practice meditation for fifteen to twenty minutes daily. Short periods of meditation in the middle of the day boost your alertness and stamina, providing more energy and rest than do much longer periods of sleep.

Give yourself blue ribbons. Reward yourself for your accomplishments. Celebrate your successes. Make your rewards commensurate with the size of your achievements. For example, when I finally earned my pilot's license after two years of flying lessons, my reward was a brand-new, top-of-the-line David Clark headset. This is the preferred choice for many professional pilots, and giving myself this reward made me feel that I had earned the right to fly with the best. People tend to repeat behavior they are rewarded for, so give yourself plenty of opportunities for blue-ribbon days.

"One of these days" does not exist. Think about it. There is no such thing. It is merely a convenient illusion, an escape mechanism to postpone the inevitable. When it comes to taking action, there is only today. So, remove the phrase from your vocabulary and replace it with one of three actions.

1. Do it today. When you have that moment of clarity and come face to face with your true ambitions, seize the moment and take action right then. When you honestly glimpse a change you must make in order to grow, instead of putting it off, validate yourself and make the change right now. Transformation can happen in an honest instant.

2. Schedule it today for a specific day in the future. Instead of saying "I'll do that one of these days," pick one. Get out the calendar and commit to your date with destiny.

3. Take the first step. Commit to just one small aspect of your larger goal. Perhaps this involves a commitment to a person who can guide you. Or maybe it means doing just one small thing that moves you in the right direction.

By taking action you will benefit instantly with a rush of validation for your efforts. And, you will be rewarded in the long run by being true to yourself. Life is too short to hit the snooze button on your dreams. It's time to wake up and take action!

Action Assignments

1. If you know you are a procrastinator, decide whether—and when—you want to change this destructive behavior. The longer you put off making the decision, the more you will reinforce the chances of turning a postponement penchant into a procrastination pathology. Putting things off becomes an end in itself. Decide now, today, during this very moment of truth, to value action instead of delay, courage instead of complacency, satisfaction and fulfillment instead of lethargy and aimlessness. Consider this first action assignment as the "altar call" for this chapter.

2. How much has procrastination cost you over the years? List at least three losses you have suffered as a result of procrastination and that you believe can be recouped if you take positive action now. Devise a plan to turn those losses into life-enriching and life-affirming celebrations. Do something today that takes you one step closer to that realization.

3. Get a witness. Tell someone you respect that you are implementing an action or change in your life. Notice, I did not say to tell them an action you are *going* to implement. Enlist their support for your desired goal and explain how you plan to achieve long-term success. Ask them to help you with encouragement and hold you accountable for your commitments.

4. Release yourself from some of the tasks you've put off. Some of the things you feel that you are procrastinating over are quite likely things you don't need to do. Reexamine the reasons why you are pursuing a goal. Are you still committed to achieving the goal, or is the goal outdated or no longer useful? Is it your goal, or is it someone else's

goal *for* you? Feel the relief that comes from shedding guilt by releasing yourself from inappropriate tasks.

5. Use the CLUB technique to help achieve something that you have let slide because you've procrastinated. It can be a personal or professional postponement. Report your accomplishment to a trusted friend, and celebrate your success.

CATCH KNIVES BY THE HANDLE

Even after you become proficient in what you do, risks never quite go away. But avoiding danger is no safer in the long run than outright exposure. Life is either a daring adventure or nothing.

—Helen Keller

When you increase your level of risk, you need to get very specific about your goal. When juggling machetes and battle-axes, for example, the goal is not simply to make a catch. It is, specifically, to catch the handle.

—Dan Thurmon

People perceive my job as being risky because I am always doing something dramatic, such as speaking in front of large audiences, juggling knives, ropewalking over flames, or doing back flips in a business suit. But no matter who you are or what you do, risk is unavoidable. Risk is relative because it is a matter of your perspective. There is no such thing as a risk-free life. In fact, "playing it safe" can be the riskiest strategy of all. If you are risk-averse, you avoid that which makes you uncomfortable. Instead of being oriented toward achieving something you see as positive, you are avoiding something you perceive as negative. In the process, you will forfeit your goals, your momentum, and control of the direction of your life. Performing in high-pressure situations, onstage in front of audiences, I've learned volumes about myself and about how to view risk in a positive way and achieve successful outcomes. Here's a story about how one such undertaking took my risk tolerance to new levels.

The Globe of Destiny

For a professional entertainer, there is no such thing as a routine day at work. I have been extremely fortunate to enjoy a life rich with a wide variety of experiences. Every day is different because every stage and each audience is unique. In fact, in many ways, each performance is a world premiere.

One day my friend John Nock called me to say, "Dan, we want you to do something with us that has never been done in any circus, anywhere."

For eight years, I had been performing annually with the world-renowned Nerveless Nocks, a Swiss family circus currently raising its eighth generation of circus performers. The "Main Event" took place in Birmingham, Alabama, at Riverchase Galleria, an enormous mall with a nine-story atrium that housed the circus every February on Presidents' Day weekend.

Perhaps you have seen the circus act in which motorcyclists enter a globular steel cage and perform high-speed routines, looping sideways, upside down, and every which way inside the sphere. At the dramatic climax, two riders perform simultaneously inside the same globe! Their communication, choreography, and timing elicit screams of terror from the audience, as the daredevils narrowly miss each other at thrilling speeds.

John's idea would take this routine to new levels of excitement. After the two riders finished their flirtation with disaster, they would stop their motorcycles, and the cage would be opened once again. Here is where I would enter, dressed in a stylish circus outfit and carrying three juggling torches. I would then stand at the bottom of the globe, juggling the torches in the air while the riders raced around me and the flames. Any mistake could result in a catastrophic accident, but the inherent risk also meant enormous potential for excitement. The audience would have an opportunity to witness circus history, and the stunt would be truly spectacular.

I would not have even considered saying "yes" had it not been for my close friendship with the Nocks. I have the highest respect for the family, their talents, their work ethic, and their practice methods. While the audience perceives them as perilous risk takers, I knew that they were disciplined, cool-headed, and immensely experienced. John would be one of the riders. The other would be Timo, whom I had never met before. He and John had done the act together, minus the torch juggler, hundreds of times. I agreed to do it and immediately felt the rush of anticipation.

I arrived the night before our first show. This would be our only opportunity to rehearse the routine and build a comfort level among all the participants before the morning's performance. My wife, Sheilia, was unconvinced that this was a wise career move on my part, but I assured her that I was working with pros and that we would not attempt the feat unless the rehearsal went perfectly.

The practice session went without any mishap whatsoever. Perhaps that's because our "practice session" was also without costumes, juggling, fire, or even motorcycles. It went like this. John, Timo, and I all met at the circus ring in our street clothes. It looked like the familiar set from most years, with the exception of the towering black steel structure that would soon become the "Globe of Destiny." That's how the performance would be billed. We all three walked up to the globe, and John showed me how to enter the cage.

"First, I will ride the Globe," said John, "then Timo. Next, we will ride together. When we finish, we'll stop the motorcycles. At that point, Lon will introduce you, the door will open, and you will enter with the torches."

We all three walked inside the Globe at this point in the rehearsal, to get a better sense of the space. It felt smaller than it looked, and I tried to imagine how the close quarters would fill up with motorcycles, riders, fire, and me!

"You stand here in the center, Dan, with the torches above your head. We will start at the same time, rock forward, then backward, then go. We will ride the side of the sphere. At that point, start juggling. When you finish, stand right here, and Timo will stop his motorcycle next to you. Move toward him so I have a little room to stop on the other side. Then we'll exit the Globe, and that will be it."

It sounded simple enough, but I couldn't help thinking how completely different the situation would be tomorrow. The audience would indeed be witnessing a premiere performance.

I assured my wife that the rehearsal went perfectly. Nobody had gotten the least bit injured. Of course, we still hadn't even tried the stunt, but I was actually feeling comfortable about the routine. It would certainly be a new challenge, but when you think about it, we really had been preparing for this challenge all our lives. John and Timo were solid in their performances, and I trusted their abilities completely. They trusted my skill with fire torches, which was essential, considering they would each be sitting astride a gas tank. All that remained was for us to put it together.

The next morning, I performed my half-hour show as the opening for the main event. This included juggling, acrobatics, audience interaction, even a bit of torch juggling atop my fourteen-foot unicycle. Then I went backstage and collected my thoughts. There was one hour to go, with the Globe of Destiny as the final act in this year's circus. I felt excited but still a little uneasy as I put on my costume, a red jumpsuit with yellow flames on the legs and chest. We were about to enter uncharted territory. As the show progressed and the finale approached, I wondered if we were truly ready. Part of me wanted to delay for just a little longer. But there is no procrastinating showtime. I soaked my torches in fuel and put in my earplugs. John had warned me that the motorcycles inside the cage are extremely loud, and I hoped the earplugs would make it easier to stay focused.

The ringmaster introduced the act, and I watched as John and Timo effortlessly floated through their initial routines, first separately and then together inside the cage. The moment was almost upon us. Lon Diamond, the ringmaster for the show, spoke in rich, resonant tones: "And now, ladies and gentlemen, you will witness circus history. You'll remember, the show started with juggler extraordinaire Dan Thurmon.

We now call again upon his unique talents as, with two motorcycle riders now inside the Nock Globe of Destiny, Dan Thurmon ignites his flaming torches!"

I did, in dramatic fashion to match his voice.

Lon continued, "Dan will now place himself at the bottom of the Globe and attempt to juggle the torches while the riders race around him at breakneck speeds."

Just whose neck was he talking about? "Ladies and gentlemen, this has never been done in any circus anywhere in the world. This is, indeed, circus history!"

The door swung into the Globe, and as I entered, my perception of time slowed dramatically. I held the torches above my head as three-foot flames billowed upward. The expressions on John's and Timo's faces told me they hadn't anticipated that the torch flames would be quite so large. In order to create a truly remarkable effect, I had placed double wicks on every torch. Seemed like a good idea at the time. We locked eyes and shook hands, partly to heighten the suspense of the performance, but mostly for us to connect and commit one last time. They revved their machines, rocking forward, then backward, and the cycles took off, whirling around and above me. I started my juggling, staying focused on just what I needed to do. After several throws at a lower level, I had the confidence to take the throws higher, first with double flips and then even higher, with triple spins that reached and surpassed the height of the motorcycles. At this level, the torches and the cycles were intermingled. With a final high throw, I ended the juggling routine without a drop. Then I moved over to allow Timo to swoop in for a landing. John came to a stop on the other side of me, and we exchanged a spontaneous three-way high five. Circus history had been made!

As we exited from the Globe of Destiny, the audience responded with cheers and applause. But for us the real thrill of this performance was the personal satisfaction that came from successfully pushing past our limitations. We repeated the stunt with greater confidence at each of the remaining eight shows. I am pleased to tell you that never once did I drop a torch, hit a motorcycle, or sustain the slightest injury.

Throughout our lives, we take on challenges that we may perceive as new or risky. We can rehearse, practice, plan, train, and procrastinate for a lifetime, or we can move forward deliberately, with conviction, and put ourselves onstage. At showtime, anything is possible. Here are some keys to orchestrating your own performance on this "Globe of Destiny" we call Earth.

First, understand yourself. What are you good at? Seek to fully understand and trust your abilities. Next, develop partnerships with others who are better than you are. Because risk is relative, we should learn from those who take challenges in stride and make them look easy. In this way we can move forward without unnecessary stress or emotional turmoil. Whom do you know who reminds you of the Nerveless Nocks? Find mentors to guide you and walk you through a mental rehearsal before your big debut. And then, if you are still overwhelmed, I find it always helps to wear a bright red jumpsuit with yellow flames.

Taking risks creates drama and excitement because, when you take a risk, it's always a world premiere. The status quo, like any fence-straddling strategy, eventually becomes boring, uncomfortable, and unfulfilling. And yet moving forward creates its own discomfort. Even a baby step into the unknown can be terrifying. Sudden, monumental changes can send us scuttling back into our cocoons, no matter how unrewarding or self-defeating that response may be.

When it comes to taking risks, most of us teeter on the threshold between normality and growth. It's always scary to test our abilities. Suppose I fail? What if I embarrass myself? Can I handle my limitations—or newfound talents and skills? Can I trust the new me? What will it be like to lose my security blanket? When we consider all these parameters, it's hardly any wonder that our first instinct is to recoil.

The great American psychologist William James assured us, "Only by taking risks from one hour to another do we really live. And often it is our faith beforehand in an uncertified result that makes the result come true." Former First Lady Eleanor Roosevelt agreed: "You must do the thing you think you cannot do." Both these great Americans had a penchant for action, not a bias for balking.

It has been my experience that when you take risks—well thought-out, calculated, timely risks—you will find yourself mysteriously aided by what Joseph Campbell refers to as "a thousand unseen helping hands." So make sure two of those hands are your own.

Two hands—hmm, that brings us back to juggling. When juggling, you work with two hands and the knowledge of natural laws such as gravity. We can't change the law of gravity; it is stable and dependable, and it affects all of us the same way. Since juggling is the act of managing multiple priorities, it is fraught with a risk—the risk of missing a catch. With knives, fire, or bowling balls, the stakes increase. If I catch one of the knives by the blade instead of the handle, I will likely cut myself. If I should drop an ax or a bowling ball on my foot, I could be seriously injured.

Juggling requires considerable practice, patience, and risk tolerance. I was fortunate to have learned the skill as a hyperactive eleven-year-old kid. At the time, my teachers were frustrated with my behavior in school and had been trying to convince my parents that Ritalin was just the ticket for me. But I'm happy to say, my folks decided against it and instead encouraged me to find other ways to channel my energy besides acting out in class.

It was at the King Richards Renaissance Faire in Bristol, Wisconsin, that I met my dear friend and mentor, Mike Vondruska. After I watched his juggling act six times in a row one day, he called me over, a bit amused at my persistence.

"Hey, kid, do you want to learn to juggle?"

I suppose I could have played it safe and walked away from the opportunity. But I was excited that this man took an interest in me, so I enthusiastically accepted his offer. When I began to learn, I discovered that I really enjoyed the challenge, and it was a great physical outlet for my overabundant energy. The practice was fun, and as I continued to improve, I found that success with juggling brought validation from others and increased my self-confidence.

But Mike taught me far more than just juggling. He taught me many valuable lessons about performing, including how to develop a routine, gather a crowd, hold that crowd's attention, and conquer my fears of risking failure in front of an audience. It was the next year, at the very same festival, when I went solo and debuted my one-man (or rather, one-boy) show.

The first lesson I learned about entertainment was simple: If you don't do well, your audience will walk away. That's the way it works with street performing. If people don't experience an immediate benefit from your show, they leave! They just get up, turn around, and walk right out of your act and your life. As a street performer, you risk humiliation and rejection. But you also gain tremendous satisfaction and confidence when the audience enjoys your act. If they stay until the end of the show, you have an opportunity to take yet another risk and ask them for money. The "hat pass," as it is called, is a defining moment for any entertainer. It is the moment we transcend the experience of having a good time together and get down to business. It is the process of building value in our audience's mind for the entertainment they have *already* experienced. It is also evidence of how we view ourselves. Ask with confidence and express your belief that you are worthy, and you will build respect and ensure a healthy hat. Ask with hesitancy, and you will instantly telegraph your lack of confidence and self-worth, distancing yourself from your audience and giving them unspoken permission to leave without dropping a dollar, or even pocket change, into your hat.

Who was taking the bigger risk? Me with the torch juggling or Mike, who let me do it while standing on his shoulders?

This is as real as it gets in performing and in life, and learning to entertain audiences under these circumstances taught me to connect quickly with people and deliver value. Each performance was risky, but the rewards grew and grew. By doing many shows each day, I learned to manage my emotions and experiment with various degrees of risk-taking. Looking back, this experience was tremendously valuable and formative.

Please understand that when I talk about taking risks, I am not talking about foolish, dangerous behavior. Certainly I do not intend for you to psych yourself up to dive off a hundred-foot cliff with only a positive attitude to protect you. If you have no experience in cliff diving, don't know how deep the water is, and have not rigorously and gradually worked your way up to such an extreme height, you would be nuts to attempt such a stunt. When I talk about risk-taking, I mean doing the things in your life that you sense you are ready for, even though you feel uncomfortable because you don't know what will happen. Often in life we stop ourselves from taking on rewarding experiences because we fear taking the risks associated with redefining our limitations, exposing ourselves to the humiliation of failure, or testing our courage.

Sure, many people experience a redefinition of their limits when they undergo a career shift or a change in their direction in life. The same is true for me. Before I was "officially" a professional speaker, my business was built around entertainment. In fact, I paid for college by performing my comedy juggling act at entertainment venues and special events. I was successful and enjoyed relationships with the top entertainment agencies, and I had a strong reputation for delivering quality performances.

When I decided to change my focus from entertainment to speaking, I believed those relationships and my reputation would serve me well and I would be able to capitalize on the value of my past achievements. I contacted all my clients and booking agents and told them about my new endeavor, expressing my hope that they would book me as a professional speaker.

What actually happened was completely different. People knew me as an entertainer, and they couldn't change that image and see me in a different light. The requests for entertainment continued to come in, but there were no requests for speeches. So I had to take a risk. I had to get uncomfortable. What I did was take an enormous leap of faith. I started saying "no" to offers for entertainment. Now, understand, this was my bread and butter that I was turning down. This was how I had provided for my family. But somehow, I knew that unless I said, "No, I don't do that anymore," I would not be able to change the way I was seen by those who knew me. Taking that risk suddenly made me very committed to the success of my speaking business.

Let's take a closer look at the relationship between risk-taking and success, and discover how risking helps us grow toward our infinite potential.

> *Take a chance. All life is a chance. The [person] who goes farthest is generally the one who is willing to do and dare. The "sure thing" boat never gets far from shore.*
>
> —Dale Carnegie

Webster's New International Dictionary defines risk as "The chance of encountering harm, loss, hazard, danger or peril; to take a perilous chance." Interestingly, all the words Webster's uses to describe risk are negative. From an early age, most of us have been conditioned to see risk-taking in a negative light. However, truly successful people see both the pros and cons associated with taking risks. They develop the experience and discernment to evaluate opportunities, measure risk against potential rewards, and *decide.*

A certain amount of daily risk is unavoidable, but we have a choice in how we view it. Because I speak all over the country, I fly a lot. Whenever you or I get on a plane, we take a risk—a calculated risk. I know that the pilots are well trained. I believe that airline security is better now since the 9/11 attacks have given rise to all sorts of new safety procedures and technologies. Still, some measure of risk will always be present, and despite knowing this, I have chosen to continue flying. For me, the logistical complications associated with not flying far outweigh the risks of using airplanes to get me from one end of the country to the other.

Life is filled with risks. Every time I stand in front of an audience, I'm taking a risk—the risk of dropping one of my clubs when I juggle, the risk of falling off my unicycle, the risk that I might forget part of my speech, the risk that the audience may not be in the best of moods, the risk that the audiovisual equipment will fail in the middle of my presentation. But because I depend on preparation and experience, I know I can stay focused, make a positive impact, and deliver a memorable message no matter what happens.

History is on the side of risk takers. People who are accustomed to success in action welcome risks as milestones, not millstones. And so can you. Here are several strategies you can implement that will help you more effectively manage any level of risk in your life.

Size up the situation. As you approach a situation, think your way through it by asking the following questions:

- Where is the risk? What is the worst thing that can happen?
- What is the likelihood that it will happen?
- What is the potential reward if I move through risk and take action?
- What would that reward mean to me? How badly do I want it?
- What is my likelihood of attaining that reward?
- Is the risk acceptable in order to achieve what I really want?

Successful risk takers are not cavalier at all about taking risks. As researcher Gerald Geis reports, "Risk takers try to turn leaps of faith into plays of percentage." As they gain success in calculating the risks involved, they begin to believe in their ability to minimize the negative consequences of risk. By examining the potential reward and the likelihood of success, you can better determine which risks are acceptable to you. By keeping your "eye on the prize," you change your thinking from avoiding the negative to achieving the positive. And you empower yourself with more powerful resources with which to succeed.

Begin small and build toward larger perceived risks. In order to whet your appetite for risk, begin with something that makes you uncomfortable but has an acceptable answer to the question "What is the worst thing that can happen?" as well as a high likelihood for success. In this way you can work up to larger risks by proving your ability to yourself. Here are some examples of smaller, acceptable risks:

- Introduce yourself to a stranger you would like to meet.
- Learn to juggle, or learn another new skill you've considered in the past.
- Take a new route to work tomorrow.
- Deliver a toast at the next dinner party you attend.
- Ask someone for forgiveness.

When in doubt, Zoom Out. As I mentioned in chapter five, I have used this technique for years to manage the anxiety that comes with performing. Regardless of your experience, that familiar and uncomfortable feeling always returns before showtime, even for professionals. It comes with the territory. The trick is to channel that energy and use it in a positive way to excite your audience.

Here's one way I do it, and it will work for you, too. When you feel overwhelmed by your responsibilities, or if you are entering into a situation that makes you nervous, this exercise will change your perspective. Visualize yourself from an outside point of view, looking down from above at yourself sitting or standing where you are at that moment. Now, take that mental picture and zoom out, creating distance between your mind's camera lens and yourself. Take the mental image farther away until you see yourself way in the distance and have a wide view of the surrounding area, buildings, or topography. Zoom out farther still, until you are not even visible, but you can only see the scene from far above, as if you were traveling in an airplane and looking down at the scenery. Now, zoom out farther still, until your camera is looking down from space at an image of planet Earth. From this vantage point, reevaluate your problems or feelings of anxiety. They will seem quite insignificant as you realize that regardless of what you do, the earth will keep right on spinning. With this "big picture" perspective, you may realize that the thing that is causing you grief is really no big deal. The problem is that you made it a big deal because you were way too close to it. Now that you've zoomed out, you have gained some objectivity and a greater sense of peace.

Associate your past experience. Even if you are about to undertake something you've never done before, you can build confidence based on your prior experiences. Here's how it works: You say to yourself, "I may not have ever tried this before, but what have I done that is similar to this experience in some way?" Take a hard look, and I know you'll be able to find some similarities from which you can draw strength and comfort. The challenge may be a new one, but it's not completely new. Your existing skills and resources are still valid. You just need to apply those skills and resources in a new way to meet your new challenge with self-assurance.

Find the fun. Often we make life too darned serious. Risk-taking should be playful, and no one knows this better than Mel Brooks, a man who has built his life and career on combining work and play. He put it like this:

> *Look, I really don't want to wax philosophic, but I will say that if you're alive, you've got to flap your arms and legs, you've got to jump around a lot, you've got to make a lot of noise . . . As I see it, if you're quiet, you're not living. You've got to be noisy, or at least your thoughts should be noisy and colorful and lively.*

How can you express your "noisy" side, flap your arms, and introduce fun into the process of risk-taking?

Reduce the risk to acceptable chunks. Bill Irwin hiked the entire 2,100-mile Appalachian Trail, from the mountains of Georgia to the forests of Maine. His only companion was his devoted dog, Orient. In a television interview several years ago, he described his difficult hike, how he weathered the cold and the elements, and how he'd wander off the trail only to be rescued by Orient. The incredible thing about Bill's story is that he is blind. He was the first blind person to successfully hike the entire length of the Appalachian Trail.

That kind of extended hike would be risky business for any of us. That Bill Irwin made the entire trip alone is a phenomenal achievement. Whenever anyone refers to him as disabled, Bill is quick to correct them by reminding them that he is "differently abled." His Appalachian Trail adventure was an eight-and-a-half-month commitment. In his book he writes:

> *Ten miles was an insignificant part of the two thousand miles it would take me to complete the trip, but I figured if I strung together enough ten-mile days, I'd get from one end of the trail to the other. Commitment and using the skills I knew I had in the time I had were the keys to success.*

When I heard Bill Irwin's story, I was reminded of the Sufi saying that we never really walk on our legs, but on our will. I believe that we all can reach our goals and move past obstacles if we commit ourselves to achieving the results. By breaking down the larger goal into smaller pieces, you can turn even the most daunting goals into accomplishments.

Visualize your success. Carl Simonton, a radiologist specializing in treatment of cancer, taught his patients to use visualization to complement his standard medical treatment. He instructed patients to "see" themselves as well. One of Simonton's patients reports:

> *I'd begin to visualize my cancer as a snake, wolverine or some vicious animal. The cure was millions of white husky dogs. It would be a confrontation of good against evil. I'd envision the dogs grabbing the cancer and shaking it to shreds.*

The patient did this three times a day for ten to fifteen minutes at a time. After six weeks, an examination revealed that his tumor had shrunk by seventy-five percent. In two months there was no trace of the disease left in his body.

I use this dramatic example to show the awesome power of the human mind to create desired outcomes using visualization. All of us have this ability. Adelaide Bry, author of *Visualization*, calls it "movies of the mind." Norman Vincent Peale called it "mental picturing." A considerable amount of research suggests that the images we hold for ourselves in our minds can become self-fulfilling prophecies. This may be the most important statement in this book, because our mindset determines our success in life. Remember, it is impossible to act in a manner inconsistent with your thinking.

Use visualization as a "fulfillment tool" for managing risk. Visualize successful outcomes for the risks you take. Make your "movies of the mind" as clear, specific, and real as your imagination allows. Form in your mind a picture of what the risk will look like, what you will need to do to minimize the risk, and what the successful outcome will be.

Replay those images in your mind as often as you can until you have dealt with the impending risk. It may take days, weeks, or months to turn mental images into physical reality, but that's how the imaging process works. Of course, visualizing positive outcomes to the risks you take is only part of the process. You will still need to take action to complement your visualizations.

"Yes" yourself—don't second-guess yourself. Maintaining a positive "can-do" attitude is central to achieving success at any level. So why do people doubt their own abilities?

Some people second-guess themselves to shirk responsibility. Others use negative thinking to hide behind doubts and fears. Most people second-guess themselves to avoid risk. In the face of unwelcome or unexpected change, they become tentative instead of tenacious. (You'll read more about that in the next chapter.) At one time or another, we all second-guess ourselves.

Attitudes are nothing more than habits of thought—and habits can be modified, changed, and ultimately stopped altogether. Our attitude is something we can control. Remember the ripple effect I mentioned in the chapter on influence? Our attitudes ripple outward, affecting ourselves and others. We can't avoid creating the ripples, but the choice is ours whether we make positive ripples by "yessing" ourselves, or negative ripples by second-guessing ourselves. The choice is ours. We can influence our environment constructively or destructively.

It is difficult for most people to recognize that the world they experience is merely a reflection of their own attitudes and behaviors. As Henry Ford said, "If you think you can do a thing, or think you can't do a thing, you're absolutely right." Whatever you believe about yourself and your circumstances directly affects your reality.

Zero in on the nature of the risk. What is the specific nature of the risk you are facing? When juggling machetes, the risk is all about the sharpened edge of the steel blade. This understanding leads me to clearly understand my objective: catch the handle.

We can all sharpen our focus by zeroing in on the risks we take in everyday life. By speaking with people who have taken risks similar to those we face, we can get a pretty good idea of what we're up against. Learning how other people handled the same risks, and what the outcomes were, helps us determine our course of action. Reading books and articles about the subject helps, too. Participating in a well-run online chat room is another way to gain valuable insights from others who "know the turf." Learning something about the nature of the risk before jumping in helps you face the unknown with a little more of the known.

Practice Safely. The first time I ever juggled knives, I knew that the most important, specific goal was to catch the handle. Yet, it was difficult to focus on that aspect, as the threatening blades drew all my attention. So, in order to sharpen my focus, I had to *unsharpen* the knives. What I did, in fact, was cover the blades with duct tape. Once this was accomplished, the risk was mitigated, and I could then concentrate on the mechanics of the trick without being distracted by the danger. This allowed me to build confidence and skill before eventually removing the tape. And when I did, I could then associate my past experience and reason that it wasn't much different, as long as my execution remained consistent. Considering this example, contemplate the risks you are about to undertake. What are the essential skills you need to master? How can you create a safe environment to practice those skills? Pilots spend many hours in flight simulators, safely honing their talents *before* taking to the sky. Similarly, you might want to "role play" a risky encounter before it actually happens.

The Rewards of Risk-Taking

> *Two roads diverged in a wood, and I—I took the one less traveled by, and that has made all the difference.*
> —Robert Frost

Stepping out of the comfort zone and forcing oneself out of the status quo and into something unknown and unfamiliar "has made all the difference" in countless people's lives. Pushing our personal and professional envelopes can take us down roads less traveled. "Nothing ventured, nothing gained" is the mantra that risk takers chant on their way toward their next adventure. "There's no free lunch" is another mantra. Risk takers know there's a price for taking risks. They also know there are rewards. And it is those rewards that put the price tag of success in proportion to the risks taken. Whether a risk is acceptable depends on the perceived value of the reward.

The rewards for risk are as varied, broad, and deep as your capacity to dream. It's a very individual matter. As you pursue success, rewards will pop up in all areas of your life: spiritual, work related, interpersonal, health related, and personal. To whet your appetite, here are a few of the possible "carrots" to encourage you. Risk takers can gain: a sense of purpose, courage, self-confidence, contentment, pride, fulfillment, respect, compassion, sensitivity, empathy, fortified willpower, increased energy, focus and vision, a reputation for achievement, and a wealth of original, unique experiences.

The Tom Hanks character in director Robert Zemeckis' Academy Award winning movie, *Forrest Gump*, put it this way:

> *My mama always said life was like a box of chocolates. You never know what you're gonna get . . . I don't know if we each have a destiny, or if we're all just floatin' around accidental—like on a breeze. But I, I think maybe it's both, maybe both happening at the same time.*

Risk-taking is a "Gumpy" thing to do, and the rewards (the chocolates) are embedded in the journey. In fact, the risks and rewards are *happening at the same time.* A classic quote by Henry David Thoreau also helps us put risks and rewards in perspective. I believe his prose has a pinch of "Gumpiness" in it as well:

> *If you advance confidently in the direction of your dreams, and endeavor to live the life which you have imagined, you will meet with a success unexpected in common hours. You'll put some things behind and pass an invisible boundary; new, universal and more liberal laws will begin to establish themselves around and within you—Old laws will be expanded and interpreted in your favor in a more liberal sense; and you will live with license of a higher order of things.*

Action Assignments

1. Make a "risk list" of eleven risks you are now willing to accept. Choose a variety of risks: mental, physical, interpersonal, and spiritual. Some items on your list may be small, others more daunting.

2. Start with the smallest risk you identified, and take a positive, calculated action to systematically conquer the perceived obstacle. Chances are, it will be much easier than you anticipated.

3. Next, choose the risk that seems most intimidating to you. Enlist the support of the risk management techniques discussed in this chapter. Set a plan in motion to stretch your risk tolerance and shift your perspective.

4. Take a few moments to visualize an upcoming risk that needs your individual attention. Visualize your preparation, what you do to minimize the risk, how you feel about the risk, who helps you, and its successful outcome. It could be one of the best "movies" you see this year. Plan to repeat your visualization a couple of times each day until you have put the risk behind you.

CHOREOGRAPH CHANGE

We need only look at nature to see that every living system, down to the most primitive cell, requires periodic renewal to survive. And we need only look at human history for countless examples of societies that clung to an old winning formula in the face of pressures to change, and perished as a result.
—John R. O'Neil

If you live your life thinking you will one day get to a point where you have peace and contentment, you will be forever frustrated. The only way to have peace and contentment in life is to find peace and contentment in the *process* of living. That process is one of unceasing change. Some people view change as negative, something that happens *to* you despite your best efforts to avoid it. These individuals experience a loss of control in response to our ever-changing world. But to those who practice *success in action,* change is what makes life exciting, fun, and rewarding. It is in the realm of change that anything is possible. Those who embrace this territory do not feel out of control. Quite the contrary. They feel in command, because they realize they can take an active role in the evolution of their world. These people have learned how to choreograph change.

> *The systems that fail are those that rely on the permanency of human nature, and not its growth and development.*
>
> —Oscar Wilde

The changes that fail are those that stop short of transformation. Have you ever made a New Year's resolution to lose a few pounds or change a particular habit, only to abandon your resolution in a few weeks? Your best intentions and sincere desires went out the window. Why was that? Perhaps it was because, although you were willing to add something new to your life, you stopped short of *reconstructing* your life and making other changes to support your new decision.

The process of welcoming change has subtractive as well as additive components. In order to accept a new future, we have to release old assumptions, outdated beliefs, and unsupportive behaviors. If we want to strengthen emerging beliefs, we have to rid ourselves of past ways of thinking and acting that interfere with our growth. In his book *The Road Less Traveled*, M. Scott Peck uses the term *bracketing*, coined by theologian Sam Keen, for the process of welcoming new information and experiences while letting go of old ones. "Bracketing," Peck says, "is essentially the act of balancing the need for stability and the status quo with the need for new knowledge and greater understanding . . . by putting some things aside to make room for the incorporation of new material."

Sam Keen describes this process in his book *To a Dancing God*:

> *Mature awareness is possible only when I have digested and compensated for the biases and prejudices that are the residue of my personal history . . . I must be sufficiently aware of my preconceived ideas and characteristic emotional distortions to*

bracket them long enough to welcome strangeness and novelty into my perceptual world . . . without this discipline each present moment is only the repetition of something already seen or experienced.

There is a famous story about a young man who was searching the world to discover the meaning of life. He traveled to distant lands, meditated in ancient temples, read classic texts, and filled himself with knowledge from many reputable sources. One day this man came to visit an old spiritual master, well known and respected worldwide for his wisdom and discipline. The master had received a letter from the young seeker requesting a meeting, and he agreed to the visit.

The old man received the student in his simple home and served tea. As soon as the young man seated himself, he began boasting about his travels, his spiritual journey, his inner awakenings, his credentials, and his expertise in their shared field. The old man said nothing as he poured tea into his guest's cup. The young man hardly noticed the hospitality and kept talking about his own accomplishments.

Suddenly the young seeker realized that his host was still pouring tea into an already overflowing cup. The hot tea was spilling over the table and onto the hardwood floor.

"Stop," cried the young man. "What are you doing? You're spilling all the tea."

The guru looked at his puzzled guest and smiled softly. "Just as the cup cannot hold any more tea once it is filled," he replied, "how can I give you the information you seek when your ego is so full?"

As the old sage demonstrated so dramatically, we cannot listen to anyone else's advice or wise counsel if we are full of ourselves, like the young seeker.

Someone once told me that ego means "easing God out." I think that applies to people who can't keep their egos in check. A healthy ego, on the other hand, makes for good self-esteem and confidence. We are all at the center of our own world, and our ego is the conscious connection between our "static" self and our evolving self.

In the story above, the young seeker wanted the advice and counsel of the old sage, but he felt threatened at the same time. He used his egocentrism and pride as a defense mechanism to protect his fragile ego from the unsettling changes he might have had to make as a result of the meeting with the master. The young man wasn't quite ready, it seems, for a positive "bracketing" experience.

All of us have opportunities to embrace change. We live in a world filled with rapidly accelerating demands for change that are occurring on many fronts: scientific, political, environmental, technological, institutional, cultural, spiritual, economic, and international. Because we are part of this amazing period of history, we must be able to manage the staggering velocity of change along with its accompanying ambiguity. Some changes are subtle, hardly noticeable, like an extra pound or two of weight gained, or the kind of fatigue that creeps up on us at the end of an enjoyable day of expended energy. Other changes are more dramatic; they catch us by surprise and shake our foundations.

On September 11, 2001, the life of every American was changed forever. My wife, Sheilia, and I know we'll never be the same. The staggering loss of lives at the World Trade Center, at the Pentagon, and in a field in Somerset County, Pennsylvania, will forever be etched in our memories.

Along with hundreds of millions of Americans, Sheilia and I stayed riveted to the TV that morning. We saw replays of planes slamming into the towering skyscrapers and watched in horror as those buildings collapsed before our eyes. We saw the crash site of United Airlines Flight 93, a Boeing 757, in a smoldering field near Pittsburgh; and we were awestruck when we saw the horrible damage to an entire wing of the Pentagon. Our heads spun for days as we tried to process what we had seen and heard.

We had witnessed unspeakable acts of terrorism on American soil by a foreign invader. Americans were in the midst of catastrophic change—and so were we. For Sheilia and me, it meant hugging each other and our son, Eddie, a little tighter. It meant rededicating our lives to God and country and to helping make America a better place to live. It meant appreciating what God has given us and appreciating what we can give others.

For a time, this became a kinder, more loving nation as people went out of their way to help one another. The impact of the tragedy was universal. To a person, everyone in our country and, indeed, throughout the civilized world, grasped the reality that historic changes were reshaping lives all across America. We shouted in unison, "The world will never be the same again!" While this statement was dramatically evident on September 11, 2001, it is also true *every single day*. The world is never the same today as it was yesterday. With each new sunrise, we are greeted with new circumstances, challenges, joys, opportunities, relationships, tragedies, and triumphs.

> *Reality is a question of perspective. The farther we get from the past, the more concrete and plausible it seems. But, as we approach the future, it inevitably seems incredible.*
>
> —Salman Rushdie

We've had time now to internalize those tragic events. They still are awesome and horrific to contemplate, but they do seem plausible and concrete now, because we have enough distance from the past to gain perspective. We know how the terrorists planned and executed their terrible mission. We will never forget the noble sacrifices and extraordinary heroism of so many Americans who died that fateful day. Although many of the images are fresh in our memories, we have gotten on with our lives, and as of this writing, we are engaged in a continuing dramatic struggle to defeat terrorism everywhere. In the process, though, many people have lost their once close identification with the events of September 11. As a nation, we have a short attention span and limited patience. The looming, uncertain future spins us into a panic, and we seek instant relief from our discomfort.

If we want to create a different global or personal reality, the process of change requires us to move confidently toward our uncertain future, guided by our principles, beliefs, and vision. Fix your gaze on what is possible, and others will begin to see what you see. Collective thought and action combine to build momentum. Change is unstoppable; it's just a question of how you handle the changes that do occur. Will you be at the mercy of the changes others prescribe for you, or will you choreograph the changes that stem from your plan for your life? It's your choice.

I want to help you embrace all degrees and magnitudes of change so you can live a happier, healthier, more successful and more productive life. It is my goal to help you muster the courage to step out of your comfort zone and choreograph the changes in your life, so you can orchestrate your own unique brand of *success in action.*

Thankfully, most of us will never have to run out of a falling building, or rush terrorists in the cockpit of a 757, or square off against insurgents in Baghdad. Most of the changes we make will not be life-threatening in nature; however, there are certain to be times when we will be pushed out of our comfort zones—or will elect to leave them on our own—in order to achieve the success and happiness we want. Although the types of changes you will encounter will vary, this is certain: change is inevitable. And because change is inevitable, there is no alternative but to accommodate it every day. I believe we have the power to choreograph ninety-five percent or more of the changes in our lives. John R. O'Neil, author of *The Paradox of Success*, accurately describes most people's resistance to change: "Because most people do not like change, change is forced upon them by crisis and discontinuity."

It doesn't have to be that way. Each of us has the power of choice. The question is, do we have the willpower to change gracefully, or will we just dig our heels in and stay as we are, even if it means being overcome by feelings of helplessness, hopelessness, and stagnation?

Spencer Johnson, MD, author of the best selling book *Who Moved My Cheese?*, writes about the learning styles of mice that are forced to adapt when their cheese is moved. The author describes the behavior of the mice: they simply respond by instinct and search out the new location of their cheese. Compare it to human behavior: we tend to question why the cheese is moved, analyze the impact it might have, and comtemplate what our next response should be. Those of us who perceive that change is coming (and prepare for it) adapt quickly to change. Those who choose to become angry (or who deny that change is necessary) do nothing and suffer the consequences of their inaction.

Myths About Change

> *Whether the change is one you have chosen or one you wish would go away, the transition forces you to leave the known and step into the new and unknown territory.*
>
> —Sabina A. Spencer

Untrue perceptions of change cause many people to become disoriented. Do you, even subtly, give credence to any of the following myths?

Myth #1:   If you are middle-aged or older, it's too late to change.

Myth #2:   If you change too quickly, it's probably superficial and won't last.

Myth #3:   If you have to change, you will.

Myth #4:   You can make someone change if your reasoning is valid and they respect you enough.

Myth #5:   Sometimes you have no choice but to change.

Myth #6:   People are only afraid of drastic change.

Myth #7:   The status quo is good enough.

Myth #8:   People are who they are, and that's the way they'll always be.

Myth #9:   All change is negative if it's not the change you want.

Myth #10:   The bottom line is that nobody wants to change.

Myth #11:   All you need to do to overcome the fear of change is to understand why you are afraid of it.

These common attitudes toward change are utterly false and lead many people to doubt their own capacity to change. I believe everyone has change-ability. We are prewired for change—it's in our DNA. It's not so much that we actively or deliberately resist change; it's that we are uncomfortable with the untried and the unknown, and sometimes it appears to take less effort just to stay where we are.

A unicycle is a lot like life: you are either going forward or you are going backward. When I demonstrate this to an audience atop my six-foot unicycle, I illustrate that in order to remain in one place, I must actually pedal forward slightly, then backward. Forward, then backward, again and again, just to maintain my present position. There is no standing still. Both the novice and the experienced individual can lull themselves into the notion that "I've done pretty well up 'til now. This is fine, so I'll just stay here for a while." To pursue this path, though, is really a futile exercise, much like idling alternately forward and backward. You will make progress in the direction of your goals, then move backward again to keep yourself in check. There is no standing still—energy is constantly flowing through your thoughts and actions.

When I first learned how to ride the six-foot unicycle, I found it nearly impossible to resist the temptation to look down. It was a long way down, after all, and if I was going to fall, I wanted to see where I was going! So, I looked down at the floor, and that's exactly where I went.

Trey Smith, an expert competitive mountain biker, was asked why he was so successful racing through the woods. His response was, "If you look at the tree . . . you've already hit it. The key is to see *around* the tree and down the path." His point was that in order to run a challenging course successfully, you have to keep your focus down the trail—where you want to go—while simultaneously managing the challenges of the changing landscape.

From time to time, life hands us events that we must handle on the fly, with little or no warning. There simply is no time to prepare. Sometimes the situation is so unfamiliar that you can't even fathom a course of action. There is no plan to follow, and it's all up to you. These are the times in life that test us the most and, in the end, define who we are. These are also the situations when it is most important to stand tall and take decisive action. Sometimes all you have to rely on are your strength of character, your heartfelt beliefs, your ethics, and your passion. And sometimes that is all you need. By connecting to your inner strength and your sense of purpose, you will find the answers you need in order to do what needs to be done. Being true to who you are and what you believe will give you the necessary faith in your ability to manage change.

Why People Resist Change

Turn and face the strange ch-ch-changes . . .
—David Bowie

People resist change for many reasons. Go through the checklist below:

Why Do People Resist Ch-Ch-Ch-Changes?

If you think a statement is true, put a "T" on the blank to the left of the statement. Place an "F" if you think the statement is false. People resist change because . . .

_____ 1. It strains their social relationships.

_____ 2. They fear economic loss if the change is unplanned.

_____ 3. Changes invariably are caused by other people who think they're helping you.

_____ 4. Change almost always causes some personal inconveniences.

_____ 5. They are afraid of the unknown, the unfamiliar, and the new.

_____ 6. Most people are defenders of the status quo.

_____ 7. They are born creatures of habit.

_____ 8. They fail to see the rewards associated with the change.

_____ 9. They don't understand why the change is necessary.

_____ 10. They perceive change as a threat to their power, status, and prestige.

_____ 11. It means *they* might have to change.

To understand why people resist change, we need to answer the question: "Resist what?" Here are the chief reasons people resist change. They are represented by the true statements on the checklist you just completed. The following statements are true and can be supported by research: 1, 2, 4, 5, and 10.

1. Social Disruption: People generally develop comfortable ways of getting along. They learn how to accept and adjust to one another. They know what to expect and learn how much of themselves to reveal. It takes time to build trust and respect, and sometimes even the slightest behavioral change can affect the security of the interdependence.

"When people form relationships," says psychologist Mark Steinberg, "they must coordinate their mutual behaviors and adapt to one another . . . the relationship they form is the product of inter-dependence, although neither loses his or her identity. Each contributes to the quality and structure of the relationship."

Good relationships become the basis for improving ourselves. By adding our uniqueness to the soul of a relationship, we do our part to strengthen it. Because changes *change* us, the relationships we are engaged in also change. Change disrupts the delicate balance of what the relationship used to be and what it must become as a result of the changes in its membership.

2. Economic loss: It is unreasonable to expect people to favor a change that negatively affects their income, investments, and cash flow. "Money may not buy happiness," said Denzel Washington during a TV interview, "but it is a heck of a down payment."

People realize that money, and access to money, is an essential ingredient in their success formula, and they are very careful about embracing changes that affect their wealth and prosperity. Money can be a source of great joy and happiness, or it can bring frustration and misery. It touches every aspect of our lives: work, leisure time, family, church, hobbies, philanthropy, investments, medical decisions, social commitments, volunteerism—the list goes on. We want to hold on to it, spend it, enjoy it—and any change that interferes with our ability to do so is automatically viewed with suspicion. For many people, money means financial freedom. Changes that affect someone's money affect that person's perception of personal freedom. This seems to be the underlying cause of resistance to change where economics is concerned.

4. Personal inconvenience: People get used to a certain way of doing things. They welcome a certain measure of routine as long as it contributes to the level of satisfaction they want to enjoy at a given time. If a change is in alignment with the demands of the moment, people are willing to accommodate the change. However, if they see the change as an inconvenience, they will whine and complain about the disruption in their otherwise predictable day.

5. Fear of the unknown, the unfamiliar, and the new. Fear begins as a thought, belief, feeling, or expectation and ends up putting us in what I call a *zone of resistance*. Many people are hesitant to step into the unfamiliar and the untried. Like pain, our fears can advise us and warn us of danger, but they can also limit our progress. Fear comes in many guises, such as "I can't," or "I'm too tired," or "I'm really not interested in doing that," or "Let's do something else."

Uncertainty and unfamiliarity bring with them a mood of vulnerability and chance. Comedian Edgar Fiedler put it quite succinctly when he said, "Forecasting is very difficult, especially when it's about the future." Every uncertainty we face, each unfamiliar venture, comes with manufactured doubts and concerns. Stepping into the unknown takes a leap of faith, particularly if we have no idea of what lies ahead of us. Our self-confidence and courage are tested. We may even tremble at the thought of venturing outside our comfort zone. We'll explore fear some more in the next chapter, when we discuss the various obstacles that can get in the way of *success in action*.

10. A threat to status, power, and prestige. People who enjoy their status and power want to keep it. They will fight any change they see as undermining their prestige and importance. They surround themselves with people who keep threatening changes at a distance. For them, the perks of importance are so seductive that they will do everything within their power to preserve the status quo. People with a penchant for power are striving for self-definition, which makes them all the more inclined to prevent perceived threats to their domain.

Mastering Change

> *To resist change is to work against the flow of life*
> *rather than surrender to and trust it.*
> —Susan Taylor

When you learn to embrace change as a natural part of your life, you'll welcome new opportunities disguised as challenges, and self-improvement disguised as vulnerability. Your fears and frustrations will diminish, and your confidence and courage will grow as you assert more control over your life. You will begin to improve your ability to choreograph change and welcome it as a teacher and an ally. As with any skill, mastering change takes time, patience, and perseverance. The Chinese character for "crisis" means two things: peril and opportunity. If we substitute "change" for "crisis," we could describe change using the same two descriptors. When we welcome change, we turn from panic to power.

In her insightful book about living with the Amish, artist Sue Bender writes:

> *Perhaps each of us has a starved place, and each of us*
> *knows deep down what we need to fill that place. To*
> *find the courage to trust and honor the search, to*
> *follow the voice that tells us what we need to change,*
> *even when it doesn't make sense, is a worthy pursuit.*

Like Sue Bender, we are all "following the voice that tells us what we need to change." I followed the voice that told me to combine my juggling, acrobatic, and unicycling skills with my speaking skills. That same voice is responsible for giving me the courage to ask Sheilia to marry me. Paying attention to that voice helped me qualify for my pilot's license, set hundreds of goals, join the National Speakers Association, and invest in a business that has become my life's work. This book is a result of listening to that voice. It is the voice of change, and it is in all of us.

Change is both crisis and opportunity. The following strategies can help you master change and turn panic-laced anxiety into powerful action. I encourage you to add each of these strategies to your change mastery plan. You'll no doubt favor some strategies more than others. Use what works for you. Become a change master.

1. Face change head-on. Whether the change is anticipated or out of the blue, it has to be managed. Ignoring it won't make it go away. Dr. Martin Luther King Jr. said, "The ultimate measure of a person is not where he or she stands in moments of comfort, but where he or she stands in times of trial and controversy."

Change teaches us something about ourselves. To face change head-on is to meet ourselves face to face. To run from change is to run from ourselves. Whether we are squaring off against the unexpected or confronting the anticipated, dealing with change takes resolve and commitment. Self-discipline and self-control help us turn the changes we need to make into character-building events, strengthening us and making us more aware of our ability to meet any challenge.

2. Keep your goals in mind. Don't let changes derail you. Stay focused on your goals and commitments. Assess the changes that occur and integrate them into your overall plan. Use goals to your advantage by using them to keep change in perspective. Stay flexible but focused. Realize that change, like goals, is part of life. Depending on the nature of the change, you may choose to modify one or more of your goals. Generally speaking, however, goals serve as our "achievement guardrails," keeping us on track and moving forward in the midst of change dynamics.

3. Shift your perspective. What thoughts, images, or memories come to mind when you hear the word "scared"? Take a few moments to think about the times you've been scared. What happened? What did you do? How did you react? Now focus on the word "sacred". What thoughts, images, or memories come to mind? When did you experience a sacred moment? Were you in church, at a spiritual retreat, on a camping trip, on the golf course, at a child's christening, at a wedding ceremony?

Although these two words have exactly the same letters, they mean two entirely different things. Transposing two letters makes all the difference in the world. This same kind of transposition can help you see change in an entirely different light. You can be frightened by change or see it as a soul-enriching event. All you need to do is shift your perspective.

4. Don't identify with the suspended foot. Moving confidently through change takes trust, focus, and perspective. The key is to continue to move forward. For example, when you climb a ladder, you lift your foot from one rung of the ladder to another so you can move up higher on the ladder. From the instant you raise your trailing foot, there is nothing for that foot to stand on until it steps onto the next higher rung. If you were to focus all your attention on the suspended foot, you would probably feel anxious and a little uncertain. After all, the foot is situated between rungs and has no visible support.

If you don't identify with the suspended foot, you realize that you are holding on to the ladder with both hands and have placed the other foot solidly on the rung beneath the suspended foot. So you have plenty of support for the climb.

This reality is amplified when I perform ropewalking. When executing this skill, you don't hold on to anything! There is only one point of contact: the one foot that stands on an ever-shifting rope. To negotiate a slack rope from one end to the other requires you to stand on one foot and raise the other simultaneously. It isn't so much walking as it is a series of one-foot balances alternating between right and left. Eventually, you will end up at the other end of the rope.

Your ability to manage change works in much the same way. If you identify with change (the suspended foot) you will probably feel anxious and uncertain about your next steps in life. Choose instead to remember that you have a solid foundation beneath you (your family, friends, past experiences, talents and abilities) to give you the support you need for your climb toward success.

5. See change from "eye to I." Visualize successful change. What the mind sees, the future beholds. The more we use focused mental imagery, which sees changes as positive events, the better our ability to program our thoughts to attract positive changes. By conscientiously applying creative visualization techniques, you are welcoming change as well as gaining access to your untapped subconscious abilities.

As I've emphasized throughout this book, our thoughts, especially our visualizations, help create our reality. As you begin using creative visualization to help manage change, trust the process, and you will transform your "eye" power to your "I" power—that is, you take the actions your mind's eye sees and make them real in the physical world.

6. Put your doubts on the short list. On a sheet of paper write down all the negative feelings and doubts you may have about the change facing you at the moment. Avoid censoring yourself. No one but you will see this page (unless you choose to show it to someone you trust). When you've finished listing your doubts and negative feelings, take a clean sheet of paper and list all the benefits this particular change can give you. Don't leave anything out. Think of all the areas in your life that this change affects. Now compare the two lists. Do the positives outnumber the negatives? Do major benefits outweigh the negative concerns you have about the impending change? Determine what the overall effects of the change are and how they will affect your life.

7. Listen inside out to what the change is telling you. Find a quiet place and relax for a few moments. Turn off the cell phone. Let people know you need a few minutes of quiet. Now close your eyes and listen. Sit absolutely motionless for five minutes. Become aware of the sounds around you. Keeping your eyes closed and your breathing slow and relaxed, cup your palms over your ears. Listen to the humming of *you* at rest. Now ask yourself this question: "What is this particular change trying to tell me?" Repeat it aloud several times if you feel it's necessary. Now listen inside out to what the change is telling you.

8. Speak to the wizard. Contact people who have been through similar changes. Share your concerns, fears, and doubts. Explain why you are seeking their counsel and advice. Learn from those who have been there before you got there. Keep the discussion centered on the dynamics of the particular change and on what worked instead of what didn't work.

9. Be a quick-change artist. One of the simplest yet most effective ways to prepare for change is to accustom yourself to change dynamics. This change strategy gives you opportunities to rehearse for change in nonthreatening ways. For example: brush or comb your hair, or button your shirt or blouse, with your nondominant hand; if you like fried eggs, scramble them or try them poached; drive a different way to work; purposely stand in the longest line at the supermarket; with someone nearby to protect you, walk around the house blindfolded for fifteen minutes; adopt a new interest like juggling or unicycling; if you're partial to red meat or chicken, go vegetarian for a couple of days; fast for a day if your health permits; draw a picture using your nondominant hand; don't wear your watch for a day; pick one of the simplest goals on your goals list and do it; turn the volume down on the TV and see how good you are at following the action; walk to the store if you usually ride; write snail mail instead of e-mail; sleep on the side of the bed you normally don't sleep on; put your dominant arm in a sling for a day; avoid watching the news for a week.

10. Sleep on it. Before you go to sleep, ask for guidance for the challenging changes ahead of you. Don't limit what God can do for you by jumping to conclusions about the answers you want. "Let go and let God," the instruction goes. The next morning, or during the night, record any insights that come to mind. If you feel that an answer was not forthcoming, sleep on it again—and again and again. Trust that the guidance will come.

11. Go back to the future. Imagine yourself one, two, or three years from now. Look back on this particular change from that vantage point. How gracefully did you handle the change? What were you able to do to turn the experience into positive change? If you could have done one thing differently, what would you have done? What did you learn from that particular experience? Describe the positive changes you made in other areas of your life because of the change. What overall advice would you give to someone else who is about to go through a similar experience?

Action Assignments

1. Think of an upcoming change in your life. It can be work related or have something to do with family, friends, or relatives. Make a list of the thoughts, behaviors, beliefs, and actions that you need to let go of in order to ensure that your change takes hold.

2. Which of the myths about change did you believe before you learned otherwise? What have you decided to do differently about any ongoing or upcoming changes now that you know the truth? List the action steps you plan to take.

3. Think back over your life thus far. Write down one experience when you can recall being scared. Describe when, where, and why. I know this can be an intense emotional undertaking, so take a couple of deep breaths and walk around the room a few times to relax. Now, recall and write down a time when you experienced something *sacred*. Describe when and where it happened, and what about the event made it feel sacred. Now reexamine your *scared* experience and, from today's perspective, rewrite it so that it has a *sacred* outcome. How does this change the way you feel about the experience?

TURN SETBACKS INTO COMEBACKS

A setback is a setup for a comeback.

—Willie Jolley

I n the fall of 1989, I was performing near Annapolis, Maryland, with my longtime friend and performance partner, Philip Solomon. Our comedy juggling and percussion act was featured at the Maryland Renaissance Festival, and the first weekend of shows had just ended. So we decided to use our time off to explore New York City.

After spending the night with my uncle Jay and aunt Dell in Warwick, New York, we joined my uncle for the three-hour early morning bus commute to the Big Apple. Jay worked in New York's textile district, and this was his daily routine.

Philip and I would be staying with our friend from high school, Tara Watford, who was an art student at NYU. After our bus arrived at Grand Central Station, we said our goodbyes to my uncle and took a subway to Washington Square Park. Knowing that Tara's apartment was in the general area, somewhere on Fifth Avenue, we planned to call her when we arrived in the neighborhood.

Reaching what we guessed was a "close enough" stop, we dragged our luggage up the subway platform stairs and into the exciting street bustle of a New York workday morning. Laden with our heavy, unwieldy bags, we quickly located a pay phone so we could call Tara.

Philip began looking through his backpack, and I watched his expression change from excitement to confusion, then dismay. His journal, containing Tara's

"Rhythm and Juggling" with Philip Solomon at the Maryland Renaissance Festival

phone number, was nowhere to be found. Somewhere along our journey, it had disappeared.

We explored our options and then tried calling information. There was no listing for a Tara Watford. We tried calling friends back home; no one knew her telephone number. I didn't even have the work number for my uncle Jay or know the name of his place of business. So we stood there, aware that we were rapidly running out of options. And then it began to rain.

All we knew for certain was that Tara lived "somewhere off Fifth Avenue"—that was the extent of our knowledge. So we located Fifth Avenue, knowing full well that finding the right building along this major thoroughfare would be like finding a needle in a haystack. But we realized that we had to be willing to start with what we knew, and see what might happen.

We began walking down Fifth Avenue, carrying our bags and looking every bit as out of place as we felt. We didn't even know what we were looking for, really, and after three blocks, we realized that just walking around wasn't going to solve our problem. It was highly unlikely that we would pass Tara on the street, and even less likely that we would find her apartment. But unless we took action and tried something, failure was guaranteed.

Philip and I turned out of the rain and into the building on our right. It was an old structure that looked as though it may have been converted into apartments. Entering with our bags, we were greeted by a woman at a reception desk. I thought to myself how ridiculous this was: trying to guess the whereabouts of our friend in the largest city in the United States. I almost walked back out of the building and back into the downpour. But Philip short-circuited my retreat by boldly walking up to the counter. He set down his bags and, with impressive confidence, asked the woman, "Could you please tell me the room number for Tara Watford?"

Yeah, right, I thought as she turned the pages in her binder. Then she stopped and answered quite matter-of-factly, "Yes, she's in eight fourteen. Let me ring that for you."

We were flabbergasted. Of all the buildings in New York City, or even all the residential buildings along Fifth Avenue, we had somehow picked the right one on the very first try! In an instant our perspective shifted 180 degrees. One moment we were hopelessly lost and alone in New York; the next, we were exactly where we needed to be, feeling energized, validated, and very lucky. Reunited with our friend, we proceeded to have an awesome time in New York. We returned to do our shows in Maryland armed with many new stories, but none more amazing than this one.

The lesson I learned from this experience was twofold. The first realization was that even when your resources are woefully depleted, they are not exhausted; there is always something you can do. You must start somewhere, and you can only begin where you are. When you are shaken or thrown dramatically off your game plan, honestly assess what you do have to work with, and then take some positive action.

The second important lesson was that even when it seemed that we were completely lost, we really were not far from where we needed to be. The obstacles were real, but in our minds they were magnified and intensified with emotion. From our perspective, it seemed that locating Tara was an impossible task. Actually, though, the place we were seeking was just a few blocks and a few bold actions away.

In life it becomes easy to magnify our problems and challenges, even to the point that the situation seems hopeless. This behavior can paralyze us, draining our spirit and preventing any forward movement. When you feel this way, it is essential to look your problems squarely in the face and recognize them for what they are, not for what you have made them out to be. You are probably not as far from the solution as you fear; in fact, the very thing you need could be right around the corner, a phone call or a prayer away.

During my seminars and performances, I have had the privilege of teaching thousands of people how to juggle. As you have already seen, juggling is an excellent metaphor for life and learning. The Juggling for Life workshop (a seminar in which I actually teach juggling to the audience members) is an opportunity to go beyond the analogy and put the principles into action. I absolutely love the process of transforming a roomful of doubtful participants into competent jugglers within a span of thirty to forty-five minutes. The excitement is palpable as the audience members learn a new skill that they had always assumed was beyond them. Amid the activity and fun, people learn firsthand these powerful techniques for adopting any new skill quickly:

- Where you place your focus is critical to success. Focus on the throw, not the catch.
- Gain feedback from your actions and make appropriate adjustments.
- You learn faster by modeling others and coaching one another.
- You have more time than you think you do. Relax.
- Celebrate the drops as a sign of progress. Dropping is a necessary part of the learning process. Failure is essential to learning.

This last point is especially difficult for a lot of people, who associate dropping with frustration and failure rather than with progress. When the balls begin to hit the floor, the participants exclaim, "I told you, I can't do this; I keep dropping." To this I respond, "Fantastic! That's exactly what you are supposed to be doing the first time you try it." When your skills as a juggler improve, you will get better, but you will still drop the ball often. No matter how advanced a juggler you become, you will drop. In fact, the more you practice, the more you drop, because you will continue to experiment with new possibilities and stretch the limits of what you can do. So become accustomed to dropping. Look forward to dropping. Celebrate your mistakes! The real question is: Are you learning from your drops? Are you turning setbacks into comebacks?

When you try to protect yourself from making a mistake, you will be timid, unsure, and focused on the wrong thing. If your feeling of self-worth relies on your being perfect, you have set your personal expectations so they yield a greater portion of misery than of satisfaction. Because we are all imperfect human beings, we make mistakes all the time. Every opportunity we have to try something new—and perhaps fail at it—is an opportunity to learn. The key is to learn how to recover quickly while keeping your forward momentum. And when you view failure from a more detached perspective, as if you were an outside observer, you will better see the reasons why you were previously unsuccessful. These new insights will enable you to take better actions, with increased knowledge and determination.

Not dropping is boring. Dropping, on the other hand, can be exciting, thrilling, and fun. And the recovery of the drop is the real skill. How quickly can you pick the object (or the objective) back up, turning the setback into a comeback? You must realistically and unemotionally ask yourself, *What are the reasons for the drops in my life? Why did the mistake happen?* Probing questions and honest answers will show you how to move forward and transcend your current level of ability.

I was on one such learning excursion when the idea came to me to use the word "drops" as an acronym to describe the five obstacles that hinder our success. On this occasion, I was in Minneapolis, at the National Speakers Association Annual Convention, with 1,800 other speakers.

After a few days of sessions, some friends and I took a break from the activities and visited the "Mall of America." This destination is a shopper's dream come true, with a store for almost anything you can imagine! On the massive directory we noticed there was even a shop that sold juggling equipment, called Air Traffic. When we found it, my friends encouraged me to go in and show off a little.

On entering, I was quickly dazzled by the array of "toys" to investigate. On the walls were every sort of juggling prop you can imagine. Kites hung from the ceiling. There were racks and racks of Frisbees and even a giant, bungee-driven water-balloon launcher that required three people to operate. I knew right away that I was in the right place, and I felt the spontaneous desire to play.

Grabbing three clubs off the wall, I began juggling. Within seconds, one of the store employees approached— a young man who began watching me intently, sizing up my skills. He seemed interested and able, so I asked him if he "passed," the juggling term for "Do you want to throw stuff at each other?"

"Yeah," he said, smiling broadly.

"Want to jam?"

"Every-others with a quick start?" he quizzed, trying to set the parameters.

"Let's go," I confirmed.

He took three clubs off the wall and in a flash, we began juggling. We passed six clubs between us, slowly at first, each feeling out the other's style and skill level. Then, once we were comfortable, we started throwing more advanced tricks. We tossed the clubs over our heads, behind our backs, doubles from the left hand, triples from the right, every which way. Some of our high throws bounced off the kites that hung from the ceiling. The energy was great. My friends stood amazed, dumbfounded that complete strangers who had never rehearsed together were able to accomplish such a complex series of throws.

Then we experimented by trying tricks we couldn't do, and we dropped clubs all over the place. Our number of drops went up because we were establishing new limits. But you know what? We caught a lot of those clubs, too. And that was exciting. We were pushing ourselves and coaxing each other to perform at a higher level. And even when we dropped clubs, we managed to pick up quickly, recovering the club and throwing it right back into the pattern, without stopping. In this way, we were able to keep the rhythm going, keep our momentum, and salvage the "pattern of throws" despite the built-in obstacles involved in attempting something unique and complex. Because we spoke the same performance language, and were equally skilled in the art, and were willing to push the envelope, we were able to minimize the effects the drops had on our overall performance.

Minimizing the drops during my Mall of America experience is the perfect metaphor for minimizing the negative effects of the obstacles we face as we seek to epitomize success in action. Using "DROPS" as an acronym for those obstacles, let's take a look at the five performance barriers that undermine our skill, courage, and patience as we try our best to become what we were meant to be. The obstacles are:

D: Distractions
R: Rushing our Pace
O: Obsolete Habits
P: Panic
S: Self-Doubt

DROPS—Distractions

Maintaining one's focus is one of those things in life that are far easier to talk or write about than to execute. Have you ever been in this situation? You are at work, thinking about an active project. The effort is coming together, and you are feeling pretty good about it. Then someone abruptly breaks into your thoughts by reminding you of an unrelated task or concern. What happens? You start to feel a little anxiety. You think, "That's right! I need to consider and act upon that, too. Maybe right now!" These thoughts may trigger others about items on your to-do list. In a matter of moments, you have gone from feeling perfectly pleased with yourself and your accomplishments to feeling that you are so far behind, you will never catch up. As the parade of disorienting distractions escalates in your thoughts, you are much more likely to drop the ball.

James Salter talks about the consequences of distractions in a profile of the great pioneering rock climber Royal Robbins:

> It is disturbing, perhaps, to think of Robbins, one
> of the greatest climbers alive, as being distracted or
> careless and losing his hold and then falling. After all,
> if he falls, what chance do we have? . . . But the reason
> has nothing to do with lack of ability. Robbins falls
> when he attempts something that is at the very limit of
> his powers, and it is his nature always to extend these

*limits. He expects distractions, obstacles, and even
falls, and prepares for them.*

This, of course, is a dramatic example of the power that distractions
have to ruin our day, but distractions have a way of doing just that if
we're not careful. A good tactic is to follow Royal Robbins' lead and
prepare for them. We will never eliminate distractions, but we can
minimize their effects on our momentum. A distraction is a distraction
only if we allow ourselves to be distracted. Otherwise, it's just stuff
that's happening around us. And that *stuff* happens all the time.

Distractions, like just about everything else, have positive applications. It's only when they interfere with what we want to do that they
annoy and harm us. When we are prepared for distractions, we can
lessen their negative impact.

One useful way to reduce the frequency of distractions is to start
every day with an organized task list. This is more than just a to-do list,
because when you take the time to plan your day, you should also set
priorities for your actions. When you are confronted with a simple
distraction, you may choose to deal with it right then, handling it the
first time it comes up. (If the ball is in your hand, throw it!) If it is more
involved, your inclination may be to minimize the distraction's effects
until you have managed higher-priority items. (Do one thing at a time,
in the proper sequence.) Either way, you will be able to keep your
momentum for the rest of the day, because you have a plan and you
are well aware of the most critical tasks.

DROPS—Rushing your Pace

Often we make mistakes when we rush headlong into something before
we are ready, or when we accelerate our pace to the breaking point.
When I got hooked on juggling, I would spend hours practicing various
tricks. I noticed that my success with various maneuvers was extremely
inconsistent. Some days even the tough tricks seemed effortless. It felt
great. Other times, I would try a trick twenty times with no success.
What is the difference? I wondered. It seemed to me that if I was able
to get the trick right once, I should be able to do it all the time.

When I was struggling, I thought that sheer repetition was the
answer. So I decided to go faster, trying a trick over and over to get it

right, racing the clock to squeeze in as many attempts as possible. But in my exuberance, I was rushing through each practice. I wanted to get as much "toss time" in as I could each day. My accelerated pace had become a liability, an obstacle to my success.

As soon as I deliberately slowed down and became less interested in *quantity* of throws, the quality improved dramatically. With this new perspective, I began to realize that not only did I have an abundance of practice time, but also the moments between the throws and catches seemed to expand. Instead of rushing my juggling pattern and creating collisions in the air above my head, I found I was able to relax and find the proper timing, which allowed all the objects to take their natural position in the pattern.

Recently I was in Montreal, studying with Cirque du Soleil, the Quebec-based international phenomenon that has revolutionized the way we experience circus. (If you have never been to a Cirque du Soleil performance, do yourself a favor and go. It will blow your mind!) Each morning in the practice gym, I observed a juggler from Peru named Gonzalo. He is extremely skilled and dedicated to his craft. But what impressed me most was not his mastery of five clubs, but his practice routine. At the beginning of each day, he would start his workout with one object. Just one. He would work diligently with the one club, throwing it from hand to hand slowly, meticulously, all the while striving for perfection of the throw. He did this for forty-five minutes before moving on to two!

When a person is given more tasks to handle or greater responsibilities to oversee, the first, instinctive reaction is simply to speed up. After all, we have the same amount of time we had before. Now, however, we are expected to accomplish more than ever. It seems to make sense—at first. What we quickly discover, though, is that acceleration by itself does not improve performance. I am reminded of this lesson every time I juggle. I remember when I first learned to juggle five balls. The pattern for five objects is essentially the same as for three. It seemed logical to me that by increasing the speed of my juggling, I would be able to fit more "stuff" into the same pattern. Eventually, I learned a more important lesson: While increasing the pace of your throws is a necessary element to juggling more objects, increased pace alone is not enough to meet the challenge.

The second thing that always happens when you add more objects to your juggling act is that the accuracy of each throw becomes extremely important. In other words, you have to make the right throw the first time, when the ball is in your hand. You don't have time to compensate for errors. Sometimes this means slowing down before you take action, in order to make sure your throw is on target.

Accelerating the pace without a clear grasp of the need for accuracy will lead you to a point where you will simply run out of gas, both physically and mentally. Continuing to substitute speed for accuracy will cause burnout. We live in a land where it is possible to achieve our dreams and goals, so we hunger for the satisfaction of accomplishment. Unfortunately, we want it all *now*! Thinking this way sets us up for disappointment, frustration, and exhaustion.

You have more time than you think you do. In fact, you have all that there is! No one on earth has more time than you do. But remember, time is relative. To experience an absence of available time, continue to rush around as quickly as you possibly can. To experience an abundance of time, resist the temptation to rush. Instead, saturate every moment with richness and meaning. The content of your experience will change your perception, and your new perspective will give you greater control and enjoyment of life.

By rushing around preparing for the future, we miss the importance of *the thing that is actually happening*. We fail to see the connection between what we're doing, what we're meant to do, and what we can do. We miss opportunities for clarity and direction, and we forget the very things that can help us find balance and gain the perspective we need in order to value each moment.

When you search for moments of joy, inner peace, and balance, you will attract activities, work, hobbies, conversations, people, and circumstances that bring joy, inner peace, and balance into your life. But, in order to benefit from them, you must eliminate your chronic hurry to experience the essence of what you want.

DROPS—Obsolete Habits

Self-defeating thoughts, habits, and actions are the three biggest obstacles in the way of people's success. That's a bold but true statement. In her superb book *If Success Is a Game, These Are the Rules*, Cherie

Carter-Scott puts the subject of obsolete habits succinctly:

> *Certainly there are such things as bad luck or*
> *unfortunate circumstances, but if you categorize those*
> *as the primary reasons why you cannot get what you*
> *want, then you are caught in an endless cycle of false*
> *causes or blaming. If there is a discrepancy between*
> *what you say you want and what you are getting, then*
> *this is a signal that you need to dig a little deeper to*
> *discover the source of your obstacles. A good place to*
> *start is with old habits that sabotage your success.*

Cherie Carter-Scott is right, of course. Old, self-defeating habits do limit our success. Let's return to the example of the juggling workshop. When I teach people the pattern for three-ball juggling, we begin with one ball, tossing it from hand to hand. This establishes the foundation of the juggling pattern. You throw across and upward, then the ball peaks and falls into the opposite hand. Then, you throw it back, across and upward, repeating this action with the other hand. After a few tries, most people develop some consistency and a smooth rhythm with their throws.

After everyone in the room has "caught on," I introduce the second ball. I demonstrate that each hand throws as before, first one and then the other, upward and across so that the balls cross in mid-air. The two throws are made in a sequence, with a specific rhythm that sounds like this: "Throw, throw. Catch, catch."

Invariably, at this point a high percentage of participants will start juggling by throwing one of the balls up and *passing* the other underneath, placing it into the other hand. This circular pattern of throwing and passing is nothing at all like what I described and demonstrated. Yet, almost immediately, many people do this on their own. Why is that? The reason is simple—it is an obsolete habit, an old pattern of behavior. In the past, these people found that by using that self-taught technique, they were able to move two balls through the air successfully without dropping.

Repeating the process ingrained the habit, and it worked—for two ball juggling. But, in order to get from two balls to three, *that* pattern must be transcended. The new pattern is a complete transformation for many, as well as an excellent opportunity for me to teach people how to change their obsolete habits.

The first step is to become aware of the fact that you are constrained by an obsolete habit. Most people who persist at the two-ball, circular pattern are not even conscious they are doing it. They are happy and smiling and think to themselves that they are doing just great. It's up to me, as their coach, to bring this to their attention. Once they see that their actions are different from what I've asked of them, they will try again, and often they continue the same old pattern. But now they have become aware they are doing it. They haven't broken the habit, but at least they are aware of their behavior. That's an important step.

Next I work with them and provide specific coaching to dismantle their pattern. I'll ask them to do only the throws, and I'll make the catches. Then we will switch, with me executing the throws while they focus only on the catches. I've developed a number of techniques to break the obsolete habit of passing balls. Some are subtle and others are more dramatic, but I will use every one until we successfully modify the throws. Once that is accomplished and we've had a successful outcome, I continue to work with this person until we routinely repeat our success. To ingrain the new behavior, repetition is necessary. When I'm confident that the student will not regress to the old pattern, I step away and allow him or her some practice time to "take ownership" of the new technique. When the student can do it consistently, we are ready to move to the next level.

The entire process I've just described takes only a couple of minutes working one-on-one with a student. But without changing the habit, progression to the next level of success with three balls would be nearly impossible.

Transforming obsolete habits in our own lives may happen quickly, or it may take more time and effort. In either case, we can use the same process. Any time we change a habit or learn something new, we go through four distinct levels of competence. I first heard a succinct description of these phases long ago from my friend and golf buddy Lee Goldsmith. (The original source of this information is unclear and debated.) Identifying and articulating the levels of learning has helped me to take on new skills more quickly and leave old behaviors behind.

- **Phase 1—Unconsciously Incompetent.** You have an obsolete habit, but you aren't even aware of it, like the person happily juggling two balls in the wrong pattern. Ignorance may be bliss, but it isn't helpful. You keep making the same mistakes again and again, and at the same time you wonder why the same problems are recurring. Certainly it's not your fault—or is it? Eventually, through introspection or someone else's observation and advice, you realize that you have a shortcoming you can characterize as an obsolete habit. Suddenly you become aware.

- **Phase 2—Consciously Incompetent.** Like our two-ball juggler, you suddenly realize that your behavior is not working to support your desired objective. You become aware of the gap between what you are doing and what you should be doing. Even with this awareness, however, you continue to persist in the old habit. After all, it is a habit, a pattern of behavior, and it has momentum. You keep acting in old ways with the knowledge that they don't work. The repeated failure is frustrating. Eventually, you make a conscious decision not to tolerate this discrepancy, so you find a way to break the pattern. Perhaps you get a coach, someone who can teach you or train you to embrace a new pattern of behavior. You may need to try methods that are subtle, creative, dramatic, or all of the above. As with juggling, repetition is the key. You'll need to force yourself to exhibit new behaviors again and again, until you are successful on demand.

- **Phase 3—Consciously Competent.** You have traded in your obsolete habit for a new and improved way of functioning. It works and you are consistently successful as long as you act deliberately. You are aware of the temptations of old habits creeping in on you, and you head them off with your new methods. You can do it, as long as you are thinking about it. This is a functional level of skill, but it demands focus, concentration, and continuous decision-making. But with time and practice and by staying committed to your new way of action, you will reach another level of execution.

- **Phase 4—Unconsciously Competent**. The new behavior has become ingrained. It is a part of you, the standard mode of operation. Obsolete habits that were a constraining factor are a thing of the past. They are easily circumvented, because your new and improved actions have taken hold completely. Because your new habits are positive, they are more successful and have created results that excite you. This has the effect of building momentum and reinforcing your new behavior. The right actions start to happen more spontaneously because you understand the pattern inside and out.

Regularly examine your assumptions and find out if they are still valid. I am reminded of a story the author Jean Deeds tells on herself. She wrote of one harrowing night alone on the Appalachian Trail, when she was listening to a bear snuffling outside her tent. She was terrified.

Her heart pounding in her ears, unable to sleep, she lay as still as possible, hoping the beast would not hear her rapid breathing and rip through the thin layer of nylon tent that separated them.

Early the next morning, Jean chanced a quick peek outside and stared directly into the face of the foraging beast: a cow, calmly chewing on grass. She laughed out loud. A hungry cow may not be something to take lightly, but it wasn't the bear she had assumed it was. She had even followed her survival training manual's instructions regarding bear encounters: lie still and play dead.

Habits, such as lack of exercise, making assumptions without verifying the facts (Jean was guilty of that, and so are most of us), worry, negative thinking, self-criticism, procrastination, complacency, taking the easy way out, poor diet, unhealthy anger, and so on, can cause us to bury ourselves in mediocrity as we listen to the "beast of change" snuffling outside.

Habits that cause us to miss opportunities for growth are millstones around our necks, obstacles that interfere with our growth. We unwittingly form habits, and eventually those habits form us. Habits, like most human experiences, are choices; self-defeating habits are self-defeating choices. It is critical that we recognize each of the habits mentioned above as a personal choice. Cardwell C. Nuckols, coauthor of *Healing an Angry Heart: Finding Solace in a Hostile World*, discusses how to harness our anger into positive energy:

Some people habitually hold anger in, which is very destructive to the cardiovascular system. Some let it out by putting down other people . . . On the positive side, others use their anger as constructive energy. I have found that a lot of folks successfully deal with anger by using it as a positive energy booster. They almost always use it as a motivational call to action.

One way to move past self-defeating habits is to realize that we are creatures of polarity. Each of the habits mentioned above has a polar opposite within us. Inside every person who acts on assumptions is a rational realist; inside every rational realist is a person who is prone to assumptions. Inside every worrier is someone who is confident; inside a negative thinker is a positive thinker. Inside everyone who is self-critical is a self-congratulator. You get the picture. Because we are filled with polarities, we can choose opposing thoughts, views, and behaviors. We can turn bad habits into behaviors that promote *success in action*. As I've said many times before, our success—or failure—is determined by our actions, and it is impossible to act in a manner inconsistent with our thinking.

We have all heard the joke about the drunk fellow who lost his car key in the middle of a dark street and looked for it under the corner streetlight "because the light was better there." Too often people allow their bad habits to keep them in the dark, by looking where they've always looked because they mistakenly believe the "light" is better there. Unfortunately, growth means stepping out of the comfortable light of mediocrity and onto the shadowy path to renewal and self-definition.

DROPS—Panic

Panic is, without a doubt, one of the most debilitating of all obstacles. Simply stated, it is the feeling that you are paralyzed with fear. In panic, you are incapable of rational thoughts; your screaming emotions are drowning out your mind, and your heart is racing. Obviously, this is not the most opportune time to juggle—or to do anything else, for that matter. Any actions you take in this state will be purely emotional or reactive behaviors. And in some cases, those behaviors can be disastrous.

In the year 2000, 3,482 people accidentally drowned in the United

States. A nonswimmer who falls or jumps into deep water quickly finds himself "over his head." Unable to find anything to grasp or kick against to stay above the water, he panics. The actions that follow are not choices at all. They are reactive behaviors, including kicking and flailing the arms wildly, gasping for air, and struggling desperately to keep one's head above the surface. Tragically, these behaviors are precisely the actions that seal the nonswimmer's fate. By flailing and struggling, he tires quickly. Gasping and yelling invite water into the lungs. Unless someone is there to rescue him, he will drown. And even when someone does try to help, a panic-stricken victim often claws and pulls at the rescuer, attempting to "climb" the person trying to save him. In far too many cases, the result is twice as heartbreaking, as the emergency situation becomes fatal for both.

Such senseless tragedies inspired one individual to take action. In 1948 Coach Fred Lanoue at Georgia Institute of Technology introduced a "drown-proofing" class, the completion of which was required for graduation by every student at the university. Coach Lanoue had developed this program first for the Navy during World War II. He emphatically believed that virtually all incidents of drowning were avoidable with the proper instruction. No person should ever drown, and no graduate of Georgia Tech would ever be unequipped for such a situation.

The class is not about swimming. It is about floating. Everyone can learn to float if they practice simple techniques that are exactly opposite to the drowning actions described above. To perform the "dead man's float," you hold your breath and remain motionless, facedown in the water, conserving energy. When you need to breathe, you exhale as you lift your head out of the water, take another full breath, and then resume the "dead man" position. With this method, you can remain in the water for a long period of time without becoming exhausted, until help arrives.

It takes discipline and practice to suppress panic and remain relaxed, especially when you are facedown in the water. Try this yourself the next time you are in the pool. This example illustrates why clear thinking is infinitely more valuable than reflexive behavior. It might just save your life.

This is why, at the onset of panic, we should disengage from what we are doing and get a fresh perspective. Doing nothing at all is often far better than doing something driven solely by panic. Disengage from the circumstances that gave rise to the panicked feeling. Develop a method for refocusing and regaining control of your emotions. This routine might include deep breathing, positive affirmations, physical activity, or contemplative stillness. Find what works for you. Practice your method with small bouts of panic so that you will have the skills ready when you really need them.

DROP**S**—Self-Doubt

While teaching people to juggle, I frequently hear comments such as "I can't do this," "I can't catch at all," or "I am completely uncoordinated." Usually, when someone tells me they can't juggle, I respond by saying, "Not with that attitude, you can't!" It's a way to break their thought pattern and bring to mind one of the guiding principles of this book: It is impossible to act in a manner inconsistent with your thinking.

Most of the time, self-doubt is more subtle than outright panic, but it can be just as debilitating. If you are thinking about doubts or fears, you will act accordingly, sabotaging your success or, at the vary least, settling for less than you are capable of achieving. From a juggling perspective, the fear of dropping prompts many people to be satisfied with small achievements. When I teach people, I'll invariably have someone in the audience who, after making his or her first three catches, wants to stop immediately so there is no further risk of failure (dropping). They quit while they're ahead. Experienced jugglers reframe the experience of dropping. They know that sometimes dropping is a good thing, a cause to celebrate rather than evidence of a personal failure. When they drop a prop, they simply pick up it up and try something else, another way of doing the trick. When they learn a new tossing sequence, they carefully observe the motion mechanics with childlike wonder. This means they don't see themselves as failures or incompetents. They simply search and find what works and what doesn't. They apply the insights they have learned, to make better throws the next time. They know that the secret of success lies in only one throw at a time. They use all their considerable skills to make the single most accurate throw, every time the object (objective) is in their hand.

Practice is one thing, but the real self-doubt kicks in right before showtime. In practice, I tend to be fearless in my juggling. I'm more aware of the way my body moves, and I express myself freely, without the constraints of hesitation or uncertainty. But when I started performing when I was twelve years old, I found *that* experience to be completely different from my practice sessions.

I was hired by the Bensonville, Illinois, Fire Department to do a half-hour performance for a neighborhood cookout, and they were willing to pay me thirty-five dollars. *A fortune!* I thought. *That's over a dollar a minute!* Immediately, my self-doubt went to work as I thought, *How can I possibly be worth that kind of money?* So I practiced. In fact, I listed every trick I knew on a sheet of notebook paper, one after the other. First I would start with three balls and exhaust my list of tricks. Then I would start a routine with four balls. I would juggle clubs next, then rings, scarves, and hatchets. Finally, I would perform my finale: juggling three torches while atop a "rola bola" balance board (a board balanced upon a cylinder), while playing a kazoo! I practiced every trick until I had them down cold. I never bothered to time my routine; I was too busy choosing the music I would use, debating my costume choices, and trying to talk myself out of the whole experience.

But when I finally got to the firehouse to do my act, my mouth became as dry as cotton, and I trembled from head to toe. But I remembered my list of tricks. And when I took the stage, my thirty-minute show lasted exactly seven minutes. *What a failure!* I thought. That was, until they paid me (perhaps out of sympathy), and I suddenly realized that now I had actually earned *five* dollars a minute!

Shortly after this early attempt at performing, a powerful thought was introduced to me. My mentor explained that fears and self-doubts lose their power when you decide that you are the one who controls your emotions. I figured that if this was true, it meant that when I performed in front of audiences, instead of feeling doubts and focusing inwardly on them, I could concentrate on the positive aspects of the experience and focus outward on my audience, sharing a moment with wonderful people. I could decide that I would be in a fantastic mood and would have a terrific time doing what I loved to do.

As a result of an attitude adjustment—and because I was truly having fun—my performances improved rapidly. The people in my audience realized I was enjoying myself, and my energy was infectious, so they became all the more responsive. They obviously enjoyed sharing positive feelings, too. In fact, they showed their appreciation by applauding and cheering my performance, and you can imagine what that did for me! The high energy, freely exchanged with the audience, took them and me to a new level of exhilaration, into an even more in-sync state of mind.

And even when I did drop, I could recover quickly with a prepared joke or spontaneous ad-lib. Even when I fell from a three-person-high pyramid, landing with a thud on the King's Stage at the Renaissance Festival, I knew I could recover with style. I struck a deliberate pose while lying on the ground, as if to convey, "I meant to do that!" Audiences want you to do well. They are your allies and are extremely understanding of your mistakes. In fact, on or off the stage, your misfortunes endear you to others if you handle things gracefully.

I realize that fear can immobilize us. It can stop us in our tracks. Some people are unable to move because they are simply too afraid to move. Others are more able to work through their fears. A great historical example of not letting fear immobilize us involves one of our great presidents. In March 1933, times were considerably tougher than now, but many of the obstacles that faced our country then are also concerns for us today as we confront new threats at home and abroad.

In early 1933, banks were closing, factories were idle, hundreds of thousands of people were out of work, and fear was running rampant. Millions of Americans waited anxiously beside their radios, wondering what the new president was going to say.

Franklin Delano Roosevelt knew he was facing an unprecedented crisis in our nation's history. He knew the paralyzing effects of fear, how it could demoralize people, how it could bring a nation to its knees. He steadied himself and spoke boldly to a citizenry that needed to hear a confident president. That day he gave one of the most dramatic and awe-inspiring speeches in American history:

> *This great nation will endure as it has endured, will revive and prosper. So first of all, let me assert my firm belief that the only thing we have to fear is fear itself— nameless, unreasoning, unjustified terror which para- lyzes needed efforts to convert retreat into advance . . .*

"The only thing we have to fear is fear itself." These unforgettable words ring as true now as they did seventy years ago. Fear could have robbed our country of its destiny then, just as it can rob us of our future now if we allow *fear* to immobilize us. Someone once told me that the word "fear" is an acronym. It stands for "false evidence appearing real." The reality is that we can move beyond self-nullifying fear through positive thinking, positive actions, and positive living.

Although fear may be an obstinate obstacle, it can also be our guide and adviser. It is perfectly natural and appropriate, even a sign of sanity, to let fear dictate your steps in dangerous situations. Fortunately, such events are rare. For most of us, major battles with fear are not driven by external forces, but rather are internal, as we grapple with shyness, self-doubt, and uncertainty. Whatever form your fear takes, your ability and willingness to face it will determine how much you enjoy *success in action.*

When I become aware of fear, I try to pause and ask myself, *Is this fear rational? Are the dangers real or imaginary?* If the dangers are real, I take the necessary corrective actions to mitigate the danger. If not, I see fear as an ally, a self-protective instinct. I am convinced that the better prepared you are, the less you will be troubled by fear. Preparation not only increases the probability of success but greatly enhances your ability to turn setbacks into comebacks and consistently deliver show-stopping performances on any stage in life.

Action Assignments

1. Obstacles can protect us as well as hinder us. Think back over the past five years of your life. Go ahead, stop reading and take a couple of minutes. Now that you've had time to think about it, can you recognize any obstacles that turned out to be blessings? What lessons did you learn from them? In what ways are you a better person for having gone through the experiences? How have the unpleasant episodes benefited you? Write thank-you notes to each obstacle. Keep the notes filed away in a drawer and retrieve them when a current obstacle becomes a controlling force in your life.

2. Name one thing you rushed haphazardly through today and, in retrospect, wish you hadn't. If you could do it over again, what would you have done differently? If it's something you can still adjust, do it! If you've lost the opportunity for deceleration, put the plan you just devised into action so you will be more prepared next time.

3. Pick two old habits that aren't working in your best interests. Get the information, help, and gumption you need to prune the habits out of your life by the end of the week. Think of each habit's polarity, and do its opposite. Remember, habits, like most human experiences, are behavioral choices. So choose wisely and enjoy the new, more empowered you as you witness your own *success in action.*

4. Someone once said, "Sometimes we turn to God when our foundation is shaking, only to find out it is God who is shaking it." When is the last time your foundation shook? What was the message to you?

10

CREATE ORIGINAL PERFORMANCES

*Most of what stands between us and our creativity is
not a negative outer environment, but a negative inner
environment.*

—Julia Cameron

It's not just what you do—it's how you do it.

—Diana Thurmon

I grew up hearing those words from my mother repeatedly: "It's not just *what* you do—it's *how* you do it." She instilled in me a belief that it's possible to approach any job, project, or task with a fresh perspective. It's desirable to be different. Just because everyone else does something one way doesn't mean you have to follow suit. In fact, it probably means there is an opportunity to express more of who you are and stand out from others in your own unique way.

I have yet to meet a person more creative than my mom. She taught

Diana Thurmon with one of her
creations at an Atlanta exhibition

Here Mom teaches mural painting
techniques for adult students (April 2005)

herself to paint out of necessity. We couldn't afford art for the bare walls of our Chicago home. As an alternative, she bought some brushes, paints, and canvases and checked out an art book from the local library. Her first painting ever was a copy of Vincent Van Gogh's *Fishing Boats on the Beach*. It was good enough, but not completely satisfying to her. She was not content to copy someone else's work, no matter how inspired. My mother knew that she had something within her that was unique and original, and with this thought, she embarked upon a brilliant forty-year career as a professional artist and art instructor.

After her first few paintings, Mom decided to try something different. To match the dark wood tones of our home, she got some mahogany boards and began painting on them. The natural surface of the wood inspired her to paint wildlife and scenes from nature. Somehow it just seemed to make sense. Others saw what she was doing and encouraged her to show her work publicly. Although she resisted at first, eventually she did present her work at art and craft shows in the Chicago area. Recalling those early days, she told me, "In the beginning I wasn't very good. I got better with practice and attention to what I was doing, but it was an original idea to paint on wood. So even early on, people responded to my work because it was unique."

Mom's entrepreneurial instincts have really influenced me. It was not enough for her to create art that she enjoyed. She thrived on producing work that others would like too—enough to pay for it! That meant providing something they couldn't get from anyone else. As a kid, I can recall making trips to lumber mills where we would purchase scrap wood—beautiful pieces of all shapes and sizes, which we then planed and finished in preparation for her artistic interpretation. We would also scour the countryside for dilapidated barns, salvaging wood to convert into original works of art. Meanwhile, Mom developed a business clientele for pet portraits. Customers sent her photos of their beloved animals, and she immortalized them (amazingly quickly, I might add) on wood or canvas. She also taught art classes out of our home basement studio.

After we moved to Georgia in 1984, Mom discovered the beauty of polished-smooth rocks (of all sizes) that she carefully selected from North Georgia rivers. She saw three-dimensional shapes of animals in the rocks and painted them to reveal the rock's "inner creatures." This period of her artistic development we refer to as the "Rock Era," and the creatures that resulted are know as "Dianamals." Now, those are some "heavy" pieces of art!

In addition to painting on natural surfaces, Mom has produced thousands of original paintings on canvas, evolving her personal style continuously over the years. Currently she specializes in creating custom murals, transforming ordinary walls into extraordinary creations.

Mom's devotion to producing marketable art taught me much, not only about the importance of creativity but also about the necessity of listening to your audience. If you want to be economically successful, you must produce something that will inspire people to pay you for it. This is not, as some might suggest, "selling out." Rather, it is the recognition that you can satisfy your need for artistic expression in any number of ways. Why not pick one that pays you well because it serves others in a way they deem valuable?

You don't have to be a painter, sculptor, photographer, juggler, actor, or musician to be creative. You can take an artistic approach to just about anything you do. Whether you are a banker, a florist, a salesperson, a construction worker, a computer technician, a parent, or a mechanic, if you take an artful approach, you'll create a life rich with texture and interest. And by making it interesting, you'll attract enthusiastic advocates who will further promote your efforts. Remember, you never know who is in your audience.

I am recognized as an "unusual" keynote speaker. My uniqueness lies in my ability to infuse my messages with action. No other speaker adds the impact of acrobatics, juggling, unicycling, and audience interaction quite like I do. As I was first getting established in the speaking industry, this distinction enabled me to set myself apart from others and grow my business through referrals. Then one day, and in only a moment's time, I was faced with an unexpected challenge that would test my creativity on new levels.

In 1997 I suffered a serious knee injury. Because the presentations that I do are so physical in nature, this clearly posed a potential threat to my career. Suddenly I didn't have the ability to deliver my high-energy, physically demanding routines. I couldn't rely on the one thing that had always made me unique as a presenter: high-impact action. I knew that the process of undergoing surgery and recovery would be lengthy and challenging. I seriously considered canceling my existing engagements, but at the same time I knew that this would have a severe impact on my income as well as on the momentum of my business. If I were to start refusing work, it would be devastating to my family and my career. Instead, I chose to adapt my message, relying only on words and some juggling. I began to share with my audiences what had happened and then present the questions, "What do you do when the thing you've always counted on in your life is no longer there for you? How can you move forward with confidence when you've lost something so essential?" Audiences were responsive because they struggle with this dilemma themselves, asking the same hard questions: What can I do when I am asked to do more with less: with fewer resources, lower budgets, abbreviated timelines? What happens if what I've come to expect is suddenly stripped out from under me? The answer, of course, is to find creative solutions. The way we handle unexpected situations is to adapt positive strategies and use what resources we still *do* have with greater effectiveness. That's what I attempted to do. Fortunately, I did make a full recovery from my knee injury. But the most positive result was that during that recovery period, my career and performance as a speaker grew tremendously. Without my usual repertoire of physical skills, I further developed and honed my speaking skills. It's really true that hardship is often opportunity in disguise. And disguised opportunities become successful outcomes when we get creative and turn adversity into advantage.

My wife, Sheilia, has a wonderful ability to see disguised opportunities. She is an inspiration because of her amazing ability to stay positive and active in improving herself and those around her. Sheilia has really helped me to elevate my vision of what I can achieve in my life. She encourages me constantly, and her influence fuels my beliefs and my actions. She expresses her own creativity through her writing and video production, creating documentary pieces that increase awareness and challenge traditional thinking about homelessness, drug addiction, and the plight of those challenged by devastating circumstances. She is passionate about her work and her volunteerism for our church and with organizations such as World Vision. World Vision's core mission is to secure housing, clean water, and food for children in developing countries, especially those children orphaned by the AIDS epidemic. It is by finding creative solutions that she fulfills her inner hunger to make the world a better place. Sheilia often quotes Mother Teresa, who said, "We cannot all do great things. But we can all do small things with great love." This is a message she lives daily, and her creativity in balancing her passion with her other responsibilities as a mother, wife, business partner, and friend simply boggles my mind.

I've included this chapter on creativity because our thoughts and ideas are the causative agents for every experience we encounter. We each have within ourselves a transforming and regenerative ability that makes it possible to turn any adversity we face into an advantage. To reach what I call "breakthrough optimization," I encourage people to make fundamental shifts in their thinking, particularly in their attitudes about their own creative abilities.

One of the most important outcomes of my seminars is the reshaping of people's beliefs in what they can achieve. I prove this in every seminar when I teach an audience member who has never juggled before how to perform the skill with me in front a live audience. I'm not kidding! Every single person I have randomly selected from the audience has been able to juggle successfully, to the amazement and applause of his or her friends and colleagues.

I believe that people can toss creative ideas around just as easily as they can juggle beanbags at my speeches and seminars. Once they become accustomed to the pattern and timing of the tosses, everything falls into place. Generating ideas works the same way. There is a pattern to thinking creatively, and a sense of timing is important, too. Let's explore this thing we call creativity in more detail and see how you can use it to succeed in whatever action you decide on to improve your life and the lives of those around you.

Creativity Gremlins

When asked to name someone who is creative, we may think of such giants as Albert Einstein, Thomas Edison, George Washington Carver, Ben Franklin, Alexander Graham Bell, Walt Disney, Michelangelo, William Shakespeare, and Pablo Picasso. From more recent times, Steven Spielberg, Jim Henson, Steve Jobs, Bill Gates, Oprah Winfrey, or David Copperfield may come to mind. "Creative" is a word generally ascribed to well-known inventors, scientists, writers, artists, and entertainers. Some people seem to be naturally more creative than others. They may have a God-given talent, but often more important than that is their belief that they are creative, and their ability to call upon those talents that lie hidden within them.

When people believe they are not beautiful or intelligent or marketable or creative, chances are, they will find ample opportunities to validate their beliefs. Often our creative ability is hindered by what I call "rutted" thinking. People lock themselves into a particular way of viewing a situation, and this blocks the spark of inspiration.

You have probably heard the story of a large delivery truck being stuck in an underpass. A team of top-notch engineers was asked to determine how best to dislodge the trailer without causing damage to the trailer or the underpass. True to their professional training, the engineers took an engineering approach to freeing the truck and busied themselves with making a series of complex stress calculations and damage assessments. A youngster, standing with his mother and watching the fiasco, walked up to one of the engineers and said, "Hey, mister, why don't you just let a little air out of the tires?"

A child's innocent but profoundly creative solution saved the engineers hours of unnecessary work, not to mention enormous expense. I don't know if the story actually happened, but it makes an important point: the human brain is creative. Unfortunately, most of us have allowed creativity gremlins to dismiss our ideas before we become conscious of them.

All the idea busters listed below have one thing in common: the fear factor. The destructive force of this negative emotion simply cannot be overstated. Fear can and often does paralyze us by stealing our cognitive resources. It is seductive, bringing a strange sense of comfort while it is busy robbing us blind. Our challenge is to recognize these gremlins as soon as they rear their ugly heads, and develop strategies for shifting our thinking into more positive, creative directions. Although this list is by no means exhaustive, here are some of the gremlins that invade our consciousness and steal our ability to operate as original and unconstrained thinkers.

The "I'm Not Creative" Mental Handcuff. The evidence is overwhelming—people who think they are creative consistently create and innovate, and people who insist they lack creative talent generally demonstrate that belief by producing average, ho-hum results. After all, it's impossible to act in a manner inconsistent with your thinking. Most "I'm not creative" people never get to explore just how imaginative and innovative they truly are. Believing they are capable of so little creative thought, most nonbelievers accept their fate and settle for mediocrity and second-rate solutions. They handcuff their imagination instead of freeing it to work its magic in their lives.

Are there really noncreative people? It seems not. Creativity researcher Gardner Murphy concludes:

> We know from watching children that the desire to create is almost universal, and that almost everyone has some measure of originality which stems from a fresh perception of life and experience, and from the uniqueness of his or her own fantasy when the youngster is free to share it.

Researcher Louis Fliegler shares similar insights:

> *All individuals are creative in diverse ways and to different degrees. The nature of creativity remains the same whether one is producing a new game or a symphony . . . Creativity is within the realm of each individual depending upon the area of expression and the capability of the individual.*

Belief is a powerful drug. It can make you creative, keep you creative, or block your creativity. Creativity requires a certain measure of autonomy and the willingness to share independent thought. It also requires a great degree of self-trust. Many people allow their fear of being seen as "different" to stifle their creativity. They feel the flow and velocity of a creative thought and perhaps say to themselves, "Uh-oh, where is this idea taking me? How's this going to look?" Their "I'm not creative" gremlin steals the insight in that moment, so they don't have to take responsibility for a revolutionary idea that could change lives all around them. It's easier to believe they are not creative than to admit they have harvested a thought that now requires action. Nor do they understand the value of their ideas.

I believe that claiming our own creative abilities is an act of faith. Creativity is God's gift to mankind, and using our creative aptitude is our gift to God. Like any ability or muscle or talent, our creativity grows stronger through use. With creative conditioning, you'll soon be poised to put all of you in what you do.

Fear of Criticism. The more unique and original an idea is, the more vulnerable it becomes to censorship and attack. Any challenge to traditional thinking usually meets with a full frontal assault launched by well-meaning people who fear any shift in the status quo. Sometimes the inhibiting effects of indifference, cynicism, ridicule, and outright personal attacks on anyone bold enough to share a new idea can be devastating to the creative process.

Most people are sensitive to overt or implied criticism, or even the threat of it. Many people become defensive, and some get downright hostile, any time they're on the receiving end of negative feedback.

Only by toughening our resolve, as well as our skin, can we foster and protect our creative output. The best advice I can give is this familiar expression: "Listen to the critics with a grain of salt." Evaluate any criticism to your ideas objectively and calmly. Own your ideas; be brave. Take pride in your creative accomplishments. Many good ideas initially fall on deaf ears—don't let them be your own.

Fear of Rejection. While criticism can be difficult to swallow, rejection is downright personal. Rejection makes us feel as though we are not accepted for who and what we are. To reject our ideas is to reject our very personhood, our self-worth as a human being. This rejection can lead to lowered self-esteem, which usually leads to self-doubt.

To protect ourselves from this devastating feeling, we censor our thoughts, words, and actions. And since creativity feeds on self-expression, originality, and imagination, the byproduct of taking a protective stance is immediate and complete depletion of our creative reservoir. And get this: this negative result is a real and powerful phenomenon that springs from something that is entirely imagined. It begins with our concern about what others might think about us simply because we have come up with a "weird" or "different" idea.

According to creativity researcher Richard Albert, "Creative people, regardless of their status and occupation, who doubt their self-worth and thus their creativeness, doubt their right to be creative . . . and their right to have independent thought. Creativity is, among other things, the demonstration of the legitimacy of one's identity and talents."

Erosion of our self-worth erodes our creativity. It's a slippery business, trying to get our ideas accepted and at the same time being able to reframe rejection. Truly successful people see rejection differently. At worst, they perceive rejection as part of the price they pay for having an original thought and being brave enough to share it. Or, in the most positive light, they see rejection as a validation that they are onto something truly unique. Most revolutionary ideas (including the notion that our planet is round) were first publicly rejected before they were accepted by the mainstream. So, if you are experiencing rejection, be joyous—you're halfway there!

The Belief that One Is Too Old to Be Creative. The "I'm too old" belief is nothing more than a myth, a self-delusion based on fear of failure. Need some proof? George Bernard Shaw won a Nobel Prize when he was sixty-nine. Thomas Jefferson invented hundreds of gadgets when he was in his seventies and eighties. George Washington Carver was still innovating at eighty. Alexander Graham Bell perfected the telephone at fifty-eight, and at seventy-four he solved the problem of stabilizing the balance in airplanes. Mark Twain was still writing in his seventies. Benjamin Franklin produced a tremendous body of written works in his eighties. Picasso painted well into his eighties. Linus Pauling, who laid the structural groundwork for DNA research, invented chemical structures when he was well into his seventies.

How about some more? George Burns created one-liners and performed onstage well into his nineties. Dancer and entertainer Fred Astaire wrote choreography and danced well into his eighties. Frank Sinatra did it his way for eighty-three years. Albert Schweitzer developed medical procedures while in his nineties. Maria Montessori devised curricula for her schools when she was in her eighties. John Glenn donned an astronaut suit in 1988 and flew a nine-day Discovery Space Shuttle mission when he was seventy-seven. Martha Graham, the intense theatrical doyenne of modern dance, choreographed until she was in her mid-nineties. Mother Teresa used her immense creativity to care for the poor until she died in her eighties.

This is so fun, I can't stop, so here are a few more: When William Edmonson lost his janitorial job in his early sixties, he began carving wood. At age sixty-seven, in 1937, he became the first black artist to have a solo show at the Museum of Modern Art in New York. The poet Walt Whitman published the ninth and final version of *Leaves of Grass* at the age of seventy-two. Howard Finster, American folk artist and former Baptist preacher, had completed over 24,000 paintings by his seventy-fifth year. At seventy-six, Grandma Moses abandoned embroidery because of her arthritis and started painting. After her hundredth birthday, she completed twenty-four more paintings. The novelist Dame Agatha Christie penned her sixty-sixth novel at age eighty-five.

As you can see, the belief that one is "too old to be creative" is not based in fact but in fear. Yet, once the belief takes hold, its power becomes quite real in the experience of the thinker. This notion springs from the same erroneous belief that older people can't lead active and productive lives. Although age may slow us down physically and athletically, it doesn't slow down our creativity, stop our innovative spirit, or adversely affect our will to tinker. It has long been known that everything that is essential to our continued growth and development— and happiness—springs from our thinking. We create our reality, no matter how old we are, from the reality within our own psychological makeup. Becoming conscious of this inner guidance and listening to its subtle messages is vital to our health and well-being—and creativity—at any age.

The "Mistakes Are Unforgivable" Attitude. For many people, the word "mistake" conjures up images of diminished self-worth and loss of credibility. In almost any type of social or professional environment you can think of, people who make mistakes are clouded with suspicion or labeled incompetent. Unfortunately—or fortunately, depending on your perspective—the creative process is built on mistakes, misfires, blind alleys, and failures of every description and magnitude. I can't count how many times I dropped clubs, balls, beanbags, and hatchets during my early days of juggling. And I still drop them with some regularity.

The "mistakes are unforgivable" attitude stifles the creative spirit and weakens the risk-taking "muscles" of anyone attempting something new. The best way to chase this gremlin away is to welcome mistakes, misfires, and drops. The mistakes I'm referring to are the ones that are well thought-out, faithfully executed, quickly modified, and thoroughly learned from attempts to push your creative and artistic limits. You've no doubt heard the expression "To err is human." When it comes to creative achievement, though, "to err" is one of the critical ingredients you need to gauge your progress.

Healthy failure is a trademark quality for many successful people. Our mistakes contain valuable information. They are essential to our education and progress. They show us what works and what doesn't work. Thomas Edison understood the essence of creativity when he remarked, "I am not discouraged, because every wrong attempt discarded is another step forward . . . I've gotten a lot of results. I know several thousand things that won't work."

So if you want to ensure success in action, increase your failure rate. Each mistake along the way serves as a course-correction device to help you catch the ideas and gain the skills that are necessary for your progress. See each mistake or misfire as an opportunity to further your personal and professional growth.

Creativity Catalysts

I shared earlier how a serious knee injury nearly ended my career. One of my favorite stories about allowing creative insights to turn tragedy into triumph is about a young French naval officer who had just qualified for flight school. Shortly after qualifying, he was injured in a near-fatal automobile accident. For almost a year, he struggled to recover from the life-threatening injuries. After several unsuccessful surgeries, doctors recommended amputation of his paralyzed arm, but the young aviator refused.

His flying days were over, of course, as his damaged arm made it impossible for him to fly. So he took to the sea. Someone had told him ocean water was the perfect therapy for rehabilitating injured limbs. In the process of acquainting himself with the nuances of the sea, he experimented with swimming and diving techniques. He became so absorbed with aquatics that he spent twenty hours a day on or in the water. He created water masks from inner tubes, snorkels from garden hoses, and flippers from wooden shelving material.

Inspired by his creative achievements and fueled by his limitless curiosity, Jacques-Yves Cousteau revolutionized underwater exploration and study. In two years he had successfully rehabilitated his arm, leaving his doctors dumbfounded. Cousteau invented underwater para- phernalia such as rubber masks and snorkels, underwater cameras, the Aqua Lung and the scuba regulator, turbo-sailing wind ships, electric sea scooters, undersea research labs, and a hundred more aquatic gadgets and devices.

He had turned a flying career into an aquatic empire. He could have believed in the gloomy prognoses of well-meaning doctors. He could have felt sorry for himself and settled for his disability, blocking his creativity completely. Instead, he chose the ocean as a creative outlet and used an injury as a fulcrum to invent a new career. He instinctively utilized several techniques to stimulate creative thought and action. You can engage the same *creativity catalysts* to jump-start your ability to transform your life into an original masterpiece.

Here are eleven such catalysts, poised and ready to springboard your ideas and spark your originality. When you feel stuck in a rut or are pressed for new ideas, implement one or all of these strategies. Let's see what they are and how to put them in action.

1. Seek Inspiration from Others. Our world is rich with examples of creative masters. The great news is that you can tap into the thought processes of geniuses who preceded you by experiencing their work with the mindset of an eager student. Choose something that really resonates with you, whether it is visual art, music, theater, film, literature, architecture, food or any other example of creative achievement. Immerse yourself in the environment. Use all your senses to see, feel, hear, touch, and taste the masterpiece. Seek to discover what about it appeals to you. What thinking does it inspire? What do you think the artist was trying to convey through his or her efforts? What can you take from this experience that will propel your own creativity? For thousands of years, artists have sought and gained inspiration from other artists. Why would you opt to create in a vacuum? Let the masters guide you.

2. Find the Third Right Answer. As is often repeated in business circles, "time is money," and instant solutions to complex problems are expected. There seems to be a widespread belief that most of life's situations have only one right answer. Unfortunately, the best answer is seldom the first answer. Most people have little patience for problems, and when they encounter them they want quick solutions. These short-attention-span solution seekers usually jump to conclusions or take the easy way out without thinking about the consequences.

Philosopher Emile Chartier warned of the dangers of such a limited perspective when he said, "Nothing is more dangerous than an idea when it is the only one you have." If you have only one viable idea, you limit your courses of action. That kind of narrow thinking is called "tunnel vision," and the tunnel usually takes you somewhere you don't want to go. People who settle for quick fixes and convenient solutions are usually motivated by fear, politics, or stubbornness.

The failure to consider alternatives and options is a trap people can avoid if they take time to consider multiple solutions. Instead of stopping at the first idea, persist a few more minutes (while you are on a roll) and find at least three—better yet, uncover ten or twenty if you can. Then you'll have a much broader perspective, and multiple choices to consider.

3. Embrace the Illogical. Creativity researcher Stanley Parnes uses the analogy of the teleidoscope, a kaleidoscope-looking device that has no movable features, to explain the value of seemingly illogical sensory input on creativity.

The teleidoscope features a complex system of fixed mirrors that generates an infinite number of designs as the viewer shifts his or her focus to different objects in the nearby environment. According to Parnes, we integrate the things we see, hear, smell, taste, and touch with what is already in our psychological memory banks, and create an endless variety of idea patterns or, as some psychologists term them, gestalts. This teleidoscopic mix creates the playground for our "illogical" connections. Parnes believes these gestalts "fuel our illogical associations and connections between remote sensory impressions and unite them to form creative insights."

Sometimes a shift of perspective is exactly what we need to produce a creative insight. The more we dissect our problem with logic, the more limiting our viewpoint becomes. But if we expand our awareness to include infinite possibilities, many of which we don't understand, we increase the odds for potential solutions to flow freely. We need these illogical connections to make sense out of ambiguity and to make ambiguity out of the sensible. Or, put another way, the more illogical a solution to an existing problem seems, the greater the probability that it will produce a meaningful connection.

When Jim Lovell, commander of Apollo 13, uttered the famous words "Houston, we have a problem," the world collectively held its breath. But as the challenge unfolded, this response became strangely empathetic to the plight of our brave adventures. The astronauts realized that the air they were breathing was becoming increasingly toxic because the filter that removed the carbon dioxide from the Lunar

Excursion Module had reached its full capacity. The small spacecraft was designed to be occupied for only a short time: during the landing, lunar excursion, and ascent from the moon's surface. But, the Apollo 13 lunar spacecraft, Aquarius, had become their temporary home when an explosion damaged the command module. The command module, named Odyssey, had been shut down in order to conserve the little power remaining in its onboard batteries for a single, desperate attempt to return to the earth's atmosphere. Time was rapidly running out. The best logical thinkers at NASA were stumped. Tragedy seemed imminent. Then, Gene Kranz, the flight director in charge of Houston support for the mission, spoke words of authority and inspiration, telling his team, "Failure is not an option."

This was a completely illogical statement. Of course failure was an option! Failure is always an option. Yet when his talented team embraced this illogical premise, they instantly shifted their thinking. The question ceased to be "Can we get our men home?" and became "How do we get our men home safely?" Tapping their creativity, they found a solution to the oxygen filter problem and designed a makeshift replacement filter system out of materials that were aboard the spacecraft. They then coached the crew to construct and install the device. To everyone's great relief, it worked, surmounting the first in a series of challenges that, from every logical viewpoint, should have doomed the mission.

When you think about it, the very idea that we could send men to the moon and return them safely to earth was, at the time John F. Kennedy announced the ten-year initiative, completely illogical. But when a nation embraced the idea, it became a matter of destiny. It was illogical for Alexander Fleming, Ernst Chain, and Howard Florey to suspect that a mold could provide a cure for infectious disease. But it did, and their discovery of penicillin changed the world. It was illogical for Benjamin Franklin to fly a kite in a thunderstorm, yet by doing so he furthered our understanding of electricity. It was illogical for Whammo to think that plastic tubing bent into a circle could be mass-marketed as a toy, yet the Hula Hoop revolutionized the toy industry and continues to be a part of our culture. Faith in God is illogical, yet it is the source of strength and meaning for billions worldwide.

Let's face it. As human beings, we have an extremely limited perspective. So much lies outside our understanding and abilities. So don't think that you have to have everything figured out before you take action. There are hundreds of examples of using illogical connections to produce perfectly sound results. Keep an open mind and a sense of playfulness when it comes to making the familiar strange and the strange familiar.

4. Break the Rules. Cher Holton, author of *Living at the Speed of Life: Staying in Control in a World Gone Bonkers*, gives a fascinating example to illustrate the potentially negative consequences that blind obedience to the rules can have on your life:

> *I heard a woman being interviewed on a television show. She was describing a frightening experience she had when she stopped at a traffic light. A car pulled up behind her, and two men got out. They ran up on either side of her car and demanded that she open the windows. They went so far as to rock her car back and forth.*
> *As she described the horrific incident, the interviewer asked what I thought was a very interesting question: "Why didn't you just hit the gas and get out of there?" Her reply: "Oh, I couldn't. The light was still red."*

Isn't that just mind-boggling? The motorist's blind obedience to rules almost cost her her life, when a creative solution was, quite literally, right in front of her. While most examples are not so dramatic, whenever we accept rules without question, we restrict our thinking and limit our options. Let me clearly state, I am not suggesting that you become a rampant law breaker. That strategy will get you locked up. My point is, rules exist for a reason. Seek to understand the reasons behind the rules, and you just might find a better way to accomplish the same objective. An unhealthy adherence to rules, codes, convention, and tradition stifles creativity and injures the entrepreneurial spirit. To ask what assumptions we are making is the beginning of the process of discovery. It releases our biases and frees our thinking. Besides, as Katharine Hepburn put it, "If you obey all the rules, you miss all the fun."

5. Think Like a Child. To people who are unfamiliar with the nature of creativity, childlike behavior may seem foolish and embarrassing. But successful people know that the child within all of us frees our inhibitions and allows us to express the joy, laughter, awe, and spontaneity that are central to creative achievement at any level. When we let our childlike nature shine forth, we unlock the rich storehouse of creativity that has been there all along. A little judicious frivolity and playfulness are good for the soul. Author Bruce Williamson says, "You're never too old for recess." Physicist David Bohn championed creative play. He said, "Creative play is an essential element in forming new hypotheses and ideas. Play, it appears, is the very essence of achievement."

Spend time with children and allow yourself to adopt their mindset and behaviors. You'll find yourself in a world of wonder, where one thought leads to another with ease and excitement. Whether you are inventing games, creating stories, or playing make-believe, these childish acts can serve as catalysts as you give yourself permission to be creative.

6. Ask Questions. Inventors, scientists, artists, writers, and performers know that everything we need to express our creative talents and abilities comes to us if we ask for it. Creative achievement comes from asking the right questions at the right time under the right circumstances. "Questions," said researcher Frank Kingdon, "are the creative acts of intelligence." George Washington Carver asked, "What other uses are there for peanuts?" He invented over three hundred applications derived from peanut oil. Hans Feuchtwanger, a Bavarian immigrant, asked, "How can I do this more cost-effectively?" He couldn't afford to serve his franks on plates and provide silverware, so he served them on long rolls, introducing the hot dog to America.

The history of creative achievement is filled with ordinary people asking some pretty oddball questions. Hanson Gregory asked, "How can I improve this cake?" and invented the doughnut. Watching a baker cook a batch of cakes, he noticed that the centers never cooked thoroughly. He poked a hole in one of the centers, and the doughnut was born. Joseph Glidden asked, "What will happen if I do this?" and stuck some wire into a coffee grinder, turned the handle, and invented barbed wire.

Asking questions like the ones above will bring creative results. Question everything. Question anything. Challenge old assumptions. Take issue with the status quo. Keep your intuitive eyes and innovative ears open. Ask who, what, where, why, and how questions. Ask them constantly.

7. Use Analogies and Metaphors. To master the use of analogy and metaphor is to master creativity. An analogy is a similarity or close resemblance between things that are different. A metaphor is a figure of speech in which one thing is likened to another by speaking of it as if it were that other: "The sun was a chariot of fire." A master of analogy and metaphor himself, Aristotle used them as if they were synonymous, and described them as "giving things a name that belongs to something else."

The distinction between analogy and its literary cousin, metaphor, lies in the use of two words: is and like. Is refers to metaphors, and like refers to analogies. For example, "The speaking business is a melting pot of interesting personalities," "My wife, Sheilia, is a powerhouse of energy," and "A creativity block is a gremlin" are all metaphors, used to strike relationships and similarities between the things named. Some examples of analogies are "Raising my children, Eddie and Maggie, is like growing beautiful flowers," and "Riding a six-foot-high unicycle is like surfing a wave."

Analogy and metaphor are indispensable tools that can lead to enormous creative insights. The story of the Westinghouse air brake illustrates the power of using analogical thinking. George Westinghouse was investigating a drilling operation site in Switzerland during one of his tours of Europe. He observed that when the Swiss tunneled through mountains, they used a compressor with a three-thousand-foot air pipe, which went from the compressor outside the tunnel to the drill at the face of the rock. This procedure, he was told, was safer and quieter than the previous one.

Suddenly Westinghouse realized a further implication of the compression method. The reason things were happening at one end was because air was being kept at a certain pressure at the other end. He understood that if the air supply were cut off, it would stop the drilling. That same concept could apply to an air-brake system, he reasoned. It was exactly what was needed on a three-thousand-foot railroad train.

If everything operated correctly in the locomotive, it would maintain enough air pressure through the train's pipe; but if anything happened to interrupt the pressure—say, the locomotive stopped working, the compressor malfunctioned, or the line was broken because a railroad car came adrift—the air pressure would decrease, and the brakes, normally held off the wheels by a spring, would be applied. Now, that's invention by analogy.

Another classic example is the story of how the automation of bell ringing in medieval churches led to the development of automated textile weaving and, ultimately, to computers. One little gizmo is at the center of this creative analogy: the punched card. Belgian carillons rang bells using punch-card technology, music played from Pianola rolls entertained our great-grandparents, Jacquard looms wove complex patterns automatically, Hollerith developed the tabulator, and IBM became a business powerhouse—all because in the Middle Ages someone developed a punch card to ring bells to the glory of God.

Gutenberg connected the idea of the coin punch and a wine press to create movable type and its offspring, the printing press. Gregor Mendel connected mathematics and biology to create the field of genetics. Fred Smith connected the airlines "hub and spoke" distribution idea with an overnight package delivery service to create Federal Express. William Harvey saw the relationship between the function of the human heart and a mechanical pump and discovered the principle behind blood circulation. Danish physicist Niels Bohr developed a new model of the atom by comparing it to the solar system. An Englishman, W. M. Folbert, saw the relationship between Austrian J. N. Maelzel's metronome and his own idea for an automobile windshield wiper that worked automatically by using compressed air supplied by the engine.

Multiply these examples by the thousands, and you will begin to get an appreciation of the ways people have used the power of analogy and metaphor to create many of the things you use and enjoy today. As you begin to use more analogical and metaphorical thinking, you will find that you are much more creative than you thought.

8. Discover your Creative Nature. To me, nothing is more inspiring than the endless beauty and variety of nature. When you need a creative jump start, why not look to the Creator's masterworks? Discover your creative nature while enjoying nature. You will never run out of material from which to draw insights, but here are a few suggestions: Take a walk through the woods and notice the details and perfection around you. Visit a botanical garden and experience an oxygen-rich environment full of beautiful plants, flowers, and trees. Climb a mountain to gain a fresh perspective on the world. Enjoy lunch next to a waterfall. Discover more about yourself and your world by watching other creatures. Explore a body of water—a lake, a stream, the ocean. Strap on a snorkel and mask and have a peek at the fascinating world under the surface of the sea. Venture inside a cave (properly equipped and instructed, of course), and open yourself to sparks of creativity in the darkness. The options are endless!

9. Create a Creative Environment. Take a look at the place where you spend your time thinking and working. What can you do to enhance your creative space to achieve greater inspiration? Consider all aspects and each of the five senses.

Sight: Do you have enough natural light? Are the images and artwork on the walls stimulating and thought-provoking? Do you see reminders of your past creative successes?

Sound: What sounds would stimulate your thinking and enhance your creativity? This may vary from day to day. Here are some options that might work for you: Put on some music—classical, gospel, jazz, funk, rock-and-roll, salsa, country—whatever floats your boat. Try the sounds of nature. Expose yourself to positive messages that are readily available as books on tape.

Smell: Smell is a powerful link to our memories and, thus, to creativity. Use this powerful ability to put yourself in a creative mindset. Light a candle. Put some flowers on your desk. Burn a little incense. Bake cookies. Brew coffee. Or open a window to take in the scents of the roses or evening jasmine from outside.

Touch: If you sit down while you create, be sure your chair is comfortable. Wear clothes that feel good on your skin and permit unrestricted movement. Take your shoes off and feel the carpet or floor beneath your feet.

Taste: Reward yourself by delighting your taste buds with flavorful, nourishing foods. Don't overindulge, but give your creative experience a little flavor!

10. Get Physical. Physical activity can trigger brainstorms of innovative thinking. This is one reason I teach juggling to my clients. Juggling is an activity that works exceptionally well because, in order to perform it, you must use both sides of your body and, therefore, both sides of your brain. This requires a relaxed focus similar to a meditative state. While practicing juggling, you stimulate many areas of your brain, firing off neurons you wouldn't ordinarily use while at rest. I hear stories all the time about how "juggling breaks" led to breakthroughs for my clients.

If juggling is not your bag, you can achieve similar results with walking, jogging, swimming, aerobics, stretching, yoga—practically anything that sets your body in motion. The benefits include increased energy, fresh thinking, relaxation, and enhanced focus. Often it is when we step back from our problems and busy ourselves with something physical that we create the opportunity for the creative solution to present itself.

11. Take a Class in Improvisation. If you have ever watched the hit TV show "Whose Line Is It, Anyway?" you will have a sense of what improvisation looks like. When performed by experts, the results are astounding and hilarious as original scenes are created instantaneously. After graduating from college, I took a class in improvisation at the Alliance Theater School in Atlanta, Georgia. I expected the class to be challenging, fun, and stimulating, and it was. But an added benefit that I didn't expect was that the games and exercises also taught me to develop and trust my original ideas. When practicing improv, you learn to make choices faster than you can think. At first it's a little unnerving, because we all have been taught all our lives to censor our thinking and actions. But when you are in the flow of exchanging ideas with others in this rapid-fire environment, you'll astonish yourself and those around you. Anyone can do it—you don't have to be naturally funny to benefit. Regardless of your background, by learning the skills of improvisation, you will reach new levels in creative thinking. Here are some of the key learning points:

- Never say "no" to an idea. When a suggestion is presented, go with it; adapt whatever is thrown at you to your own interpretation.

- Trust your instincts. When it comes to volleying ideas, the phrase "grip it and rip it" comes to mind. Don't hold back. Let your ideas fly with enthusiasm. Often the energy and commitment behind the idea is what "sells" it to an audience.

- Take the less obvious choice. Humor and heightened interest come from making surprising choices. When presented with a problem, never go with the most obvious solution. Look deeper, and you'll create more compelling interest from your audience.

Remember that creativity is a journey. You may begin with one set of questions and an idea of what you want to discover, but keep in mind that a billion variables are changing all the time. The paint on life's canvas never dries completely. Be open to where the paint takes you, and delight in each day's unveiling of your own magnificence.

Action Assignments

1. It's not just what you do but how you do it. How can you make your current job a unique performance by expressing your originality? List three things you currently do or could do to put more of *you* in what you do.

2. Quickly review each of the five creativity gremlins in this chapter. Which one is most frequently responsible for stealing some of your creative insights? Make a commitment and plan to out-maneuver this gremlin. Look for opportunities this week to use your creativity to transcend your fear-based limitations.

3. Think of one pressing issue that needs your creative attention. Ask *who, what, where, why,* and *how* questions to stimulate the flow of ideas. Once you've recorded your questions, look for goals hidden within the questions. Review the goal-crafting tips in Chapter Four. You'll be surprised at how easily the solutions come once you take action.

FIGHT FOR YOUR BALANCE

There is a growing trend toward defining success in terms of a balanced life, in which worldly pursuits share space with "intangibles" like rich and mutually supportive relationships and family roles, a healthy body that can cope well with stress, participation in community life, and opportunities to fulfill creative and altruistic urges.

—John R. O'Neil

The first step to maintaining one's balance is the decision that balance is not merely a desirable luxury but an essential requirement for a successful life. It is worth all our efforts, because balanced living today is the way to circumvent tomorrow's regrets.

—Dan Thurmon

While writing this book, I've watched our daughter change so much. Maggie, nearly three years old now, has become my darling daredevil. She climbs atop the furniture, performs twirling improvised dances, and even stands comfortably in my hands as I hold her high above my head. Her ability to balance her tiny body

Early balance lessons—five-month-old Maggie makes it look so easy.

is quite remarkable.

Thinking back to the time Maggie was just getting the hang of walking, I can remember her sheer determination as she would teeter around like a drunken sailor, stumbling from one side to another, overextending her body and fighting with all her will to maintain control, only to wipe out dramatically on the carpet. The process was very amusing to her and to us! Despite all the setbacks and spills, she persisted with enthusiasm, each time pulling herself back to her feet and boldly launching her body forward until, at last, she developed the muscle control and confidence to succeed.

As I watch my daughter, I often think about the subject of balance as it relates to life. In order to be there to spend time with her, my son, and my wife, I am orchestrating a different sort of balance, one that involves airplane trips and hotel rooms, office work, writing, friendships, church, golf games, exercise, and mowing the lawn, among other things. Much of the time I pull it off with grace, and the patchwork of life comes together seamlessly. Sometimes, though, I confess, the velocity of life seems too much to handle, as I am torn between the various forces competing for my time, attention, and energy. As I meet with audiences across the country, the subject of maintaining a better balance resonates with nearly everyone I encounter. I see an almost universal longing for a life that has greater meaning and fulfillment.

Life is all about balance. We are in a constant state of being off balance, then regaining some semblance of balance, only to get knocked off again. It often seems that no matter what we do, we can't ever seem to get completely comfortable. And even in those rare moments when we appear to have reached some sort of equilibrium, it doesn't last—it's as fleeting as it is elusive.

Balance is a skill we are always learning, yet we will never fully master it. That's because perfect balance is an illusion. The notion of being "balanced" implies that we reach a position in life where everything evens out and we enjoy an effortless, harmonious state of being. Dream on.

We marvel at the gymnasts, dancers, yoga practitioners, and circus performers whose amazing feats of balance look so effortless. Picture in your mind a tightrope walker suspended high above the ground. The audience watches in breathless anticipation as he moves along, effortlessly maintaining perfect balance. *Or does he?* Take a closer look and you'll see that in order to stay balanced on the wire, he is constantly making countless tiny, critical adjustments. He lifts his "free" leg as a counterweight, shifts his head and shoulders, raises and lowers his arms, adjusts the balance pole. There is *never a moment* that the performer is at rest. In fact, he is never truly "in balance." He is perpetually *out of balance,* making adjustments that bring him through a moment of balance, only to readjust time and time again. Most of these movements are so subtle they are imperceptible to the audience. He makes it look effortless. But the ropewalker knows there is no such thing as maintaining balance without continuous effort and adjustment. Balance is something you work for, and at times *fight* for, step by step and moment by moment.

What is the lesson for all of us as we seek a balanced life? Simply put, we will never achieve perfect balance. We pass through the moments of balance, but we cannot stay there, because life is fluid. What we can achieve is an awareness that allows us to recognize when we are tumbling in an undesirable direction, and a mastery that enables us to make the small but critical adjustments that will bring us back toward center. If you wonder, "How can I ever reach a balance between all the aspects of my life?" you are asking a flawed question. Perhaps a better question is, "What adjustments must I make to stay on the tightwire?"

The way I illustrate this visually when I'm speaking to audiences is to talk about it while sitting on top of a six-foot unicycle. Imagine this:

I'm up there speaking about balance and zipping across the room, up and down the aisles and inches away from audience members. It's a great way to keep their attention and illustrate my point. And in the process of executing such a routine, I constantly have to assess my balance and make the necessary adjustments.

Although she wasn't referring to staying atop a unicycle, Indira Gandhi captured the essence of this idea when she said, "You must learn to be still in the midst of activity and to be vibrantly alive in repose." And when you're up on a six-foot unicycle, you must be "vibrantly alive in repose," or you will topple over as fast as you can say "Oops!" Every time you mount the unicycle you risk falling on your face. If you fear the activity, though, your hesitancy will impede your progress. It is impossible to act in a manner inconsistent with your thinking, so first you must manage your internal dialogue and thought processes. You learn quickly to use both your head and your feet.

To achieve success and happiness in life you must master a similar discipline, using both your head and your feet. Achieving stillness in the midst of activity—even in the middle of chaotic circumstances—and vibrancy in repose is the focus of this chapter. For most people, gaining a sense of balance means distancing themselves from the demands placed on them by work, family, and environment. We tend to think in terms of conflicts between competing demands instead of seeing life as a unified whole, made up of complementary parts and integrated responsibilities.

Is Balance Worth Fighting for?

I've learned a lot about balance while riding unicycles, standing on my hands, and walking a slack rope (a variation of the tightwire, in which a rope is suspended between two points and, because it is not completely taut, moves from side to side as you walk it!). Each of these physical skills requires practice and determination, and in each case you must first learn to fall before you learn to succeed. There is a safe way to fall (or "bail") from an attempted balance. When you recognize that you are out of the range of motion that feels comfortable, you make a conscious decision to abandon your attempt and make a controlled and deliberate leap to safety. This might mean jumping from the slack rope to the ground—aborting your balance and choosing a safe descent instead of an "uncontrolled dismount." Similarly, when experiencing the uncomfortable sensation of being off balance on a six-foot unicycle, you might respond by springing from the seat to the ground, distancing yourself from the uncooperative apparatus. But there is another option to the off-balance dilemma. My ability as a performer increased measurably when I developed the skill and confidence to respond to off-balance moments by working through the struggle instead of leaping to safety. Sometimes this involved stretching myself into an awkward or vulnerable posture in order to regain control. When walking a rope suspended over flames or riding a unicycle fourteen feet tall, the motivation to fight through the tense moments increases dramatically. When the stakes are highest, the option of jumping to safety is no longer available to me, and I readily find the third level of commitment, for there is no turning back.

I deliberately chose the action word "fight" to describe our quest for balance. In order to make changes that improve your state of balance, you must perceive them as worth fighting for. What are the consequences of failing to regain control of your life? What does the worse-case scenario, the plummet from your personal tightwire, look like for you? The potentially negative consequences of unbalanced living include unemployment, divorce, loneliness, obesity, cancer, alienation, regret, bitterness, addiction, and just general misery. I don't mean to scare you, but I do hope to get your attention and illustrate that balance in life is not a luxury but a vital necessity. The stakes are high, and failure can be far more devastating than a poorly executed unicycle dismount.

On the flipside, when you acquire the ability to recognize and adjust your orientation in life, you will achieve a more balanced state of being and maintain that condition more often than not. Even when you are pulled off balance, you will understand that it is happening and that you have a choice: to maintain your present course or make adjustments.

Placing Your Focus

Have you ever tried to balance a broom, baseball bat, or yardstick in the palm of your hand? Well, let's give it a try. That's right, I want you to try it right now. You can learn volumes about balance by trying this physical skill, so give this activity your attention and your best effort.

First, find an object that is long (at least twenty-four inches) and thin and light enough for you to hold comfortably in your hand. The longer the object is, the easier it will be to balance, since you will have more reaction time to make adjustments. A short object, such as a pencil or spoon, is much more difficult. Incidentally, because of this fact, a taller unicycle is technically easier to ride than a shorter one, because the adjustments to your balance happen at a slower pace than they would otherwise. My fourteen-foot unicycle is eerily slow to respond to the rider's input. I say that it is "technically" easier because, although there is more time to make adjustments, the psychological challenge intensifies. But, let's return to the challenge at hand.

Ready? Then, let's give it a go. Follow these steps precisely: Place the object to be balanced on end, in the palm of your dominant hand, and use your other hand to position the object upright and as vertical as possible. Now, look down at your dominant hand and let go with the other.

If you complied with the instructions above, you no doubt experienced an immediate failure. I set you up to fail, because it is nearly impossible to balance an object while looking down at your hand. So now that you know what not to do, we'll move on to a more useful technique.

As before, place the yardstick, broom, or whatever you have on end in your dominant hand. This time, before letting go with the other hand, shift your focus to the top of the object. Not midway up. Not near the top. I want you to focus on the very tip-top. Now let go of it and keep your focus fixed where it is. Almost immediately the object will start to fall off balance, and this means it's time for you to make an adjustment. As you see the top begin to move in one direction, gently follow it with your hand. Don't look at your hand, mind you. Just move it and keep watching the top of the object. As you monitor the peak of the object, continue to follow it smoothly with your hand.

This may take some practice, but chances are, you have already significantly improved since your first attempt. That's because you now have the proper perspective. So why did I ask you to do this? Of course it's an analogy. The key to balancing any object is the same as the secret to juggling: keep looking up. In other words, it's impossible to feel balanced if you are going through life looking down at the minutiae, obsessed with the trivial items you encounter every day. If you focus all your effort on those things, you can't also keep your eye on the big picture, and before you know it, you've fallen out of balance.

So where should you focus? Focus on what matters most in your life. Focus on your goals, your relationship with your Creator, your family, your essential responsibilities at work, your mental and physical health, or your personal needs of the moment. The solution to your state of imbalance will be different each time, and it's up to you to find the appropriate adjustment that will bring you back to center. To understand what truly matters and deserves your attention, you must be able to look up and see the big picture. As the apex of your life drifts askew, you reposition beneath it to restore equilibrium. This dance never ends, but it does become more subtle and spontaneous with practice.

Small Adjustments

One of the keys to sustaining balance is the understanding that it takes small adjustments, not bold, dramatic gestures, to maintain our equilibrium. A moment ago, when you were trying the balance exercise, you probably experienced some anxiety as you focused on the object in your hand and watched it fall away from you. If you are like most people I teach, you probably responded by jerking your hand underneath the falling object with such force that it "backfired," sending the object tumbling in the opposite direction. Don't worry; this is a very normal reaction.

I can remember the first time I tried to walk the slack rope. As I started to feel myself fall to one side, I responded by throwing my weight in the opposite direction with such enthusiasm that it pulled me off balance in the other direction—and straight down! Fortunately, I was only two feet off the ground. The same thing happens whenever I teach unicycle or balancing skills to beginners. During the first several attempts, the students generally overcompensate for misalignments until they learn to relax and find the "stillness in activity." At that point their adjustments become subtler and far more effective.

Whether you are attempting to hold a broomstick in your hand or manage the various aspects of your multifaceted life, overcompensation is one of the quickest ways to short-circuit your balance. It is a well-intentioned, reflexive response to the discomfort we experience when our world is off kilter. The disharmony that comes with imbalance is so uncomfortable that we want to end it, or at least make it better as quickly as possible. So we often take actions that are attempts at a "quick fix" of the symptoms of our ailment instead of moving gently in the direction of a cure.

For example, consider your health. You would no doubt agree that your physical and mental fitness is a vital component of a balanced life. When you are off balance in this area and experiencing a lack of physical health, whether it is excess weight, low energy, sickness, shortness of breath, or some other symptom, other areas of your life will also suffer. You may be less productive at work, less happy, and unable to be supportive in your vital relationships. Additionally, your spiritual growth may suffer because of your condition, and you may not have the energy to handle your obligations, much less engage in personal interests that bring you enjoyment. If you recognize that you are suffering and feel sufficient remorse and pain, you may decide that a change in lifestyle is necessary. This is the first level of commitment. Moving to the second level of commitment, you begin to take action. You decide that from this day forward, things will be different. And wanting to accomplish your transformation as soon as possible, you decide to go all out. You resolve to reform your eating habits completely, visit the gym three times a week, stop smoking cigarettes, get more sleep, drink more water, and start training to run the marathon that's coming up in six months!

Making so many radical adjustments at once is, of course, a recipe for failure. It is unlikely that you will be able to execute your well-intentioned plan. Even if you should, your exuberant devotion to this one area of life would likely pull you off balance in another direction. I suggest a different approach. Start with one small adjustment. Make one change that you can implement and sustain. Once this change takes hold in your life, you will see the impact it has on your overall balance. Then you can make other corrections to further your progress. Considering the dilemma of suffering health, the first small adjustment might be to take a twenty-minute walk every other morning, to eliminate one specific item from your diet, or to go to bed a half hour earlier each night.

Don't feel that you have to restructure your entire life. Instead, implement a small adjustment; choose something attainable. Then watch the apex of your life shift, and process the effect this adjustment has on your life. Did it create the desired result? If so, you may want to try to take it a step further.

Off Balance On Purpose

Sometimes, being off balance is a good thing. After all, in order to accomplish anything in life, you must be deliberately off balance. In my programs I illustrate this on my six-foot unicycle, as I demonstrate the method for reaching your chosen destination. The first step is to place your focus where you want to go. Then you must lean forward, throwing your center of gravity out in front, so that you begin to fall toward your face. Once your momentum is headed in that direction, you begin pedaling in order to keep from crashing. The sensation, when you perform it correctly, is similar to leaning forward while skiing downhill, or like surfing a wave.

So if we are experiencing *success in action* and we are actively pursuing a goal, we are bound to be off balance. Unless you are willing to lean forward and experience the thrill of falling, you will not move in that direction. (Picture me on my unicycle, leaning forward and racing across the stage.) In fact, if you are apprehensive about trying new things, you may find yourself drifting backward. (Now envision me leaning and pedaling in reverse in order to illustrate this point.) And even when it appears that all we are doing is staying in one place, choosing to preserve our skills right where they are, we are in fact moving forward then backward as we keep ourselves in check. In unicycling terms, this is called "idling." (Imagine me atop the unicycle, maintaining my ground by pedaling forward one rotation, then back one rotation to stop my progress, then forward, then back, in order to stay in one place.) "Treading air" to stay in one place on a six-foot unicycle actually requires more effort than does riding across the room!

Many people live their lives idling. They start moving in one direction, but then as soon as they begin to get traction, they backpedal to avoid leaving their comfortable position. Forward and backward they go, expending great amounts of energy going nowhere, in order to avoid venturing into unfamiliar territory. Some of the reasons for this behavior include thoughts like these:

- "I'm already successful and content at this level."
- "I just want to stay where I am."
- "What I'm doing now makes sense to me."
- "I just want to be comfortable."
- "I don't want to get too good too quickly—they just couldn't handle me out there!"

The reality is that there's no such thing as standing still—perfect balance is an illusion. Life is fluid, and energy is always flowing through our thoughts, actions, and interactions with others. In order to make a move—or accomplish something, we must lean forward and throw ourselves into the challenge.

Author and speaker Dick Biggs points out in his book *If Life Is a Balancing Act, Why Am I So Darned Clumsy?*, "Don't worry if a particular day is out of balance due to a heavy workload or family emergency. Strive for weekly, monthly, quarterly, or even yearly balance. If you try to live a perfectly balanced life every day, you will fail."

Seeing the complementary nature of the different roles and responsibilities that compete for our attention helps us make more positive adjustments to the demands placed on us. Instead of feeling pushed and pulled by competing conflicts, we can consider each of our obligations as important parts of the overall symphony of our lives.

If life were a symphony, the different responsibilities and roles we played could be represented by the different sections that constitute an orchestra. When it comes to seeking balance, most people want to know how they can keep their lives and their work properly separated. If orchestra leaders asked how they could separate the sound of the wind instruments from that of the percussion section, the result would be noise, not music. A better question to ask about balance is, "How can I harmonize my life?"

In a professional orchestra, the percussion section doesn't compete with the wind instruments, and the strings don't drown out the percussion section. Each section harmonizes with the others. I believe we can harmonize and balance the "sections" of our lives in much the same way.

Juggling has taught me this, too. None of the balls I toss tries to compete with the others. I send each one on a certain trajectory with well-timed tosses in just the right direction. The balls work in unison if my focus and actions, my eye and hand coordination, are in proper alignment. I don't see any ball as competing for my attention, although I need to be aware of each one's location. The sequence and timing of the tosses creates a harmonious pattern that supports everything within my vision and influence. I think of my life in exactly the same way. Adopt this mindset, and you will have a new way of processing the challenges that face you.

As you'll recall from chapter one, your "life pattern" consists of five objects, or objectives, that you handle simultaneously. These five spheres of influence are your work, your relationships, your health, your spiritual growth, and your personal interests. Let's review the visual illustration of what a harmonious and balanced life pattern might look like.

When you are at your best, you are not pursuing many different things all at the same time. Instead you are skillfully shaping the five spheres of your life to create a functional, beautiful synthesis of action. Only by taking a higher point of focus can we grasp the reality that all five spheres of influence are interrelated and cross-connected, each to all the others. There are no isolated experiences. You cannot enforce a change in one aspect of your life pattern without affecting every other aspect. If the five spheres are not in harmony—that is, when you pursue conflicting objectives—you experience internal tension, frustration, and often failure. These disquieting results are alarms signaling that it may be time to make an adjustment in one or perhaps multiple areas.

The great news is that you are in control of the pattern. It is entirely up to you. As you look at the above illustration, you no doubt have an understanding of certain areas where your life is in balance. Almost certainly you can also identify situations where you are experiencing conflict. Like errant juggling balls, the spheres of your life are headed for a collision, and should you maintain the present trajectory, the results will be painful and damaging to your work, relationships, health, spiritual growth, and personal interests. A dysfunctional pattern disrupts all aspects.

By living my life with this mindset, I have learned to make choices that enhance multiple spheres simultaneously. For example, I play drums in my church band (personal interests and spiritual growth). I exercise while I play outdoors with my kids (health and relationships). Best of all, I have a job that enables me to incorporate all five spheres at once! Engineering an environment that supports balanced success requires that you develop certain skills, maintain a sense of purpose, and muster the conviction to trust your gut when deciding how you spend your time.

When considering a life change, it is vitally important that you examine the impact it will have on each of your spheres. Instead of taking a one- or two-dimensional approach to change by treating the symptom, or outward manifestation, of the problem, you will need to embrace this new, multidimensional approach to change. And you will need to hone certain skills. These are the skills of connecting, disconnecting, engaging, disengaging, and synthesizing. Sharpen these talents (which you already possess to some degree) and you will move through life with greater purpose, fulfillment, and effectiveness.

Connecting and Disconnecting

When you make a connection to something or someone, whether a person, responsibility, interest, or commitment, you bring that person, thing, or pursuit into your world. A connection is not a one-time encounter. It is a conscious decision that this new element will become part of your life, part of your pattern, for some period of time.

Connecting is the easy part. We are very good at taking on new relationships, new responsibilities, and new experiences. It's easy to say "yes" to new connections, creating an ever-expanding pattern that towers higher and higher above our heads. This is why making connections and bringing new things into our lives should not be taken lightly or haphazardly. You always have the choice. In every encounter, you are the one with the authority to determine whether you will connect. If you connect, you've just added something to your pattern, and it will remain part of your life until you remove it. If you don't connect, you have decided that this particular person, interest, or experience does not have a place in your life—at least not right now.

Not connecting is different from disconnecting. By not connecting, you decide in advance to pass on the experience. But disconnecting is the way you remove something from your pattern that has already been there for a while—maybe for a day, maybe for a very long time. This tends to be a much more difficult proposition. Making connections is easy and exciting. But when we add something to our lives, rarely do we first make room by removing something or, said another way, by clearing a space for it in the pattern. Disconnecting is uncomfortable, whether it involves saying good-bye to an old friend or an old habit.

But it is in the realm of disconnecting that we find the power to regain control of our lives. It is by using this power that we consciously sculpt a balanced life. You can't have it all. As the old saying goes, "If you stand for everything, you'll fall for anything." I would add to that, if you attempt to do everything, you accomplish very little.

Disconnecting promotes clarity. Disconnecting brings freedom. When you have an overabundance of activity in your pattern, it creates stress, chaos, and a feeling of being overwhelmed. Even if you engage in something infrequently, it still occupies space in your pattern and your thoughts. By consciously removing it, you streamline your thinking and clarify your purpose.

We also need to disconnect from the parts of our patterns that breed conflict or disruption among our most important objectives. If you are pursuing a relationship, for example, that is a hindrance to your health or spiritual growth, you must either change the nature of that relationship or disconnect from it altogether. If you enjoy a personal interest that takes a toll on your performance at work, your health, your important relationships, or your spirit, then this may also be a good candidate for disconnection.

As you exercise the skills of connecting and disconnecting, you will achieve a newfound confidence and pride in your ability to see and shape the pattern of your life.

Engaging and Disengaging

Connecting and disconnecting are the skills we use to shape our patterns in broad strokes, determining what will and what will not occupy an important place in our lives. Engaging and disengaging, however, are the instruments we use to manage our activities from moment to moment. By disengaging from one task and engaging in another, we shift our focus, attention, and energy completely from one item to the next.

An expert juggler knows that he or she cannot simultaneously keep track of every movement of every object in the pattern at every single instant, especially with five, six, or seven items in the air at once! The key to juggling is this: when it appears that you are doing many different things all at the same time, what you are actually doing is one thing at a time, in the proper sequence.

You can only influence the ball that is in your hand. And the task at hand is to make the best throw possible, to take action and achieve the most positive result. This means that we discipline ourselves to focus completely on the present moment. Do nothing haphazardly, but instead move through life with conscious awareness of where you are and what you are doing. Don't distract yourself from what is most important. Stay in the moment, stay engaged, and execute to the best of your ability.

This is easy to say and difficult to practice in our hyperdrive culture. We are constantly distracting ourselves with cell phones, voice mail, electronic messages, and the insanity of "multitasking." Again, the decision to engage is yours to make. When your cell phone rings, you have a choice. You can take the phone call and engage with whoever is on the other end. But if that decision derails your momentum from completing the work you are doing, or if it awkwardly interrupts the face-to-face conversation you are having with a person who is important to you, then you can decide not to accept the engagement. Just don't answer the phone! Don't engage, and instead keep your focus right where it is. Try this and you'll feel a sense of power. Your cell phone is a tool to assist you, not distract you. After you have completed your task and have a moment to refocus, then check your voice mail and return the phone call, on your terms. This way you stay proactive and in control of your pattern and your life.

When we take on a new task, we must first disengage from what we are doing or thinking. Again, consider the challenge of the juggler with many objects aloft. In order to make the next throw, he must look away from the throw he just made. I use this metaphor because it is so applicable for the way we execute throughout our day. Once we take action and make the best possible effort, advancing or completing the task, it is now out of our hands and out of our direct control, at least for the moment.

People become overwhelmed with stress when they fail to disengage. Perhaps you have had the experience of being at work but thinking about your family at home. This brings feelings of guilt and resentment as you think, "Why do I have to be here when I am needed there?" Later, when at home with your family, you may have the opposite thought and feel burdened by the work left undone and the looming challenges that await you the next day. What is going on in this scenario is twofold. First, you are viewing your work and your relationships as separate pursuits when in fact they are part of the same thing. Your work enables you to provide for your family. Second, and more important to this discussion, you are experiencing inner conflict because you cannot or will not disengage.

When we go to work, we are most effective when we are able to disengage from our other concerns and engage our energy and attention on our work-related tasks. When we get home, we serve our relationships best by disengaging from our work-related issues. When you disengage from one element, you are not diminishing its importance or relevance to your life. You are just making yourself available to be present and experience the thing that is actually happening right now in front of you.

There is a huge difference between disengaging and disconnecting, and it is important to make that distinction clear. When you go to work and you disengage from your family, you remain connected to them. They are still in your pattern. In fact, as I stated, the work you are doing is actually a part of your relationship with your family. That is true in this example and in any other you can contemplate, whether it relates to your health, personal interests, spiritual growth, work, or relationships. They are all interconnected. There are no isolated experiences. When you disengage your focus from one part of your life, you remain connected. You will engage it once again when it requires your attention and comes back into your field of view. You remain connected until you decide to remove it from your pattern altogether.

The speed with which you engage and disengage determines your ability to move confidently forward and remain in control of your life. Those who are most effective at managing multiple projects, relationships, and interests are the ones who have mastered the skills of engaging and disengaging. You have heard it said, "If you want something done, give it to a busy person." This is true because the busy person knows how to disengage from one thing and engage another in the blink of an eye. Those most successful at leading full yet balanced lives have developed these skills and practice them every day.

The Art of Synthesis

When we attempt to engage two tasks at the same time, we create a synthesis. Recall the first time you ever tried driving your car while dialing on your cellular phone. If you are like me, you probably thought it would be easy. After all, you had years of experience with both tasks— driving and dialing a telephone. But if you are like me, you also realized that in that moment, when you combined the two tasks (and started steering with your knee), it wasn't easy at all. This challenge was different. Even though you had experience with each task independently, when you combined them, you created something new. It takes practice, and it's a little scary how many people are out there practicing right now!

Any time you add a new task to what you already know how to do, or you execute two tasks simultaneously, you create a synthesis. In the example above, you were not doing two things at once (driving and using your phone). You were performing one task, but now it was a new task you created through synthesis, called "driving your car *while* using your phone." Do you see the difference? When you add something new to what you already know, you create a new "one thing."

Because it requires practice, we should choose carefully when we attempt new combinations. Sometimes, in a safe environment, it is appropriate for us to stretch our abilities and handle multiple tasks at the same time. Other times, when safety is an issue or it is critical that you get it right the first time, the correct course of action is to disengage from other tasks and focus on the most important one exclusively.

With practice comes an increased ability to handle more challenges. The more you do, the more you can do. Synthesis is another tool in your toolbox for managing your pattern. But it is not always the right one. It is up to you to determine when you should synthesize and when you should disengage one task to execute another task more effectively.

In the case of using cell phones while driving, the Harvard University Center for Risk Analysis estimates that this combination of tasks contribute to automobile accidents resulting in 2,600 deaths, 570,000 injuries, and 1.5 million instances of property damage each year. Clearly, this is one area where synthesis is difficult to safely accomplish.

There is no perfect model or template for a balanced life. Balance, like beauty, is in the eye of the beholder. Your personal approach will be unique to your character and objectives. When the daily rush of unfulfilled tasks seems too much for you to handle, remember that balance is part of the natural order of things. It is in the universe's makeup. Nature itself strives for and eventually achieves balance and harmony; thus, our quest for balance is legitimate and ingrained. It is part of the music of the spheres, ranging from the smallest subatomic particles to the planets and stars. Your five spheres combine orbits to create your personal reality. They respond to your influences; they grow and change with your attention and effort. So let's discuss how you put it all together, from both a personal and a professional perspective.

I am incredibly blessed to work for myself, and that freedom enables me to be the architect of my lifestyle. In your present life situation, you may not be able to make the same choices, and I'm not suggesting you should. These are merely examples of the adjustments that have worked for me. You are the one who gets to design your life! As you do, remember, if you don't fight for your balance, no one will.

Balance at Work

What is a job? So often we describe our occupation without understanding the larger purpose that work plays in our lives. The word "job" has taken on a negative connotation, as we view our work as an unpleasant role we must take on in order to survive. I know some people who refuse even to say the word and instead spell it as if it were some form of profanity. "That's my J.O.B." Yuck! With that mindset, it's no wonder that many people dread going to work. They suffer intolerable commutes and live for the weekends or all-too-rare vacation days. Job dissatisfaction leads, in many cases, to stress, unhappiness, and resentment.

Instead of viewing work as a "necessary obligation," I suggest a shift in thinking. As Abraham Maslow's pivotal theory on the hierarchy of needs suggests, the work that you do serves multiple needs in your life, on a graduating scale of fulfillment. Once your most basic psychological need is satisfied and it no longer occupies your thinking, then you naturally begin to strive to attain the next, more advanced need.

The most basic need we fulfill is survival. We work in order to make money. That's a fact. Without money, we cannot eat, provide shelter for ourselves and our families, or obtain clothing. Once this need is fulfilled, we move on to the second level of Maslow's hierarchy: the need for safety. We must feel reasonably comfortable and protected. The third need is for belonging. We work in order to feel connected to others, satisfying social needs for acceptance, love, and communication. As human beings, we have a longing for validation of what we think and what we do.

As job-related achievements bring success, we move up to even higher levels of fulfillment. As our job takes on greater personal meaning and responsibility, we enjoy increased self-esteem. It is also the means by which we serve others. If we pursue work simply for our own satisfaction, we are diminishing the importance of our efforts. Service to others can be a powerful, compelling mission that brings significance to your work. But the highest level of Maslow's hierarchy of needs is self-actualization. Our ultimate quest in life is to truly understand ourselves. To experience the highest level of fulfillment with your work is to know that you are following your true purpose. Are you doing the work that you were meant to do? Are you putting all of *you* in what you do? When we find our true calling and pursue it with complete commitment, then we will find that our work is not work at all. It is an enjoyable, exciting, constantly unfolding adventure, one in which you grow along personal, professional, and spiritual lines. For all of us this is the ultimate quest in life: to be aligned with our purpose. Unfortunately, many never know or even comprehend that satisfaction, as they are simply doing their J.O.B.

Internationally acclaimed Fortune 500 consultant and author David Whyte has explored work as an opportunity for the deepest discovery of our personhood:

> *Some [people] have experienced fulfillment for only a few brief hours early on in their work lives and then measured everything else, secretly against it . . . Some have felt eager and engaged by their work for years and then walked into their office one fine morning to find their enthusiasm gone, their energies spent, their imaginations engaged in secret ways, elsewhere . . . For them, if they are to have any chance at balance— or individual freedom—they must understand that the consummation of work lies not only in what we have done, but in who we have become while accomplishing the tasks at hand.*

Men and women all across America are drowning in boring, stultifying, mediocre work. They are chronically overstimulated by trivialities and are lacking in genuine challenges. Burnout is one of the chief ingredients for a chaotic, dysfunctional, and disharmonious life.

Naturally, people in this situation seek convenient solutions to make the problems go away. When people feel bad enough and sad enough, their need to feel better becomes almost a craving, so they do whatever is necessary to get temporary relief. What constitutes a quick fix differs from person to person, of course, but it ends in the same result: immersion in unfulfilling work just to get by. This type of soulless immersion masks a more chronic underlying unhappiness with the work itself, with oneself in particular, and with the world in general.

One of the key components to happiness in life is the discovery and pursuit of a meaningful vocation. Work can be challenging or numbing, exciting or dreary, rewarding or disappointing. It's your choice, and it just might be one of the most important choices you will ever make!

Balance at Home

In my life, my family is the foundation of my strength, spiritual growth and purpose. That's a core belief, and I do my best to stay connected to that belief at all times. Over the years I've made decisions about how to structure my life and ensure that I have the time and energy to devote to my wife and children. I travel extensively in my business, delivering presentations across the country, and whenever possible I try to take my family, transforming a business trip into a family adventure.

Our son, Eddie, had made forty commercial airline flights by the time he was two years old. He has been to more than a dozen states and several international destinations. Right now, with two children, it's more difficult to travel as a family, but we still do it when it makes sense. Other times I plan my solo trips to maximize the time that I have at home. I also try to handle the majority of my work while I am on the road. That way, when I get home I can spend much of my time focused on my family. And when I do work, I can usually do so from my home office.

Balancing the personal me with the professional me in that setting gets very interesting at times, but we've created solutions that have

Sheilia and Eddie in the cockpit. As a non-ticketed lap baby, Eddie made forty commercial flights before he was two years old. This earned him the unofficial distinction of Delta Air Lines' "most frequent free-loader."

worked well and help me to keep my priorities in balance—most of the time. Since I don't commute or spend eight hours a day at an office away from home, I can structure my day to have meals with my family, and I can enjoy playtime with my kids during breaks, then return to my work.

Of all human relationships, none are as important, vital, and enduring as those of home and family. Family ties, parenthood, and close friendships are and always will be my chief priorities.

Sometimes it's easy to forget how important the people in our lives are, until we face an unexpected tragedy or illness. The sudden death of someone we love can rock us off balance and shake our foundations. Emerson said, "You cannot do a kindness too soon, for you never know how soon it will be too late." One thing is for certain: If you neglect your family, you are paying too high a price for whatever success you think you are achieving.

Dean Ornish, the world-renowned researcher of coronary heart disease, was featured on the covers of *TIME, Newsweek,* and other magazines for his groundbreaking work on the healing power of intimate, supportive relationships. In his book *Love and Survival,* he examines the impact of love and intimacy on a person's overall health and psychological well-being. Since the kind of in-depth, intimate relationships he writes about are not usually found in work settings, I want to include his findings here, particularly since I'm making the case for a more wholesome, healthy, balanced, harmonious *you.* From his analysis, Ornish concludes:

> *When we feel loved, nurtured, cared for, supported and intimate, we are much more likely to be happier and healthier. We have a much lower risk of getting sick and burned out and, if we do, a much greater chance of surviving. In fact, if we do not have anyone we feel close to, no one who'd take care of us, no one we could turn to in time of need, we may have three to five times higher risk of premature death and disease from all causes.*

The intimacy and love Ornish refers to come from close relationships with family and friends. Ornish goes on to say:

> *It may be hard to believe that something as simple as talking with friends, feeling close to your parents, sharing feelings openly, or making yourself vulnerable to others in order to enhance intimacy can make such a powerful difference in your health and well-being, but study after study indicates that they often do.*

As it turns out, the quality of our relationships has a powerfully protective effect on our health, happiness, and well-being. The more supportive, cohesive, and loving our relationships, the healthier we are, and the easier it is for us to get back into balance.

You are the architect of your life. You can define success however you choose, and the attainment of that success is determined by the actions you take. Those actions are driven by your thoughts, which you create and manage moment to moment. Establishing compelling goals for your life is vital in order to help you keep your focus, measure your progress, and recognize when you have achieved what you are after. As you pursue those goals, you will encounter change, risks, and setbacks along the way. But with your *success in action* mindset and positive orientation, you can embrace those factors, lean forward, and navigate through uncertainty. In the process, you will not only reap the rewards of a more fulfilling life, but you will inspire those around you and come to know a new and improved sense of balance.

Action Assignments

1. Think of the times when you have been "still in the midst of activity and vibrant in repose." Pick one of the times when you've been still while chaos reigned all around you. What were the circumstances? How did you respond? What was the outcome? Describe your state of mind. What did you learn that helped you in subsequent, similar circumstances? As you look back on the incident now, what would you have done differently? Recall a time when you were "vibrant in repose." Ask yourself the same questions above.

2. It is time to streamline your life and experience the power of disconnecting. Identify something that has been occupying space in your life pattern for far too long, and give yourself permission to let it go! This could be a habit, a relationship, an obligation, or a goal. Make a conscious decision that this item is no longer serving a useful purpose in your life, and give yourself a little more space.

3. Prioritize your personal interests. Identify the hobbies, subjects, and activities that you enjoy that also support your growth in the other four life spheres. In other words, which personal interests also help you build strong relationships, grow spiritually, improve your health, and embolden your work efforts? Place your energy and time enjoying the interests that support your quest for better balance.

4. Consider a life change you are currently navigating or contemplating. Imagine the new, improved you. Once the change is completed, what will the new pattern look like? Complete the statements below:

Having made this change, my life has improved in many ways. For example:

My work is now_____

_____

My relationships are better because_____

_____

My health is_____

_____

My spiritual growth is_____

_____

My personal interests are now_____

_____

You have now added motivation and fuel to propel you forward in making this life change. This is a multidimensional approach to change, which has power rooted to the very core of who you are as a person. Post these positive benefits where you will be reminded of them, and take the necessary steps to enlist the guidance, information, and support to keep you moving in the right direction.

Epilogue

YOUR INFINITE POTENTIAL

Congratulations on successfully completing this book! You deserve to feel a rewarding sense of accomplishment. But the real question is, what happens now?

I will never forget the rush of satisfaction I experienced when I first learned to juggle, when it finally came together, and I was at last able to sustain the three-ball pattern. It felt fantastic. Then, before long, another notion rushed into my head. You guessed it: *How about four?*

I immediately tried juggling four balls, using the same technique I had learned for three. This approach was not the least bit successful. Balls collided, caroming off one another, crashing down on my head and bouncing all over the room. When I asked my mentor, Mike Vondruska, what the problem was, he gave me some excellent advice. He said, "Dan, when you add the fourth ball, you need to learn a new pattern. You aren't just adding to what you already know. The addition of one more changes everything."

Mike taught me that when juggling four balls, the objects don't cross in the middle, as they do with three. Instead, even numbers are juggled by dividing the objects equally between hands—two in the left hand and two in the right. Instead of changing sides, the balls circle back into the hand that launched them.

> *Now that you have completed this book, you have new tools to implement. But you aren't just adding to what you already know. The addition of this new inform-ation changes everything. You need to learn a new pattern.*

Armed with this new knowledge, I rushed back home to master it, scooping up four balls with increased enthusiasm. I tried juggling four once again, and still it didn't work. I quickly discovered that it would take practice to succeed.

And here's where it got interesting. As I continued to practice four-ball juggling, I began to notice a curious side effect: My three-ball juggling got a lot better. The truth is, I never got the hang of four . . . until I tried five. It seemed I needed to push for the next level before I could master the one I was working on.

> *If you think what you are doing now is difficult, then it's probably time to try the next harder thing. When you do, this level will get easier. And once you stretch your abilities, you will never be the same as you once were.*

When I was in grammar school, my teachers always said I wasn't living up to my full potential. They were right, of course—I'll never reach my full potential, and neither will you, because your potential is *infinite*. You will never learn it all! But in the process of pursuing *more* of your potential, you will harvest rich rewards, learning volumes about yourself and positively influencing the lives of those you touch.

Thank you for allowing me the privilege of being a part of your journey. I wish you all the best of *success in action*!

Acknowledgements

This book would not be a reality but for many wonderful people who have been in my life. For their influential gifts, including time, guidance, encouragement, friendship, and inspiration, I would like to acknowledge the following people.

Thanks to my wife and soul mate, Sheilia, for your love and encouragement. You bring out the best in me and help me appreciate life to its fullest. Thanks to Eddie and Maggie for understanding that sometimes Daddy has to work and travel. Thanks for the warm welcomes, great hugs, and special moments we enjoy together. You're the greatest gift God ever gave me.

Thanks to my family:
Mike and Diana Thurmon, Ed and Carlene Witowski; my sisters Wendy Warder and Sandy Manzari; my soul brother Philip Solomon; Stanley and Claire Wojtak, Jim Warder, Mike Manzari, Bill and Evelyn Thurmon, and Richard and June Proctor.

Thanks to those who helped shape my career and my life, including:
Mike Vondruska, Bill Clary, Jon Schwartz, Andy Kosiarek, John and Carol Goddard, Jon Cowles, Eric Somerville, Howie Marmer, Lee Goldsmith, Van Brown, Eddie Coker, Spencer Humm, Cindy Westaway, Doyle Patrick, Alison McLaughlin, Lester McNeeley, Frank Birdsall, Doug McCart, David Silverman, Debra Kerney, Mike Cash, Tricia Light, and George McMillan.

Thanks to my friends and colleagues of the National Speakers Association, especially:
Ken Futch, Shirley Garrett, Curt Boudreaux (who bought the first copy of this book years ago), Shep Hyken, Bruce Wilkinson, Giovanni Livera, Bil and Cher Holton, Nido Qubein, Mark Sanborn, David Greenberg, Austin McGonigle, D.J. Harrington, Jane Riley, Joe Gandolfo, Chris Clarke-Epstein, Lenora Billings-Harris, Gene Griessman, Greg Smith, Dick Biggs, Mike Stewart, Jeffrey Gitomer, Carol Hacker, Ed Scannell, Jeff Justice, Dave Reznik, Eric Chester, Renee Walkup, and Mark Mayberry.

Thanks to all the wonderful clients who have made it possible for me to do what I love . . . and get paid. I especially appreciate the friendship and support of:
Blane Haywood, Randy Merritt, Scott Sandlin, Scott Humphrey, John Bradshaw, Bob Spahn, Brian Cooksey, Danny Crutchfield, Erik Kadlec, Steve Sieracki, Jack Middleton, John Rader, Zach Platek, Tim Tassopoulos, Mark Conklin, Ty Yokum, Andy Lorenzen, Lisa Gibson, Kate Good, Tamela Coval, Jodi Goldstein, Carl Ruff, Stephanie Kingsbury, Tammy Siewruk, Mo Kimball, Julie Efaw, Patty Sauer, Mike Klemm, Ron Miles, John Rasper, Suzi Northcutt, Carlos Muniez, Susan Stewart, Suzanne Gylfe, Ami Kaplan, Dick Jones, Dick Wilde, Pam Glotzbach, Charlie Dunn, Tommy Housworth, Camille Thompson, Ed Adler, Andrea Gold, Martin Downing, Mike Parks, Beth Neal, Jay Flynn, Sharon Ruttenbur, Pam Elledge, Cathy Crider, Mark Williams, Kenna Thomas, Lyric Resmondo, Charlene Zaske, John Michael, Sheryl Camp, Gloria Jacobs, Debbie Haukenberry, Bob Bulmer, Bob Groening, Mark Castel, Christopher

Long, Jim Fowler, Patti Allen, Missy Weld, Tina Boudreau, Lisa Dunavin, Benita Falk, Michele Carrere, Carol Posey, Canada Steffel, Kaaren Cheney, Michele Rubino, Katrina Kaposts Smith, Angie Bolton, Doug Ehrlich, Peter Smallman, Jack Murphy, Glenna Newberry, Bill Rodgers, Nicole Hay, Sue Buri, Patrick Diemer, John Rasper, Pam Bennett, Mark Williams, John Pringle, Phelps Hope, Kenneth Jones, Pamela Hargis, Patrick Sobers, Jeanie Northcutt, Marilyn Gardner, Amy Kitchen, Kathy McCullum, Teresa Sandman, Belinda Miller-Foey, Karen Brandell, Amy Kosnikowski, Shellie McDaniel, Ellen Wentz, Blaine Nelson, Lynn Ellis-Stallings, Vicki Champion, Vicki Escarra, Henry Alvarez, Sue Koch, Karen Moore, Esther Eagles, Carol Parker, Cami Miller, Ray Shrader, Jay Janowicz, Marjorie Cook, Kim O'Dell, Rodger Wunderlich, Pam Newland, Natalie Gaburick, Nancy Lively, Wayne Edwards, Kimberly Grant, Michael Tompkins, Mark Wiltshire, Kathy Van Pelt, Mary Ann Schuster, Marilyn Ligon, George Cates, Christine Rizk, Benita Falk, George Hilliard, Sally Scott, Jeremy Figoten, Danny Harris, Sandy Jeske, Mike Premo, Nathan Slovan, Trey Reilly, Joy Miccio, Randi Sumner, Jennifer Stickler Leverette, Lauri Robinson, Dorothy Streich, Jesus Leal, Bill Hooker, Reed Lynn, Alice Fieler, Mark Naber, Danne Obert, Tony Schroder, Steve Corson, Carolyn Stonehouse, Sharon Pattschull, Shane Taylor, Todd Taylor, Paul Mangano, Jim Spahn, Jennifer Lester, Steve Erickson, Jerry Ardizzone, Diane Miller, Michele Champion, Julie Dietrich, Allayne Brackbill, Jeff Bigelow, Lisa Warren, Susie DeWeese, Anita Neal, Angelo Harris, Bud Watford, Sandy Block, Randy Ell, Ruth Lyons, Stephanie Lalliss, Andrea Wilson, Karen Martin, Earl Smalley, Lisa Dunavin, Janet Chiarella, Gary Lombard, Connie Harmon, Nancy Wenzel, Bil Wolinger, Renee Rooker, Tina Weede, Judy Butterfield, Suzanne Pratt, Terry Danner, Ellen Westbrock, Debbie Katkin, Carol Devine, Bonnie Browning, Debbie Garner, Tony Garston, Steve Thomas, Susan Henderson, Christine Lawry, Gayle Solomon, Rich Tatgenhorst, Dianne McGarey, Scott Martin, Anne Rohr, Chris Wolski, Tom Tidmore, Kaarin Raup, and Mike McGraw.

For their artistic contributions to this book, I'd also like to thank: Michael Carr, Leslie Raines, Tom Abraham, and Tony Brischler.

About the Author

Dan Thurmon began his entrepreneurial career when he was eleven years old after learning to juggle at a Renaissance Festival. That one event uncovered a passion for engaging and inspiring audiences that has only grown over time. As an entertainer, Dan has appeared at thousands of events across the country and overseas. He has shared the stage with acts such as The Commodores, Dave Koz, The Neville Brothers, Bella Fleck, Frankie Avalon, and Kool and the Gang. He has also appeared many times on national television, including *The Late Show* with David Letterman. Dan has also performed for U.S. Armed Forces in Iraq, Afghanistan, and four other countries."

As he built his entertainment business, Dan was able to self-finance his education, travel the world, and learn what it takes to consistently deliver superior performances on and off the stage.

Dan is president of Motivation Works, Inc., an international speaking and entertainment firm. He teaches audiences how to manage the demands of their busy lives with increased focus and decisive action. His unique speaking style, *Speaking with Visual Impact*™, utilizes all of his skills, blending meaningful content with emotionally charged performances.

Dan is a graduate of the University of Georgia with a degree in Marketing. He has also studied business management, music, theater, acting, dance, gymnastics, and aviation. In 2003 Dan achieved the highest earned award of the National Speakers Association, receiving the elite designation of "Certified Speaking Professional." He has delivered over a thousand presentations across America, Europe, and Asia for organizations including IBM, General Motors, Deloitte and Touche, The Coca Cola Company, and AT&T. Dan currently lives in the Atlanta area with his wife, Sheilia, and their children, Eddie and Maggie.

Motivation Works, Inc.
Our Mission is to inspire and teach people to transcend the ordinary, find balance and achieve breakthroughs in all areas of life. We accomplish this Mission by delivering educational presentations and support materials that consistently meet these three goals.

1. Raise the spirits and fuel the minds of audiences.
2. Elevate the vision of what is possible to achieve.
3. Stimulate new and better ways of thinking and performing.

ORDER FORM

☐ Please send me _____ copies of Success in Action at $24.95. Add $4.00 for U.S. shipping. Allow 15 days for delivery.

(Call for information on bulk order discounts and Canadian/International shipping.)

☐ My check or money order for $ _____ is enclosed.

☐ Please charge my: ☐ VISA ☐ MasterCard

Card no. _____

Expiration Date _____

Cardholder _____

Credit Card Billing Address_____

City _____State _____ Zip _____

Signature _____

☐ Shipping Address

Name_____

Organization_____

Address _____

City _____State _____ Zip _____

Telephone _____ Fax _____

Email _____

Mail or Fax Order to:
Motivation Works, Inc.
2055 Scenic Highway North, Suite C-311
Snellville, GA 30078
Phone: 770 982-2664
Fax: 770 982-2665
Email: order@danthurmon.com
Web: www.danthurmon.com

ORDER FORM

❑ Please send me _____ copies of Success in Action at $24.95. Add $4.00 for U.S. shipping. Allow 15 days for delivery.

(Call for information on bulk order discounts and Canadian/International shipping.)

❑ My check or money order for $ _____ is enclosed.

❑ Please charge my: ❑ VISA   ❑ MasterCard

Card no. _____

Expiration Date _____

Cardholder _____

Credit Card Billing Address_____

City _____State _____ Zip _____

Signature _____

❑ Shipping Address

Name_____

Organization_____

Address _____

City _____State _____ Zip _____

Telephone _____ Fax _____

Email _____

Mail or Fax Order to:
Motivation Works, Inc.
2055 Scenic Highway North, Suite C-311
Snellville, GA 30078
Phone: 770 982-2664
Fax: 770 982-2665
Email: order@danthurmon.com
Web: www.danthurmon.com